Published by
Rajneesh Foundation International
Rajneeshpuram, Oregon 97741 U.S.A.

Bhagwan Shree Rajneesh

THE
BOOK
OF THE
BOOKS

Volume II

Discourses on
The Dhammapada
of Gautam the Buddha

Editor: Ma Prem Asha
Design: Ma Prem Tushita
Direction: Ma Yoga Pratima, M.M., D.Phil.M. (RIMU), Arihanta
Copyright: © 1983 Rajneesh Foundation International
Published by:
  Ma Anand Sheela, M.M., D.Phil.M., D.Litt.M. (RIMU), Acharya
  Rajneesh Foundation International, President
  P.O. Box 9, Rajneeshpuram
  Oregon 97741 U.S.A.

First Edition: December 1983 — 10,000 copies

Extracts from *The Dhammapada: The Sayings of the Buddha*,
translated by Thomas Byrom, are reprinted with kind
permission of the publishers, Alfred A. Knopf, New York,
and Wildwood House Ltd., London. Text © 1976 Thomas
Byrom.

Printed in U.S.A.

ISBN 0-88050-514-1

Library of Congress Catalog Number 82-50462

CONTENTS

INTRODUCTION

Gautam the Buddha.

The name always conjured up a vision of a man, head framed by a golden halo, sitting under a tree in a lotus posture, dispensing incomprehensible and mysterious profundities that none of the mortals gathered at his feet could ever hope to understand. And any book I opened on Buddha simply reinforced that image and compounded my confusion even more.

Then life led me to Bhagwan Shree Rajneesh, to my own Buddha. And one day, to those of us gathered at His feet, He began to speak on Buddha and on Buddha's scriptures, on the Dhammapada.

It's not that the mystery became less mysterious; on the contrary, it grew and grew, day by day. But it transcended the mysterious: it gave birth to the miraculous. And the miracle was that it was at last so straightforward, at last so clear. It was absolute magic—mysteriously simple, miraculously real.

"What I am saying here," He said one morning, "you can read in the Bhagavad Gita, in the Bible, in the Koran, in the Dhammapada, what I am saying you can find easily in the Upanishads, in the Tao Te Ching—but you will not find the fragrance. Those are flowers—old, dead, dried up. You can keep a roseflower in your Bible; soon it will be dry, the fragrance will be gone, it will be only a corpse, a remembrance of the real flower. So are the scriptures. They have to be made alive again by another Buddha, otherwise they cannot breathe.

"That's why I am speaking on the Dhammapada, on the Gita, on the Bible—to let them breathe again. I can breathe life into them. I can share my fragrance with them, I can pour my fragrance into them. Hence, the Christian who is really a Christian, not just by social conditioning but because of a great love for Christ, he will find Christ alive in my words again. Or if somebody is a Buddhist he will find in my words Buddha speaking again —in twentieth-century language, with twentieth-century people. . .

"And then all the scriptures become alive for you. Then reading the Bible, you are not just reading a book— then Moses speaks to you, Abraham speaks to you, Jesus speaks to you, face to face!"

Here, then, is the rich and incomparable fragrance of Bhagwan Shree Rajneesh, breathing new life and love and laughter into words twenty-five centuries old.

And here, too, is Gautam the Buddha.

Speaking to you.

Face to face!

Swami Krishna Prem

THE
BOOK
OF THE
BOOKS

volume
two

These discourses, based on
The Dhammapada of Gautam the Buddha,
were given by Bhagwan Shree Rajneesh
at Shree Rajneesh Ashram,
Poona, India
July 1-10, 1979

How can a troubled mind
Understand the way?
If a man is disturbed
He will never be filled with knowledge.

An untroubled mind,
No longer seeking to consider
What is right and what is wrong,
A mind beyond judgements,
Watches and understands.

Know that the body is a fragile jar,
And make a castle of your mind.
In every trial
Let understanding fight for you
To defend what you have won.

For soon the body is discarded.
Then what does it feel?
A useless log of wood, it lies on the ground.
Then what does it know?

Your worst enemy cannot harm you
As much as your own thoughts, unguarded.

But once mastered,
No one can help you as much,
Not even your father or your mother.

The Wisdom of Innocence

ONCE I WAS ASKED: "WHAT IS PHILO-sophy?" I said, "Philosophy is the art of asking the wrong questions." The blind man asking "What is light?"—this is philosophy. The deaf asking "What is music? What is sound?"—this is philosophy.

If the blind man asks, "How can I get my eyes back?" this is no more philosophy, this is religion. If the deaf goes to the physician to be treated so that he can hear, then he is moving in the direction of religion and not in the direction of philosophy.

Philosophy is guesswork, it is speculation; knowing nothing, one tries to invent the truth. And the truth cannot be invented, and anything invented cannot be true. The truth has to be discovered. It is already there...all that we need is open eyes—eyes to see it, a heart to feel it, a being to be present to it. The truth is always present but we are absent, and because we are absent we cannot see the truth. And we go on asking about the truth, and we don't ask the

4

right question: How to be present? How to become a presence?

We ask about the truth and that asking is also going away from it, because the asking implies that an answer is possible from somebody else. Asking implies that somebody else can tell you what the truth is. Nobody can tell you it, it can't be told.

Lao Tzu says: "The truth that can be said is no more truth. Once said, it becomes a lie."

Why? Because the person who knows, knows it not as information; otherwise, it would have been very easy to transfer the information to anybody who was ready to receive it. The truth is known as an inner experience. It is like a taste on the tongue. If a man has never tasted what sweetness is, you cannot explain it to him—it's impossible. If a man has not seen colour, you cannot explain to him what it is.

There are things which can only be experienced, and through experience understood. God is that ultimate experience, which is utterly inexpressible, untransferable. It cannot be conveyed. At the most, a few hints can be given; but those hints are also to be received with a very sympathetic heart, otherwise you will miss them. If you interpret them with your mind you are going to miss them, because what can your mind do as far as interpretation is concerned? It can bring only its own past. It can bring only its own chaos. It can bring its conflicts, doubts, confusions. And all those it will impose on the truth, on the hint given to you, and immediately everything is distorted. Your mind is not in a state to see, to feel.

Religion simply means creating a space in your mind which is capable of seeing, which is capable of non-conflict, which is capable of being one without any split, which is capable of integrity, clarity, perceptiveness. A mind which is full of thoughts cannot perceive; those thoughts go on interfering. Those thoughts are there, layer upon layer. By the time something reaches your innermost core, if it ever reaches, it is no more the same as it was delivered by someone who had known. It is a totally different phenomenon.

Buddha used to repeat each hint thrice. Somebody asked him, "Why do you repeat one thing thrice?"

He said, "Even thrice is not enough. When I say it for the first time, you only hear the words. Those words are empty, just empty, hollow shells, with no content. You cannot hear the content the first time. The second time, you hear the content with the words, a fragrance comes, but you are so dazed, you are so mystified by its presence, that you are not in a state to understand. You hear, but you don't understand. That's why I have to repeat it thrice."

I go on repeating again and again for the simple reason that you are so asleep—it has to be repeated, hammered. Maybe in some moment, some auspicious moment, you will not be so deep in sleep, you may be close, very close, to awakening, and something may enter into you. You may be able to hear. Yes, there are moments when you are very close to awakening—not awake, not asleep, just in the middle, somewhere in between.

Each morning you know, there are a few moments when the sleep is no more but you are not yet awake, you cannot say you are awake. You can hear, in a very vague way, the sounds of the birds, and the milkman and the wife talking to the neighbour and the children getting ready to go to school, and the traffic noise, and a train passes by—but in a very vague way, not totally, partially. And you go on dozing off into sleep. One moment you hear the noise of the train passing by, another moment you have gone deeper into your sleep.

Now the sleep researchers say that it happens continuously in your sleep: if you sleep for eight hours, you are not on the same level continuously; your level goes on changing, peaks and valleys. The whole night you are going up and down. Sometimes you are very deep in sleep where even dreams disappear. Patanjali has called it *shushupti*—dreamless sleep. And sometimes you are full of dreams. And sometimes you are just on the verge of awakening. If something shattering, shocking happens, you will be awake, suddenly awake.

That's the effort of all the Buddhas: waiting for that right moment when you are very close to awakening, then a little push and your eyes open and you can see.

God cannot be explained but can be seen, can be experienced—can*not* be explained. Any explanation for God is nothing but explaining him away. Hence, the more priests, theologians, professors there are, the less religion there is in the world. The more popes and the more shankaracharyas, the less religion there is in the world—because these people go on explaining and God cannot be explained. They have stuffed your minds with so many explanations; now those explanations are in conflict. Now it is almost impossible to figure it out, what is what, which is which. You are in utter confusion. Man has never been in such confusion before, because humanity has never been so close before. The earth has *really* become a village, a global village.

In the ancient days the Buddhists knew only what the Buddha had said, and the Mohammedan knew only about what Mohammed had said, and the Christian knew only about Jesus. Now, we have become inheritors of the whole heritage of humanity. Now, you know Jesus, you know Zarathustra, you know Patanjali, you know Buddha, you know Mahavira, you know Lao Tzu, and hundreds of other explanations, other hints, and they are all jumbled up in you. Now it is very difficult to pull you out of this confusion. The only possible way is to drop this whole noise, not in parts but in toto. That's what my message is.

And by dropping it, you will not be dropping Jesus or Mohammed or Buddha; by dropping it you will come closer to them. By dropping it, you will simply be dropping the priests and the traditions and the conventions and the exploitation that goes on in the name of tradition and convention. By being clear of all this, forgetting the Bible and the Vedas and the Gita, you will attain to a clarity, a cleanliness. Yes, you need a spring cleaning, you need a total unburdening of the heart. Only then, in that silence, will you be able to understand.

Buddha says:

How can a troubled mind
Understand the way?

THOUSANDS HAD GATHERED AROUND BUDDHA, just as you have gathered around me—thousands of seekers had come to Buddha and they were asking all kinds of questions. And Buddha was not interested in their questions at all; he was not interested in answering them. He was interested, certainly, in showing them the way, but the problem was that they were so much troubled with their questions *and* the answers that they had collected, they were so much disturbed by all the knowledge that they had been

8

carrying all along, that it was impossible, almost completely impossible to show them the way.

Hence this sutra:

How can a troubled mind
Understand the way?

So rather than giving them more answers, more explanations, more knowledge, Buddha started taking away their knowledge, their ready-made answers, their *a priori* conceptions, their prejudices.

India has never been able to forgive Buddha for that. Immediately after he died the traditional mind of this country started uprooting all the plants that he had planted; all the rosebushes were burnt. Buddha was completely thrown out of this country. The greatest son of this land had no shelter here; the teaching had to seek shelter in foreign lands.

This is not accidental, this has happened always. Jesus was condemned by the Jews, crucified by the Jews, and Jesus was the greatest Jew who has ever been on the earth, the greatest flowering of the Jewish consciousness, the uttermost expression, the crescendo, the Everest. But why did the Jews deny him? They should have been happy, they should have danced and celebrated, but they could not —they could not forgive him. Because his presence made them feel very mediocre; that was his crime. He had to be punished for it, for being so high, for being so beyond, for being so superior, for being so graceful, for bringing such love. For his presence he had to be punished, because his presence was making people feel ugly by comparison. He had to be removed so the mediocre mind could feel at ease.

Jesus was *not* killed by Jews, he was killed by the mediocre mind. It happened to be the Jewish mediocre mind in the case of Jesus; the same happened with Buddha. Buddha has not been forgiven by the Hindus, and he was the greatest Hindu ever. He was the purest Hindu possible, the very quintessence of Hinduism. What the Upanishads were saying, he had actualized it. He was the realization of the deepest longings of this land, but he was uprooted from here, he was thrown out of here.

Buddhism disappeared from India; not even a trace was left behind—utterly washed away. Why? He was tremendously respected in Tibet, in China, in Korea, in Japan, in Thailand, in Burma, in Ceylon. The whole of Asia loved the man, so unique is his teaching, so pregnant are his words. But India simply forgot all about him—the Indian mediocre mind. It has nothing to do with the Indian—again the mediocre mind. The mediocre mind never allows the genius; the mediocre person is happy with other mediocre people. The stupid people are happy with other stupid leaders. The more stupid the leader is, the more people are happy—because he looks so like them.

I have heard:
A new superintendent was appointed in a mad asylum. The old was giving his charge over, he was retiring, and a small feast was arranged for the old to be thanked for all his services, for the new to be received by the inmates. All the mad people gathered.

The old superintendent was a little puzzled; he had never seen them so happy. All the mad people were so happy, so joyous, that he could not resist the temptation of asking them—and he was to leave the same day, so he had to ask immediately, otherwise it would always remain a curiosity in his mind and he would never know the answer.

He asked the mad people. "Why are you looking so happy?"

They said, "Because of the new superintendent—he looks just like us! You were a foreigner amongst us, you were sane. He looks mad!"

And that was a truth: the new superintendent was almost insane. But the insane people were very happy. Somebody had now come who would not make them feel insane.

This has always been the situation on the earth—this earth is the madhouse. And whenever a sane person happens, we misbehave with him. Thousands of people had come to Buddha to ask, "Where is God? What is God?" And especially the brahmins, the pundits, the scholars, who were fully informed, well-informed about the scriptures, they used to come to him to ask, "Do you believe in God? Define your belief, explain your concept."

And Buddha insisted again and again:

> *How can a troubled mind*
> *Understand the way?*

He used to say, "Please don't ask about God. Your asking about God is just like a blind man asking about light—it *cannot* be explained. I am a physician," he insisted, "I can treat your eyes, I can give you your vision back. And then you will be able to see by yourself, and the light has to be seen by you yourself. My seeing the light is not going to help. I may see the light, I may even describe it, but it is not going to give you any idea of what it is."

In fact there is *no* possible way to explain to the blind man what light is. Light is an experience, something existential, unexplainable. And God is the ultimate light, the light of all the lights, the light behind all the lights, the source of all

11

lights. How can God be explained to you if you are blind?

Hence Buddha never talked about God. And the pundits and the brahmins would go back to their places saying, and spreading rumours that "This man does not answer the question because he does not know. Otherwise, why can't he say simply yes or no? We asked a very simple question, 'Do you believe in God?' He could have said yes or no; if he knows then the answer is simple. But he talks in a roundabout way; we ask about God and he talks in parables. He says, 'How can it be said? How can it be explained?' The real fact is he does not know. The real fact is that he is an atheist in disguise; he is deceiving people, corrupting people."

Hindus have invented a very cunning story about Buddha. They say:

God created the world. At the same time he created hell and heaven—hell for those who were to be punished and heaven for those who were to be rewarded for their virtues. But it happened that thousands of years passed and nobody entered hell, because nobody committed a sin. Of course, the Devil was very tired of waiting and waiting and waiting —with no work, with no business! Not even a single soul had turned up!

Tremendously angry, he approached God and said, "Why have you made this hell, for what? And why have you put me there in charge? We are tired, my whole staff is tired. Nobody ever comes up. We open the shop and we sit the whole day and not a single customer! We keep the doors open—not a single soul ever enters. What is the point? Please make us free from this job."

God said, "Why didn't you come earlier? I had completely

forgotten about it. I will make arrangements. Soon I will be born in the world as Gautam the Buddha, and I will corrupt people's minds. I will corrupt their minds so much that you will be overcrowded. You just go back to hell and wait."

And that's how it happened, the story says: God came to the world as Gautam the Buddha, corrupted people's minds, destroyed their beliefs, uprooted their conventions, shook their faith, created doubt in their minds, suspicions, and since then hell is so crowded that the Devil goes again and again and says to God, "Now, stop! Please stop! We are tired, so many people! We are running a twenty-four hour service, day in and day out; even in the night the doors can't be closed. People simply go on coming!"

A very cunning story. Do you see the delicate cunning-ness in it? In one sense Buddha is recognized as God's *avatara*. Hindus are more cunning in that way than Jews. They simply denied that Jesus was the son of God, they rejected Jesus. Hindus are more sophisticated in that way, more polished, more cultured—of course, a more ancient civilization. And the more ancient the civilization becomes, the more cunning it becomes. See the cunningness: Buddha is accepted as the tenth incarnation of God, and yet God takes incarnation into the world to corrupt people's minds. So although Buddha is God, beware, don't listen to him! You see the strategy, the trick! They don't deny Buddha godhood—in fact it was almost impossible to deny Buddha godhood.

H.G. Wells has said that Gautam the Buddha is a paradox: the most godless man and yet the most godly. He never talked about God, he never told people to believe in God.

God is simply missing from his teaching. It is not a necessary hypothesis, it is not needed. The *most* godless and yet the most godly...nobody seems to be so godly as Buddha, so graceful as Buddha—just a lotus flower, the purest consciousness conceivable. As fresh as dewdrops in the early morning sun.

They could not deny that; they had to accept that he was God. But they could not accept his approach because his approach, if accepted, would destroy the whole established religion, the whole establishment. He takes away all the beliefs; in fact he makes it a very important thing, very essential, that a man of belief will not be able to know ever. He does not mean become a disbeliever, because disbelief is again belief in a negative way. Neither be a believer nor be a disbeliever.

Buddha's approach is that of an agnostic. He is neither a theist nor an atheist—he is an enquirer. And he wants you to remain open to enquire. Go with no prejudice, go with no ready-made idea—because if you go with a certain idea, you will project your idea onto reality. And if you have some deep-rooted idea in your mind, you will see that idea being fulfilled in reality and it will be only a hallucination, a dream projected by you. You have to go utterly empty. If you really want to know the truth you have to be absolutely empty, you should not carry any idea, any ideology; you should go naked, nude, empty. You should function from the state of not knowing. The state of not knowing is the state of wonder.

There is an ancient saying of Jesus, not recorded in the Bible, but Sufis have preserved it. Sufis have preserved many beautiful sayings of Jesus. The saying is so tremendously important that one wonders why it was not recorded in the

Bible, but if you ponder over it the reason becomes clear.

The saying is: Blessed is the one who marvels, because his is the kingdom of God. Blessed is one who wonders... this has not been recorded in the Bible—why? because the Bible wants to create a certain religion, a certain sect; it wants to propagate a certain ideology. And the man of wonder has to drop all ideology.

Blessed is the one who wonders, because only in wondering can you be like a child, innocent. And only in that innocence can you know that which is.

> How can a troubled mind
> Understand the way?

SO WHENEVER A PERSON WOULD COME TO Buddha and enquire, great questions about life and life's mysteries, Buddha would say, "You wait, you meditate. First let your troubled mind become untroubled. Let this storm of your mind go past. Let silence come, because silence will give you the eyes. I can show you the way to be silent, and then you don't need anybody's guidance. Once you are silent, you will be able to see the way and you will be able to reach the goal."

And our minds are really troubled. A thousand and one troubles are there. First, everybody is in a state of schizophrenia, more or less; the differences are only of degrees. Everybody is split because the exploiters, both religious and political, have depended on this strategy: divide the man, don't allow man integrity, and he will remain a slave. A house divided against itself is bound to be weak. So you have been taught to fight with the body; that is the root strategy of division, of dividing you: "Fight the body, the body is your enemy. It is the body that is dragging you towards hell. Fight, dagger in hand! Fight day and night! Fight for lives together! Only then one day will you be able to win over it. And unless you are victorious over your body, you are not going to enter into the world of God."

For centuries this nonsense has been taught to people. And the result is that everybody is divided, everybody is against his body. And if you are against your body, you are bound for trouble. You will fight with your body, and you and your body are one energy. The body is the visible soul, and the soul is the invisible body. The body and soul are *not* divided anywhere; they are parts of each other, they are parts of one whole. You have to accept the body, you have to love the body, you have to respect the body, you have to be grateful to your body—only then will you attain to a certain kind of integrity, a crystallization will happen. Otherwise you will remain troubled. And the body will not leave you so easily; even after hundreds of lives the fight will be there. You cannot defeat the body.

I am not saying that the body cannot be won over, mind you, but you cannot defeat the body. You cannot defeat it by being inimical towards it. You can win over it by being friendly, by being loving, by being respectful, by trusting it. That's exactly my approach: the body is the temple, you are the deity of the temple; the temple protects you, shelters you against rain, against wind, against heat. It is in your service! Why should you fight? It is as stupid as the driver fighting the car. If the driver fights with his car, what is going to happen? He will destroy the car and he will destroy himself in fighting with it. The car is a beautiful vehicle; it can take you on the farthest journeys.

The body is the most complex mechanism in existence. It

is simply marvellous! And blessed are those who marvel—begin the feeling of wonder with your own body, because that is the closest to you. The closest nature has approached to you, the closest God has come to you, is through the body. In your body is the water of the oceans, in your body is the fire of the stars and the suns, in your body is the air, your body is made of earth. Your body represents the whole existence, all the elements. And what a transformation! What a metamorphosis! Look at the earth and then look at your body—what a transformation, and you have never marvelled about it! Dust has become divine—what greater mystery is possible? What greater miracles are you waiting for? And you see the miracle happening every day. Out of the mud comes the lotus...and out of the dust has arisen our beautiful body. And such a complex mechanism, running so smoothly—no noise. And it is really complicated.

Scientists have made very complicated machines, but nothing to be compared with the body. Even the most sophisticated computer is just a toy compared to the inner mechanism of the body. And you have been taught to fight with it. That creates a split, that keeps you troubled, that keeps you in a constant civil war.

And because you fight with yourself, which is utterly stupid, your life becomes less and less one of intelligence and more and more one of stupidity. And then you want great transformations—you want jealousies to drop and you want anger to disappear and you want no greed in you. It is impossible! With such misunderstanding from the very beginning, how can you create the space where transformations happen, where anger becomes compassion, where hate becomes love, where greed becomes sharing, where sex becomes samadhi? How can you hope, how can you expect such great transformations, with such a troubled state?

The fundamental thing is to drop the split, to become one. Be one! And then all else is possible, even the impossible is possible.

> *How can a troubled mind*
> *Understand the way?*

The way is very simple and very direct. Even a child can understand it. It is as simple as two plus two equals four, or even more simple. It is as simple as the song of a bird, as simple as a roseflower—simple and beautiful, simple and of tremendous grandeur. But only an untroubled mind can understand it, only an untroubled mind has the capacity to see it. Otherwise you will live in greed and you will live in anger, and you will live in jealousies and possessiveness, and you will live in hatred. You can pretend, you can become a saint on the surface, but you will remain a sinner deep down. And the greatest sin is to divide yourself; the greatest sin is not committed against others: it is always committed against yourself. This is a state of suicide, creating this division between your body and yourself. Condemning the body you can become only a hypocrite, you can only live a life of pretensions.

In a first-class railroad compartment, two beautifully dressed ladies are discussing clothes while a gentleman in the corner pretends to be asleep. When one lady says she finds the cost of clothes impossible nowadays, the other suggests she should follow her example and take a boyfriend on the side: "He will give you five hundred a month for a little present—your husband would never do that."

"But what if I can't get a friend with five hundred dollars?"

"Then take two with two hundred and fifty each."

The gentleman speaks up: "Listen, ladies, I am going to sleep now. Wake me up when you get down to twenty bucks."

People *are* pretending in every possible way. The person who is pretending to be a saint may be just the opposite, and the person who is pretending to be awake may be asleep, and the person who is pretending to be asleep may be awake . . . *all* kinds of pretensions! Because the society creates the context where it allows you only either to live an utterly condemned life, the life of a criminal, or the life of a hypocrite, of a pretender. The society gives you only two alternatives: either be honest and be a criminal, or be dishonest and be respectable. It does not allow you the third alternative. Why does it not allow you the third alternative? Because the third alternative creates a Jesus, a Buddha, a Krishna, and their presence makes the crowd feel very mediocre, very insulted, humiliated.

So please don't decide by seeing people's appearances. More are the chances, almost ninety-nine point nine percent, that whatsoever they appear on the surface they will not be deep down. You can be certain about it, I say almost completely certain because only point one percent can you miss— which is not much. Only once in a while will you come across a Buddha, whose appearance is the same as his inwardness. Otherwise you will come across people who are one thing on the outside and another on the inside. Don't be deceived by appearances.

An actress picks up an out-of-work tramp and takes him to her apartment because he has very large shoes on, and she

19

has been told that men with big feet have big pricks. She gives him a steak dinner with plenty of pepper and beer, and then drags him off to bed.

In the morning the man wakes up alone and finds a ten-dollar bill on the mantlepiece, with a brief note: "Buy yourself a pair of shoes that fit you."

But that's how we all go on deciding...from the outside. In fact, because we don't even know our own insides, how can we look into other people's insides? We don't know the art of looking in. First you have to practise the art with yourself. First you have to go into your interiority, your inner world. You have to go deeper and deeper into your consciousness, to the very center of it. Once you have penetrated the core of *your* being, you will be able to see into anybody else's core of being. Then nobody can deceive you! Because then you don't see the appearance: you see the reality.

> *How can a troubled mind*
> *Understand the way?*

THE TROUBLED MIND CANNOT UNDERSTAND anything! It is not a state where understanding is possible. Understanding does not mean knowledge. A troubled mind can become very knowledgeable—you can go to the universities and you can see the professors—very knowledgeable—but they are more troubled than you, far more in inner conflict than you. Their knowledge does not help them at all. Knowledge has never helped anybody, it only burdens. It gives you respectability, certainly. It is a great ego-trip, and the ego feels very puffed up; but the more the ego is puffed up, the more you will be in trouble inside because the ego is a false phenomenon. And when you become too attached to the false, you start losing contact with the real; when you start growing roots in the false, you forget to grow roots in the real.

The man of knowledge is as unconscious as you are. The ignorant and the knowledgeable are not in different boats; they are fellow-travellers. The difference between them is only of information—which is not a difference at all, which is not a difference that makes any difference. I may know only a few things, you may know a few more, somebody else may know a thousand and one things, and somebody else may be just a walking Encyclopaedia Britannica—that makes no difference at all.

A Buddha is not a man of knowledge: he is a man of understanding—not full of information but full of insight. Full of vision, not full of thoughts. A clarity, a mirrorlike clarity, and a great awareness.

You are moving like a somnambulist, a sleep-walker; you don't know what you are doing, you don't know why you are doing it; you don't know where you are going, you don't know *why* you are going. Your life is accidental, and an accidental life is an unconscious life; it is like a robot.

A man at the theater with his wife goes out to the toilet at the intermission, but goes through the wrong door and finds himself in the garden. As it is too well-kept to think of using the ground, he lifts a plant out of a flower-pot and uses that, then replaces the plant.

He goes back and finds the next act has already begun. "What has happened so far in this act?" he asks his wife in a whisper.

"You ought to know," she says coldly. "You were in it!"

Man lives in unconsciousness. He is not aware, not at all aware. You can watch any person, you can watch yourself, slowly slowly, and you will see so many unconscious acts happening that it will be almost unbelievable how you have lived up to now. You are lying for *no* reason at all! And when you catch yourself redhanded lying, you will be surprised—why were you lying in the first place? Because there is no reason. You are not going to gain anything out of it. Just a habit. Just a mechanical routine. You become sad for *no* reason at all.

Now there are a few researchers who say you can make a calendar of your moods, and I find their research significant —you can really make a calendar of your moods. Just go on noting down for one month: Monday in the morning, how you felt, and in the afternoon and in the evening and in the night...just at least eight times per day, go on noting every day at the exact same times how you feel. And within three or four weeks you will be surprised that on each Monday at the same time you feel exactly the same.

Now this cannot be because of any circumstances outside, because each Monday they are different. It is something inner—although you will find excuses outside, because nobody wants to feel responsible for his own misery. It feels good to make others feel responsible for your misery. And you can find excuses; you can invent them if they are not there.

That's where people have become very very creative. In fact their whole creativity consists in creating excuses: "Why am I sad?" and you can find a thousand and one reasons. "The wife said this and the children are not behaving well and the neighbours and the boss in the office and the traffic and the prices are rising high..." and you can find a thousand and one things, they are always there, and you can paint the whole world very gloomy, dark, and then you can feel at ease that it is not your responsibility that you are sad.

But the *same* world, and Tuesday morning you are feeling very bubbly, very joyous, radiant—again you can find excuses: "This is a beautiful morning, and the sun and the birds and the trees and the sky, and all is so full of light—such a beautiful morning!" You can find excuses for all kinds of moods, but if you make a diary of four to eight weeks you will be really shocked that everything that happens to you is almost completely dependent on you. You have an inner wheel that goes on moving, and the same spokes go on coming on top again and again.

Yes, there are circumstances outside, but they are not causes; at the most they trigger. A certain mood that is bound to happen is triggered by a certain circumstance. If this circumstance were not there, then something else would have been the triggering point—but it was bound to trigger it.

People who have lived in isolation have become aware of this fact. Buddha used to send his disciples for isolation. In the new commune we are going to have underground caves so I can send you for one month's isolation—absolute isolation, you disappear from the world, so you cannot blame any circumstances outside because there is nothing outside...you and the wall of the cave. And you will be surprised: one day you are happy, one day you are unhappy, one day you are feeling very greedy, one day you are feeling angry and there is nobody who has insulted you, irritated you. One day you will find you are telling lies to yourself! because you cannot find anybody else.

"Could I buy you a drink?" he asked, by way of striking up a conversation.

"No thank you," she said. "I don't drink."

"What about a little dinner with me in my room?"

"No, I don't think that would be proper," she said.

Having had no success with the subtler approaches, the young man pressed directly to the point: "I am charmed by your refreshing beauty, mademoiselle, and will give you anything your heart desires if you will spend the night with me."

"Oh, no, no, monsieur, I could never do a thing like that."

"Tell me," the young man said, laughing, "don't you ever do anything the slightest bit improper?"

"Oui," said the French girl, "I tell lies."

You watch how many times in the day you tell lies—and for *no* reason at all—and how many times you become angry, for no reason at all, and then you will see that you are living in an inner world, a subjective world of your own. Understanding means understanding these fundamentals of life's functioning. And if you understand these fundamentals, transformation is not difficult. In fact, understanding itself becomes the transformation.

> *How can a troubled mind*
> *Understand the way?*
> *If a man is disturbed*
> *He will never be filled with knowledge.*

THE WORD 'KNOWLEDGE' DOES NOT MEAN WHAT *you* mean by knowledge. When Buddha uses the word 'knowledge' he means wisdom, not information; he means knowing, not knowledge.

If a man is disturbed...

is in conflict, is in confusion, is in a divide, is split inside, if a man is a crowd within...

He will never be filled with wisdom.

Wisdom needs unity, wisdom needs integration, wisdom needs a crystallization of awareness, of watchfulness, of watching your acts, your moods, your thoughts, your emotions...of watching everything that is happening in your inner world. By just watching it, a miracle starts happening. If you start seeing that you tell lies for no reason at all, just that very awareness will become a hindrance. Next time you are just on the verge of telling a lie a voice within you will say, "Watch, beware—you are moving into the trap again." The next time you are falling into sadness, something inside you will make you alert, will alarm you.

This is the path of transforming your energies—*ais dhammo sanantano. Ais maggo visuddhia*—this is the way of purification, this is the eternal law of transformation.

> *An untroubled mind,*
> *No longer seeking to consider*
> *What is right and what is wrong,*
> *A mind beyond judgements,*
> *Watches and understands.*

So the first requirement for a sannyasin is:

> *An untroubled mind,*
> *No longer seeking to consider*
> *What is right and what is wrong...*

A tremendously important and revolutionary statement. Buddha is saying: Don't consider what is right and what is wrong, because if you consider what is right and what is wrong you will be divided, you will become a hypocrite. You will pretend the right and you will do the wrong. And the moment you consider what is right and what is wrong, you become attached, you become identified. You certainly become identified with the right.

For example: you see on the side of the road a hundred-rupee note; it may have fallen from somebody's pocket. Now the question arises: To take it or not to take it? One part of you says, "It is perfectly right to take it. Nobody is looking, nobody will ever suspect. And you are not stealing —it is just lying there! If you don't take it, somebody else is going to take it anyway. So why miss it? It is perfectly right!"

But another part says, "This is wrong—this money does not belong to you, it is not yours. In a way, in an indirect way, it is stealing. You should inform the police, or if you don't want to be bothered with it, then go ahead, forget all about it. Don't even look back. This is greed and greed is a sin!"

Now these two minds are there. One says, "It is right, take it," the other says, "It is wrong, don't take it." With which mind are you going to identify yourself? You are certainly going to identify with the mind which says it is immoral, because that is more ego satisfying. "You are a moral person, you are not ordinary; anybody else would have taken the hundred-rupee note. In such times of difficulties, people don't think of such delicacies." You will identify yourself with the moral mind. But there is every possibility you will take the note. You will identify yourself with the moral mind, and you will disidentify yourself from the mind which is going to take the note. You will condemn it deep down; you will say, "It is not right—it is the sinner part of me, the lower part, the condemned part." You will keep yourself aloof from it. You will say, "I was against it. It was my instinct, it was my unconscious, it was my body, it was my mind, which persuaded me to do it. Otherwise, I knew it, that it was wrong. I am the one who knows that it was wrong."

You always identify yourself with the right, the moralistic attitude, and you disidentify from the immoral act—although you do it. This is how hypocrisy arises.

St. Augustine has said in his confessions: "God, forgive me, because I go on doing things which I know I should not do, and also I don't do things which I know I should do."

This is the conflict, this is how one becomes troubled. Hence Buddha gives you a secret key. This is the key that can take you out of all identification: don't be identified with the moral mind—because that too is part of the mind. It is the same game: one part saying good, another part saying bad—it is the same mind creating a conflict in you. Mind is always dual. Mind lives in polar opposites. It loves and it hates the same person; it wants to do the act and it does not want to do the act. It is conflict: mind is conflict. Don't get identified with either.

Buddha is saying: Become just a watchfulness. See one part is saying this, another part is saying that. "I am neither —*neti neti*—neither this nor that—I am just a witness." Only then is there a possibility that understanding will arise.

> *An untroubled mind,*
> *No longer seeking to consider*
> *What is right and what is wrong,*
> *A mind beyond judgements,*
> *Watches and understands.*

To go beyond judgements of good and bad is the way of

watchfulness. And it is through watchfulness that transformations happen. This is the difference between morality
and religion. Morality says, "Choose the right and reject
the wrong. Choose the good and reject the bad." Religion
says, "Simply watch both. Don't choose at all. Remain in
a choiceless consciousness."

Religion is very very different from morality. Morality
is very ordinary, mundane, mediocre; morality cannot take
you to the ultimate, it is not the way of the divine. Morality
is only a social strategy. That's why one thing is right in
one society and the same thing is wrong in another society;
one thing is thought to be good in India and the same thing
is thought to be bad in Japan. One thing is thought to be
good today and may become wrong tomorrow. Morality
is a social by-product; it is a social strategy to control. It
is the policeman inside you, the judge inside you—it is a
trick of the society to hypnotize you according to certain
conceptions that the society wants to be imposed upon
people. So if you are born in a vegetarian family, then the
non-vegetarians are the greatest of sinners.

One Jaina monk once told me that "I love your books, but
why do you mention Jesus, Mohammed and Ramakrishna
with Mahavira? You should not mention them in the same
line! Mahavira is Mahavira—how can he be compared and
put in the same way, in the same category with Jesus,
Mohammed and Ramakrishna?"

I said, "Why not?!"

He said, "Jesus drinks wine, eats meat—what greater sin
can one commit?"

Mohammed ate meat and got married to nine women!
One has to renounce the woman—and not only one but
nine! A perfect number. In fact, there are no more numbers;
nine is the last number, then again repeats the same. . . .

"Mohammed got married to nine women, was a meat-eater—how can you put Mohammed with Mahavira? And how can you put Ramakrishna with Mahavira? He used to eat fish."

A Bengali is bound to eat fish.

His only criticism of my books is that I have put these people together.

Now ask a Christian...I once asked a Christian missionary, "What do you say about this Jaina monk—he has said this? Have you any objection?"

He said, "Certainly! How can you put Mahavira with Jesus? Jesus lived for humanity, sacrificed himself for humanity—what has Mahavira done? Mahavira is utterly selfish; he thinks only of his own salvation. He cares nothing about others! He never healed a blind person, he never raised a dead person from death. He was just meditating for twelve years in the mountains, in the forests—what more selfishness...? And the world is suffering and people are in great pain, and he didn't come to console them. What more luxury can there be? Just meditating by the side of a river in the forest—what *more* luxury! What has he done for the poor humanity? Jesus sacrificed himself—he lived and died for others. His whole life was nothing but pure sacrifice. How can you put Mahavira with Jesus?!"

And he too seems to be right. Now how do you decide? Buddha never healed the sick, the blind, the deaf, the dumb —just meditated. Seems to be selfish! He should have opened hospitals, or at least schools; should have distributed medicine, should have gone to the flood areas and served people ...he never did anything like that. What kind of spirituality is this? According to a Christian, it is pure selfishness.

Now who is right? And who is going to decide? We live according to our prejudices.

The Jaina monk is wrong and the Christian missionary is wrong, because both are judging—and to judge is wrong. Jesus is Jesus! He lives in his own way. Buddha is Buddha; he lives in his own way. Unique personalities, unique expressions of God. Neither is a copy of the other, and neither needs to be a copy of the other. And it is beautiful that the world has variety. If there were only Jesuses and Jesuses again and again, they would look like Ford cars coming out on an assembly line—each second a Ford car coming out, the same, exactly the same as each other. It is beautiful that Jesus is one and simply one and unrepeatable. And it is good the Buddha is alone and unrepeatable.

A really religious person has a non-judgemental approach. The moralist cannot avoid judgements; he becomes a judge. Now, this Jaina monk, an ordinary person, stupid, is ready to judge Jesus, Ramakrishna, Mohammed. Knows nothing, understands nothing, has never meditated—has not known himself yet. That's why he had come to me.

He had come to me to understand what meditation is and how to meditate. Meditation has not happened yet, but judgement is there—and he is ready to judge even a man like Jesus, is not even ashamed of what he is doing, is not shy, is very arrogant. And so is the case with the Christian missionary! He knows nothing of meditation, what Buddha was doing, what Mahavira was doing. He knows nothing of the subtle ways in which a Buddha functions. Just his becoming enlightened is the greatest service to humanity possible—nothing more can be done. He has certainly not cured physical eyes, but he is the man who has cured thousands of people's spiritual eyes—and that is real service! He has made thousands of people hear, listen, understand—*that* is real service.

But this Christian missionary, because he runs a primary school and a hospital, thinks himself somebody who is authorized to judge. The moralist always judges, the religious person never judges. He lives in a non-judgemental consciousness.

> *A mind beyond judgements,*
> *Watches and understands.*

He simply watches and understands. If Buddha had come across Jesus, he would have understood; if Jesus had come across Mahavira, he would have understood. Just watching, seeing, and there is understanding.

> *Know that the body is a fragile jar,*
> *And make a castle of your mind.*

BY 'MIND' BUDDHA MEANS CONSCIOUSNESS. BY 'Mind' Buddha means Mind with a capital M—not this ordinary mind that you have but the Mind which happens when all thoughts have disappeared, when the mind is utterly empty of thoughts. Make a castle of your mind because this body is going to die—don't depend on it.

> *In every trial*
> *Let understanding fight for you*
> *To defend what you have won.*

And remember continuously, because the struggle is long, and the journey is arduous. Many times you will fall and forget, many times you will start judging. Many times you will start getting identified with this or that, many times the ego will assert itself again and again. Whenever the ego asserts itself, whenever identification happens, whenever judgement arises, immediately remember: watch, simply watch, and there will be understanding.

And understanding is the secret of transformation. If you can understand anger, immediately you will be showered with compassion. If you can understand sex, immediately you will attain to samadhi. 'Understanding' is the most important word to remember.

> *For soon the body is discarded.*
> *Then what does it feel?*
> *A useless log of wood, it lies on the ground.*
> *Then what does it know?*

Don't depend on the body and don't remain confined to the body. Use it, respect it, love it, care for it, but remember: you have to leave it one day. It is only a cage, it will be left behind, and the bird will be gone. Before that happens, take care of the bird too. Cleanse your consciousness because that will be going with you. Your understanding will go with you, not your body.

So don't waste too much time in decorating it with cosmetics, with clothes, with ornaments—don't waste too much time with the body, because the body belongs to the earth and the earth will claim it back. Dust unto dust. You don't belong to the earth: you belong to some beyond, to some unknown. Your home is in the unknown; here you are only a visitor. Enjoy the visit and use it as much as possible to grow in understanding and maturity, so that you can take home your maturity, your understanding, your wisdom.

> *Your worst enemy cannot harm you*
> *As much as your own thoughts, unguarded.*

32

When thoughts are unguarded, unwatched, your mind is your greatest enemy.

> *But once mastered,*
> *No one can help you as much,*
> *Not even your father or your mother.*

But the same mind, if mastered—mastered by watchfulness, mastered by meditation—is transformed. It becomes the greatest friend. Nobody can help you as much as it.

The mind is a ladder: unguarded it takes you downwards, guarded it takes you upwards. The same ladder! The mind is a door: unguarded it takes you outward, guarded it takes you inward. The same mind unguarded becomes anger, hatred, jealousy; guarded it becomes compassion, love, light.

Be watchful, be awake, be alert, be non-judgemental. Don't be a moralist: create a religious consciousness. And by 'religious consciousness' is meant a choiceless awareness. Let this phrase sink deep in your heart: choiceless awareness. This is the very essence of Buddha's teaching—*ais dhammo sanantano.*

*would you speak more about
the new phase of your work?*

what is the key to this puzzle?

God is dead. . . ?

*can you say something
about guilt and fear?*

July 2

Drink to the Full and Dance!

The first question

Bhagwan,
Would you please speak more about the new phase of your work? Sri Ramakrishna, Sri Raman, and even J. Krishnamurti, appear one-dimensional. Did Gurdjieff attempt a multi-dimensional approach? Was it the cause of his being so greatly misunderstood?

Ajit Saraswati,

I T IS BUT NATURAL TO BE MISUNDERSTOOD IF you really want to help people. If you don't want to help them, you will never be misunderstood—they will worship you, they will praise you. If you only talk, if you only philosophize, then they are not afraid of you. Then you don't touch their lives.

And it is beautiful to know complex theories, systems of thought. It helps their egos, it nourishes their egos—they become more knowledgeable. And everybody likes to be more knowledgeable. It is the subtlest nourishment for the ego.

But if you *really* want to help them, then the problem arises. Then you start changing their lives, then you start trespassing their egos, then you start interfering with their centuries and centuries old habits and mechanisms. Then you create antagonism: they are afraid of you, they are inimical towards you. And they will try in every possible way to misunderstand you, to misrepresent you.

One-dimensional people are beautiful flowers, but not of much use. Krishnamurti has been talking for forty or more years, and people listen! And the same people have been listening to him for forty years...and not an iota of change in their consciousness. Certainly they have become very knowledgeable, argumentative, logical. If you discuss with them—they are the best people to discuss anything with— they go into the most subtle, delicate worlds of thought. They can analyse everything: awareness, meditation, consciousness.... They have become very efficient, very clever, but they remain as mediocre as ever, as stupid as ever, with only one difference: now their stupidity is garbed behind their so-called knowledge that they have gathered from J. Krishnamurti.

Krishnamurti has remained just an intellectual phenomenon, because he never took the trouble to enter into people's lives. It is dangerous to enter into people's lives— you are playing with fire.

Sri Raman is perfectly okay: sitting silently in his temple, people can come, offer flowers, worship, and he will simply watch. And, of course, he has a beauty and a grace, but it is one-dimensional; it does not affect life in its totality. At the most, people can be moved by it emotionally; just as J. Krishnamurti moves people intellectually, Sri Raman moves people emotionally.

And the same was the case with Ramakrishna. Many

people's emotions were touched, and they would cry tears of joy. But it is not going to transform you. Those tears of joy are momentary; back home you will be the same.

Gurdjieff certainly is a pioneer. With Gurdjieff begins a totally new concept of spiritual life. He has actually called his way 'the fourth way'—just as *I* call my way 'the fourth way' he also calls his way 'the fourth way'. He was immensely misunderstood—because he was not interested in imparting knowledge to you, he was not interested in consoling you. He was not interested in giving you beautiful theories, visions, hallucinations. He was not interested in your tears, in your emotions and sentiments. He was not interested in being worshipped by you, he was interested in transforming you.

And to transform a person means you have to take a hammer in your hands, because many chunks of that person's being have to be cut. The person is so topsy-turvy that everything is wrong as it is, and it has to be put right. And he has invested so much in his wrong way of life that anybody who wants to change his style of life—not only the circumference but the center too—he becomes afraid of, he is scared of. Only a few courageous people can enter into the world of a man like Gurdjieff. Tremendous courage is needed, a courage to die, because only then is one reborn.

Gurdjieff was a midwife. He was not a teacher, he was a Master. Krishnamurti remained a teacher. Raman remained a beautiful individual—enlightened, but just a faraway, distant star. You could watch and you could appreciate and you could write poetry about it, but that's all. It remained a distant phenomenon. You could never hope to reach him; the distance was vast. And there was no effort from his side to bridge it. And what could you do? How could *you* bridge it? If you had been capable of bridging yourself with

a man like Raman, there would have been no need to make
the bridge. A man of that capacity would be able to transform himself on his own; he would not need a Master. Unless
Raman tried to make the bridge, the bridge was not possible.

And he was aloof, distant, cool. He was not involved. He
knew all misery is false. And, certainly, it is so—but not
for those who are in misery. The man who is awake knows
that the person who is crying and weeping in his sleep is
seeing a dream, true. As far as the man who is awake is
concerned, it's perfectly true. But even though it is a dream,
a nightmare, for the person who is fast asleep it is a truth.
And the man who is fast asleep cannot make any effort to
connect himself with the awakened man. Obviously, it is
impossible. He cannot even be aware that somebody is
awake; he is so much engrossed in his nightmare. Only the
awakened can make the effort. But to disturb somebody's
sleep, even though he is in a nightmare, is dangerous.
Nobody wants to be disturbed, nobody wants to be
interfered with.

People have strange ideas—sleepy people, idiotic people,
but they have strange ideas of freedom. They have *no* freedom! They *can't* have. They can't afford it in their sleep.
How can a sleepy man have any freedom? But they have
ideas, great ideas of freedom, and a man like Gurdjieff
interferes. His compassion is far greater than the compassion
of J. Krishnamurti, Raman, and Ramakrishna.

Ramakrishna is beautiful—singing the praise of God,
praying, worshipping, dancing. He is something of the
beyond. He reminds you that much more is possible in life
than is happening to you—but that's all. Through him just
a little remembrance can reach you. But your life is such
that that remembrance is not going to create any mutation;
it will be forgotten. You will enjoy it. Again and again you

would like to go to the man and see him dancing and singing and praying...and you will feel good.

This is what Buddha calls 'counting the sheep of others'. He is a beautiful flower, but by looking at a rose you cannot become the rose; neither can you become a Ramakrishna by looking at Ramakrishna.

Great effort is needed. You have to climb the mountain against all hazards. Unless a Master tries to approach you in your deep sleep, unless he stirs your being, holds you hard and takes you out of your ignorance, it is impossible, it is almost impossible. But you will be angry at this man—who wants to be disturbed? One has become accustomed to a certain way of life; mind always likes the old, the known, the familiar. Even though it is miserable, still the mind is afraid of the new, because with the new you have to learn again how to behave, how to be. And who wants to learn? You are so efficient with the old, your ego is so satisfied with the old—why bother?

And when you come across a man like Gurdjieff, he shatters all the nonsense that you have gathered. He shatters mercilessly! Sometimes he has to say things which are not really true, but just to shatter your ideas he has to say them.

A friend has asked: "How was it possible that a man like Gurdjieff, a man of such great understanding, did not understand the idea of kundalini energy?"

He called it kundabuffer. He was very much against the idea of kundalini. He used to say that the worst thing that could happen to a person in life is the arousal of kundalini. The questioner, naturally, is bewildered.

But you don't understand the real meaning of Gurdjieff. He called it kundabuffer because of the nonsense that theo-sophists have created in the world. They talked so much about kundalini, the serpent power! And it was all gibberish;

they knew nothing about it. They were just fabricating, they were just inventing theories and ideas. It was *all* guesswork.

In fact, out of a hundred books that are written about kundalini, ninety-nine are absolute nonsense. And the people who had gathered around Gurdjieff had come through theosophical philosophy, hypotheses, doctrines. He was shattering their knowledge; he was not saying anything against kundalini. How could he say that? He knew far better than Blavatsky, Annie Besant, Alcott, Leadbeater—he knew far better than these people. These people were only experts in creating doctrines, and really they were great experts. They had created almost a world movement—about auras and colours and kundalini. . .new words from the ancient spiritual lore. And they created worlds, imaginary worlds, around those words.

Gurdjieff is right to call it kundabuffer. And Gurdjieff is right in saying that the worst thing that can happen to a man is the arousal of kundalini. But remember always that he was talking to his disciples, in a particular context. He was shattering the knowledge of his disciples about kundalini power—because the first step of a Master is to destroy your knowledge, because your knowledge is basically false, borrowed.

Before you can be made familiar with the truth, the untrue has to be taken away. And sometimes the Master has to be very merciless. And sometimes the Master has to say things which are not really so. Kundalini is not a wrong idea, but for ninety-nine percent of people, Gurdjieff is right.

Now, there are again people like Gopi Krishna, who are writing books on kundalini and the serpent power, and the great genius that comes through it. It has not even happened to Gopi Krishna! What kind of genius has he? At the most, the only proof that he has given of his genius is some absolutely worthless poetry, just like the poetry schoolchildren write. He has been a clerk his whole life. His poetry smells of his whole life's clerkship—it stinks! It has no beauty, it has no grandeur—it has nothing of the superb.

And now he is propounding around the world that when kundalini arises your latent power of genius becomes manifest. How many yogis have won the Nobel Prize? And how many yogis have contributed to the world's scientific knowledge, art, poetry, painting, sculpture? How many of your people whose so-called kundalini has arisen have contributed in any way to the world's richness?

What Gopi Krishna is talking about is not kundalini but kundabuffer. Gurdjieff would have put him right with a single blow. But he attracts people. People are very much attracted by mystical nonsense, by occult stupidity, by esoteric gibberish. Just start talking with people about chakras, centers of energy, and kundalini passing through them, and they are all-attentive. You just try it! There is no need to know anything about it—just invent...because Jaina mystics have not talked about kundalini, Buddhist mystics have not talked about kundalini, Christian mystics have never known anything about it, Sufis are absolutely unaware of this energy called kundalini. Only Hindu yoga talks about it.

There *is* something in it, but not exactly the way it is told to people. The knowledge that is floating around about kundalini is all nonsense, and Gurdjieff was right to condemn it. He was condemning the whole theosophical movement. Theosophists were very much against Gurdjieff. They knew nothing, but they created a great movement. They were more or less political people, scholars, logic-choppers, but not in any way realized souls.

Gurdjieff shattered many beliefs. He shattered one of the *most* fundamental beliefs of the whole of humanity. He said, "There is no soul. You are not born with a soul—the soul has to be created by great effort. And only very rare people have been able to create it. The millions of people walking on the earth are all soulless."

Now, can you create a greater shock?—just telling people: "You are soulless. There is nothing inside you—hollow, nobody inside you. You are not yet born; you are just a body, a mechanism. Yes, you have a possibility, a potentiality, to become a soul, but then you have to do much work for it, great work for it, and only then is it possible to have a soul. It is the ultimate luxury to have a soul."

Now, down the ages, priests have been telling you that you are born with a soul. That has created a very wrong state of affairs. Because everybody has been told he is born with a soul, he thinks, "Then why bother? I am already a soul. I am immortal. The body will die but I am going to live." Gurdjieff said, "You are nothing but the body, and when the body dies *you* will die. Only once in a while does a person survive—one who has created soul in his life survives death—not all. A Buddha survives, a Jesus survives, but not you! You will *simply* die, not even a trace will be left."

What was Gurdjieff trying to do? He was shocking you to the very roots; he was trying to take away all your consolations and foolish theories which go on helping you to postpone work upon yourself. Now to tell people, "You don't have any souls, you are just vegetables"—just cabbage or maybe a cauliflower; a cauliflower is cabbage with a college education—"but nothing more than that." He was really a Master par excellence. He was taking the very earth away from underneath your feet. He was giving you such a shock that you had to think over the whole situation: are you going to remain a cabbage? He was creating a situation around you in which you would have to seek and search for the soul, because who wants to die?

And the idea that the soul is immortal has helped people to console themselves that they are not going to die, that death is just an appearance, just a long sleep, a restful sleep, and you will be born again. Gurdjieff says, "All nonsense. This is all nonsense! Dead, you are dead for ever. *Unless* you had created the soul...." Now see the difference: you have been told you are already a soul, and Gurdjieff changes it totally. He says, "You are not already a soul, but only an opportunity. You can use it, you can miss it."

And I would like to tell you that Gurdjieff was just using a device. It is not true. Everybody is born with a soul. But what to do with people who have been using truths as consolations? A great Master sometimes has to lie—and only a great Master has the right to lie—just to pull you out of your sleep.

For example, you are fast asleep and I shake you and shake you and you don't budge. And then I start shouting "Fire! Fire!" and you start running out of the house. Outside we will settle the matter. I will say that there is no fire...but this was the only way to wake you up.

Once you have known the soul, Gurdjieff will whisper in your ear, "Now don't be worried. Forget all about what I was telling you. But it was needed. It was a device. I had to shout 'Fire!' otherwise you were not going to get out of your sleep."

But these people are bound to be misunderstood. To understand a man like Gurdjieff is an almost impossible job.

You can understand him only if you go with him, if you go along with him. And the work that Gurdjieff did was a very secret work—it can't be otherwise. Real work can be done only in a mystery school. It is hidden, it is underground. It is *not* public and it cannot be public.

In the middle ages the mystics disappeared behind the garb of alchemy; they had to disappear because of the Christians. The Christians were destroying all kinds of sources which were in any way in conflict with Christian ideology. They were not allowing anybody to practise anything else; even to talk about anything else was not permitted: "Christianity and only Christianity is the way."

The mystics had to disappear. They created a beautiful deception: they created the idea of alchemy. They started saying, "We are alchemists; we have nothing to do with spirituality. All that is rot. We are seeking and searching for the secret of immortal life, of eternal youth. We are trying to find ways and means to transform base metals into gold." And just to deceive the public they made chemistry labs. If you had entered into an alchemist's world, you would have encountered jars and medicines and herbs and test-tubes... and you would have seen a kind of lab where much chemical work was going on. But this was only a facade; this was not the real work—the real work was happening somewhere else deep down in the school.

The real work was to create integral, crystallized human beings, to create wakefulness. The real work was meditation, but Christianity does not allow meditation. It says prayer is enough. It does not allow inward search. It says worshipping God is enough, going every Sunday to the church is enough, reading the Bible is enough. It has given you toys—and that's how it has happened in other countries too.

In India too the mystics have lived in disguise.

Just the other day I was reading a Sufi story—and Gurdjieff is basically rooted in the Sufi tradition. He is a Sufi. He learnt his secrets from the Sufis.

I was reading a Sufi story:

A disciple came to the Master and said, "I am in trouble. The trouble is that the richest man of the town is going on a pilgrimage. He has a beautiful daughter, and I have a great reputation because of all the discipline that I have gone through and the character that I have cultivated. I have such a reputation in the town that he wants me to take care of his beautiful daughter while he is on his pilgrimage. And I am afraid—I know my temptations. And the girl is really beautiful; in fact I have always been infatuated with her. I have been avoiding. . . ! This is too much: for six months or nine months she will be living with me. I cannot trust myself. What should I do?"

The Master said, "I know a man who knows the secret. You go to him."

And he told him to go to another village where a madman lived. He said, "But what can that madman. . . I know about that madman, I have heard much about that madman. He is utterly mad! How can he help me?"

The Master said, "You just go, but go very watchfully. Watch everything that is happening there."

He went to the madman. A very beautiful young boy was pouring wine and the madman was drinking.

Now, Mohammedan countries have been, down the ages, homosexual, very much—so much so that it is only the Mohammedan paradise which is gay. It is far more advanced than any other paradise. In the Hindu paradise there is no place for a gay person. In the Christian paradise, no, not at all. Even the Jewish God is very much against homosexuality, very angry. But the Mohammedan God is very lenient. Not only are beautiful women provided for the virtuous, but beautiful boys too.

This beautiful young boy pouring wine and the madman drinking...this man felt great hatred, condemnation. But because the Master had said, "Watch and go and ask him for advice...." he forgot all about his problem. First he asked, "Please tell me what is happening? What are you doing?"

The madman laughed and he said, "This boy is my son. And, come close...my glass contains only water—what he is pouring is not wine."

The man asked, "Then why are you pretending that you are drinking wine? Nobody sips water the way you are sipping. The flask from which he is pouring water is not used for keeping water—then *why*?"

The madman laughed and said, "So that nobody entrusts his beautiful daughter to me when he goes on a pilgrimage. This is a device!"

He must have read the thought; he must have been telepathic. He must have seen this man through and through. "So that nobody entrusts his beautiful daughter to me, so nobody bothers. So that I am left alone. But please don't tell my secret to anybody, otherwise I will have to move from this town to another town. My madness is a rumour created by me. My characterlessness is a rumour created by me. And if *you* really want to work on yourself," said the madman, "you should do likewise. Go back. Start behaving foolishly, stupidly, madly, immorally—at least pretend!—and nobody will bother you."

Gurdjieff lived a life which was very mysterious; it was

not public. His school was a hidden school. What was happening there, people were simply guessing.

And that's what is going to happen in the new phase of my work. My commune will become hidden, underground It will have a facade on the outside: the weavers and the carpenters and the potters...that will be the facade. People who will come as visitors, we will have a beautiful show-room for them; they can purchase things. They can see the creativity of the sannyasins: paintings, books, wood-work.... They can be shown around—a beautiful lake, swimming pools, a five star hotel for them—but they will not know what is really happening. That which will be happening will be almost all underground. It has to be underground otherwise it cannot happen.

I have a few secrets to impart to you, and I would not like to die before I have imparted them to you—because I don't know anybody else now alive in the world who can do that work. I have secrets from Taoism, secrets from Tantra, secrets from Yoga, secrets from Sufis, secrets from Zen people...I have lived in almost all the traditions of the world; I have been a wanderer in many lives. I have gathered much honey from many flowers.

And the time, sooner or later, will come when I will have to depart—and I will not be able to enter again in the body. This is going to be my last life. All the honey that I have gathered I would like to share with you, so that you can share it with others, so that it does not disappear from the earth.

This is going to be a very secret work. Hence, Ajit Saraswati, I cannot speak about it. I think I have already spoken too much! I should not have said even this.

The work will be only for those who are utterly devoted.

Right now, we have a big press office to make as many people as possible aware of the phenomenon that is happening here. But in the new commune the real work will simply disappear from the world's eyes. The press office will function—it will function for other purposes. People will go on coming, because from the visitors we have to choose, we have to invite people who can be participants, who can dissolve in the commune. But the real work is going to be absolutely secret. It is going to be only between me and you.

And there will not be much talk between me and you either. More and more I will become silent, because the real communion is through energy, not through words. As you will be getting ready to receive the energy in silence, I will become more and more silent. But I am keeping a great treasure for you. Be receptive....

And as my work goes underground and becomes more secret and more mysterious, more and more rumours and gossip are bound to spread all over the world. People become very suspicious of anything secret. And because they cannot find any clue, they start inventing their own ideas about what is happening there. So be ready for that too.

But don't be worried about it. It is going to be a mystery school—such schools existed when Zarathustra was alive; he created such a school. Many such schools existed in Egypt, India, Tibet. When Pythagoras came and visited this country he noted the fact of the mystery schools. He was initiated into many mystery schools in Egypt and in India. Jesus was trained by the Essenes, a very secret mystery school.

All that is beautiful and all that is great in human history has happened only through a few people who put their energies together for the inner exploration. My commune is going to be a mystery school for inner exploration. It is the greatest adventure there is, and the greatest dance too.

The second question

Bhagwan,
What is the key to this puzzle?
The Buddha says, Speak less: and silence
  feels beautiful,
For what have I to say?
Tales of the past, dreams of the future,
Giddy gossip or reasoned argument,
All taste phoney to the tongue.
Silence is beautiful,
And yet...
The sound of merry chatter over teacups
Echoes the carefree chirping of the birds—
Energy flowing in a joyous cosmos.
Bhagwan, tell me,
What is the key to this puzzle?

Nirgun,

DON'T TAKE GAUTAM THE BUDDHA TOO seriously. Silence *is* beautiful, certainly it is beautiful. But who has told you that gossipping is not beautiful? In fact, the more you enjoy gossipping, the deeper will be your silence.

These are polar opposites and they balance each other.

49

If you work hard in the day, you will sleep a deep sleep in the night. Polar opposites: hard work brings a deep sleep. Illogical! The logical thing would have been that you rested the whole day, practised rest the whole day, and then you sleep a deep deep sleep in the night. That would have been logical, but God is illogical.

That seems to be perfectly right: the whole day you practised rest—naturally you should have more rest in the night than anybody else who has not practised it! And the man who has been doing just the opposite—hard work, tilling the ground, digging in the earth, working in the garden, chopping wood, carrying water from the well—the whole day he was perspiring, working hard, a tiring work, by the evening he is utterly tired—logically he should not be able to sleep at all because he practised the opposite. But this is not how life functions.

Life functions through the polar opposites. Life is not logical: life is dialectical. It is a dialectics: thesis, antithesis, and they both balance and become synthesis; then synthesis functions again as a thesis and creates its antithesis. . . and so on and so forth. Life is not Aristotelian but Hegelian.

It is perfectly good to gossip. And when you gossip, gossip totally—let it be a meditation! Knowing perfectly well that it is gossip, still it can be enjoyed. In fact, it can be enjoyed more because it is just gossip! And then fall silent.

The chirping of the birds is beautiful, but have you watched that when suddenly it stops there is great silence? The silence is deepened by the songs of the birds. The silence that follows the storm is the deepest, the most profound.

Nirgun, don't take Buddha too seriously. He can be taken too seriously—he is a one-dimensional man. What I am saying. . . if you had asked the same question of Buddha, he would not have said the same thing. He would have said: "Nirgun, you are coming to the right point. Stop gossipping and stop talking. Say only the minimum, the absolutely necessary." He would have suggested being very telegraphic. If it can be done in ten words, then don't do it in eleven words. If you can cut words more and more, so much the better.

But my own experience is that if you cut all your gossipping, all your talking, your silence will be superficial, your silence will be just a kind of sadness. It will not have depth. From where will it get depth? It can get depth only from its polar opposite.

If you really want to rest, first dance—dance to abandon. Let every fiber of your body and being dance, and then follows a relaxation, a rest, which is total. You need not do it: it happens on its own.

I am not saying that gossipping should be done to harm somebody; then it is no more gossip, it is violence; then it is no more gossip, it is something else camouflaged as gossip. Gossip should be a pure art, with no motivation—joking for joking's sake, gossipping for gossipping's sake. And then it will keep you cheerful.

And when it stops...and how long can you gossip? There is a natural limit to everything. *The sound of merry chatter over teacups* cannot continue for ever. Soon the teacups will be empty and the chatter will disappear...and then there is a profound silence.

It is good that the birds have not heard Buddha, that the trees have not heard Buddha.

Nirgun, I would not like you to become a Buddhist. I know Buddhist monks: they become very serious, too serious, so that their seriousness is a kind of disease. They cannot laugh, they cannot joke. In fact, if they read my discourses on Buddha and they come across juicy jokes, they will just close their eyes. They will not even be capable of reading them. Their whole being will withdraw, they will shrink away. They will not be able to forgive me.

Don't be too serious at all. My message is that of rejoicing. That's where I am different from Buddha—Buddha *is* a serious person. Not a single statue exists in which he is shown laughing, or even smiling. Yes, there are Chinese and Japanese statues of Buddha in which he is shown smiling and laughing sometimes—sometimes even a belly-laughter, his belly shaking. But those are Chinese and Japanese Buddhas.

In fact, if you see a Chinese statue of Buddha and an Indian statue of Buddha you will not be able to conceive *any* relationship between the two; they are so totally different. The Indian Buddha is very serious. His body is athletic: he has a big chest and a very very shrunken belly—no belly at all. And if you see the Chinese Buddha it is just the opposite: you will not find the big chest at all; it is completely lost because the belly is so big. And you can see even in marble statues that the belly is shaking with laughter. His face is totally different: it is round and gives you the sense of a child. The Indian Buddha's face is very Roman—it was made after Alexander had visited India; it is Greek and Roman. The features are not Indian. Look again at an Indian statue of Buddha: the features are *not* Indian. Alexander and his beauty impressed people so much that they imposed Alexander's face on Buddha's body.

And he is very serious, utterly serious. You cannot conceive him ever laughing. But when Buddhism reached China it met a very profound philosophy—the polar opposite. The dialectics happened there. Buddhism became the thesis and Taoism became the antithesis: the meeting of Buddha and

Lao Tzu. The Chinese statue of Buddha is a cross; it is half Gautam Buddha and half Lao Tzu. Both are mingled into each other: that belly belongs to Lao Tzu, that laughter belongs to Lao Tzu, and the silence belongs to Buddha. It has been the greatest meeting that has ever happened in the world. Out of it is born the most profound, the most significant phenomenon in all history: Zen.

Zen is neither Buddhist nor Taoist, or it is both together. It is a strange meeting. In fact, Lao Tzu and Buddha, if they had met physically, would not have agreed on *any* point. Lao Tzu was a man of laughter. He used to move from one village to another sitting on his buffalo—must have looked like a clown. And he was almost always laughing, rolling on the ground—at the whole ridiculousness of existence, at the absurdity of life.

Buddha and Lao Tzu are polar opposites. Maybe that's why both these philosophies became attracted to each other. Both were incomplete; the meeting made them more complete. Neither will Lao Tzu agree with Zen nor will Buddha agree with Zen.

I have heard a story:

In heaven, in a cafe, Buddha, Confucius and Lao Tzu, all the three are sitting, chit-chatting. And the woman, the owner of the cafe, a beautiful woman, comes. She brings the juice of life. Buddha immediately closes his eyes. He says, "I cannot look at it! It is not worth looking at—life is misery. Birth is misery, life is misery, death is misery. Remove it from my sight otherwise I cannot open my eyes!"

Confucius opens his eyes half-way—he believes in the golden mean, the middle way—just the half. Looks with half open eyes and says, "I cannot deny it without tasting it." He is a man of more scientific leanings. "How can you

53

say anything unless you experiment? You should not declare such things off-hand. So," he says, "just give me a sip." He tastes it and he says, "Buddha is right: it is bitter, it is miserable, and I completely agree and I am a witness to Buddha. But I will again say that Buddha is wrong—without tasting it, nothing should be said. Although he is right because I can approve him—on *my* witnessing he is right. But on his own he is not right."

Lao Tzu takes the whole flask and before the owner woman can say anything, he takes it down in a gulp. The whole flask he drinks, and he becomes so drunk that he starts dancing. He does not say a word—bitter or sweet, misery or bliss. When he comes a little bit to his senses, Buddha and Confucius ask him, "What do you say?"

He says, "There is nothing to say...life should be drunk to its totality, then only does one know. And when one knows, there is nothing to say. It cannot be put in *any* category. Misery or bliss are categories—life is beyond all categories. But one should know it in its wholeness, and only I know it in its wholeness. You have not even tasted it. Confucius has only tasted it, but one should not decide by the part about the whole. Only *I* can say what it is, but I am not going to say because it is not sayable. If you really want to know, I can order another flask. Drink it to the full and dance—that is the only way!"

That is the only way to know anything.

The meeting of Buddhism and Taoism is the strangest phenomenon in the world. But it was bound to happen; there is a certain inevitability in it—because such polar opposites attract each other. Just as negative and positive poles of magnetism or negative and positive electricity attract each other.

Buddhism travelled from India to China. Taoism never travelled to India, because Taoism was so utterly drunk with ecstasy, with joy—who cares? Buddhism travelled, had to travel. The seriousness became very very heavy. Once Buddha was gone, once the light was gone, then it was just like a rock on the chest of the followers—it became too heavy. They had to move to find something non-serious to balance it.

Nirgun, don't be serious about it. Enjoy your gossipping, enjoy the small things of life, the small joys of life. They *all* contribute to the enrichment of your being. And always remember: non-seriousness is one of the most fundamental qualities of a really religious person.

A sincere young man went to an understanding old rabbi for advice. "The problem is my sexual appetite. When I shake hands with a woman it is aroused—even when I pass a pretty woman on the street it is aroused. It disturbs me because I love my wife very much."

"Don't worry, son," said the rabbi. "It doesn't matter where you work up an appetite as long as you dine at home."

This rabbi is a wise man, non-serious, taking life playfully. My sannyasins have to take life very playfully—then you can have both the worlds together. You can have the cake and eat it too. And that is a real art. This world and that, sound and silence, love and meditation, being with people, relating, and being alone . . . all these things have to be lived together in a kind of simultaneity, then only will you know the uttermost depth of your being and the uttermost height of your being.

The third question

Bhagwan,
What do you say about the famous statement of
Friedrich Nietzsche that God is dead?

Neeraj,

FRIEDRICH NIETZSCHE SAYS GOD IS DEAD—THAT means he was alive before. As far as I know, he has never been alive. How can God be dead if he has never been alive? God is not a person, so he cannot be alive and he cannot be dead. To me, God is life itself! God is synonymous with existence. Hence you cannot say God is alive or God is dead. God is life! And life is for ever...it is a continuum, it is eternal, no beginning, no end.

Nietzsche was really saying that the God that people had worshipped up to then had become irrelevant. But he was very much accustomed to making dramatic statements. Rather than saying: "The God that people have worshipped up to now is no longer relevant," he said: "God is dead." And in a way, dramatic statements penetrate people's consciousness more. If he had said it in a philosophical way it may have missed the target; but it became the most important statement made in these hundred years. No other statement has had such significance, or has had such an impact on human thinking, behaviour, life.

The Christian God is dead, the Jewish God is dead— that's what Nietzsche was saying. But there have been so many Gods and all have gone down the drain; if you make a list you will be surprised how many Gods have been worshipped. One man has made a list; I was reading the list: not even a single name that he mentions is known. Near-about fifty Gods he mentions. The Egyptian Gods are no more there; not even in Egypt does anybody know about them. There was a time when for those Gods even human beings were sacrificed, wars were fought, crusades, murders, rapes; villages were burnt in the name of those Gods. Now even the names are not known. I read the whole list; out of the fifty not a single name is known. There have been many Gods invented by people; and when those people become tired of those Gods, they invent new toys and they throw the old ones.

These Gods go on being born and dying, but these are not the true God. 'True God' simply means life—*ais dhammo sanantano*—the inexhaustible law of existence. How can it die? There is no way. Forms change . . . .

It seems God visited the New York subways recently. Someone had scrawled on the wall: "God is dead—signed Nietzsche," and underneath it was written: "Nietzsche is dead—signed God."

That seems to be far truer. But an even better message for you:

A London subway has this cheerful message: "God is dead, but don't worry—Mary is pregnant again!"

The fourth question

Bhagwan,
Can you say something about guilt and fear?

Latifa,

FEAR IS NATURAL, GUILT IS A CREATION OF THE priests—guilt is man-made. Fear is in-built, and it is very essential. Without fear you will not be able to survive at all. Fear is normal. It is because of fear that you will not put your hand in the fire. It is because of fear that you will walk to the right or to the left, whatsoever is the law of the country. It is because of fear that you will avoid poison. It is because of fear that when the truck driver sounds his horn, you run out of the way.

If the child has no fear there is no possibility that he will ever survive. His fear is a life-protective measure. But because of this natural tendency to protect oneself...and nothing is wrong in it—you have the right to protect yourself. You have such a precious life to protect, and fear simply helps you. Fear is intelligence. Only idiots don't have fear, imbeciles don't have fear; hence you have to protect the idiots otherwise they will burn themselves or they will jump out of a building, or they will go into the sea without knowing how to swim or they can eat a snake...or anything they can do!

Fear is intelligence—so when you see a snake crossing the path, you jump out of the way. It is not cowardly: it is simply intelligent. But there are two possibilities.

Fear can become abnormal, it can become pathological. Then you are afraid of things of which there is no need to be afraid—although you can find arguments even for your abnormal fear.

For example: somebody is afraid of going inside a house. Logically you cannot prove that he is wrong. He says, "What is the guarantee that the house will not fall?" Now houses are known to fall so this house can also fall. People have been crushed by houses falling. Nobody can give an absolute guarantee that this house is not going to fall—an earthquake can happen...anything is possible!

Another man is afraid: he cannot travel because there are train accidents. Somebody else is afraid: he cannot go into a car—there are car accidents, and somebody else is afraid of an airplane....

If you become afraid in this way, this is not intelligent. Then you should be afraid of your bed too, because almost ninety-seven percent of people die in their beds—so that is the *most* dangerous place to be in. Logically you should remain as far away from the bed as possible, never go close to it. But then you will make your life impossible.

Fear can become abnormal, then it is pathology. And because of this possibility, priests have used it, politicians have used it. All kinds of oppressors have used it. They make it pathological, and then it becomes very simple to exploit you. The priest makes you afraid of hell. Just look in the scriptures—with what joy they depict all the tortures, with really great relish. Scriptures describe in detail, in great detail, each and every torture.

Adolf Hitler must have been reading these scriptures; he must have found great ideas from these scriptures describing hell. He himself was not such a creative genius as to invent the concentration camps and all kinds of tortures. He must have found them in religious scriptures—they are already there, priests have already done the work. He only practised what priests have been preaching. He was a really religious man!

Priests have only been talking about a hell that is waiting for you after death. He said, "Why wait so long? I will create a hell here and now. You can have a taste of it."

I have heard that once a man died, reached hell, knocked on the door; the Devil looked at him—he looked German. He asked him, "From where are you coming?"

The man said, "From Germany."

He said, "Then there is no need to come here—you have already lived it! Now you can go to heaven. And you will find our place very boring because you had a far more improved edition of hell; we are still living in the bullock-cart age—old tortures. You know far more sophisticated instruments, ways, means."

Gas chambers are still not known in hell. In a single gas chamber, ten thousand people, within seconds, can become smoke. And you will be surprised to know that although we are living in the twentieth century, man is still an animal. Thousands of people used to go to see. Glass was fitted, fixed in, one-way: you could see what was happening inside, but the insiders could not see who was looking in from the outside.

Thousands of people would stand outside watching through the glass: people disappearing in smoke—simply disappearing in smoke—thousands of people dying within seconds. And the people who were enjoying outside, can you call them human beings? But remember, it has nothing to do with Germany: this is so all over the world. Man is exactly the same everywhere.

The priests became aware very early that the fear instinct in man can be exploited; he can be made so much afraid that he will fall at the feet of the priests and will tell them, "Save us! Only you can save us." And the priest will concede to save them if they follow the priest; if they follow the rituals prescribed by the priest, the priest will save them. And out of fear people have been following the priests, and all kinds of stupidities, superstitions. . . .

The politician also became aware soon that people can be made very much afraid. And if you make them afraid, you can dominate them. It is out of fear that nations exist. The fear of America keeps Russians slaves to the communists, and the fear of Russia keeps Americans slaves to the government. Fear of each other . . . the Indians are afraid of the Pakistanis, and the Pakistanis are afraid of the Indians. It is such a *stupid* world! We are afraid of each other, and because of our fear the politician becomes important. He says, "We will save you here, in this world," and the priest says, "We will save you in the other world." And they both conspire together.

It is fear that creates guilt—but not fear itself. Fear creates guilt via the priests and the politicians. The priests and the politicians create in you a pathology, a trembling. And, naturally, man is so delicate and so fragile, he becomes afraid. And then you can tell him to do anything and he will do it—knowing perfectly well that it is stupid, knowing perfectly well deep down that it is all nonsense, but who knows . . . ? Out of fear, man can be forced to do anything.

A young woman who can't prevent herself from coughing and sneezing at the theater asks a doctor for a remedy before going to a first night. "Here, drink this," he says, offering her a glass. She drinks it, mouth awry, and asks what it was, imagining some type of bad-tasting cough medicine.

"That's a double dose of Pluto water," he answered. "Now you won't dare sneeze or cough."

... You don't get it. You have never tasted Pluto water—try, and neither will you be able to dare to sneeze or cough. Do an experiment: you can ask Ajit Saraswati for Pluto water, only then will you understand the joke—it is very existential. Because you didn't get it I will have to tell another:

One morning, a big she-bear raided Joe's cabin, scattered everything, ate everything, tore up everything, and ambled away.

Joe trailed her, shot her, and then noticing how much she resembled a woman, he satisfied his passion with her carcass. Just then he noticed another hunter cowering in the branches of a nearby tree. Realizing his deed had been observed, Joe pointed his gun at the man, made him climb down and said, "Have you ever made love to a bear?"

And the hunter said, "No, but I am getting ready to try."

Man can be forced to do anything—just to save himself. And because the pathology that the priests have created in you is unnatural, your nature rebels against it, and once in a while you do something which goes against it—you do something natural—then guilt arises.

Latifa, guilt means you have an unnatural idea in your mind about how life should be, what should be done, and then one day you find yourself following nature and you do the natural thing. You go against the ideology. Because you go against the ideology, guilt arises, you are ashamed. You feel yourself very inferior, unworthy.

But by giving people unnatural ideas you cannot transform them. Hence, priests have been able to exploit people, but they have not been able to transform them. They are not interested in transforming you either. Their whole idea is to keep you always enslaved. They create a conscience in you; your conscience is not really *your* conscience—it is created by the priests. They say, "This is wrong." You may know from the deepest core of your being that there seems to be nothing wrong in it, but they say it is wrong. And they go on hypnotizing you from your very childhood. The hypnosis goes deep, seeps deep in you, sinks deep in you, becomes almost part of your being. It holds you back.

They have told you sex is wrong—but sex is such a natural phenomenon that you are attracted towards it. And nothing is wrong in being attracted towards a woman or a man. It is just part of nature. But your conscience says, "This is wrong." So you hold yourself back. Half of you goes towards the woman, half of you is pulling you back. You can't make any decision; you are always divided, split. If you decide to go with the woman, your conscience will torture you: "You have committed a sin." If you don't go with the woman, your nature will torture you: "You are starving me."

Now you are in a double bind. Whatsoever you do you will suffer. And that's what the priest has always wanted—for you to suffer. Because the more you suffer, the more you go to him for his advice. The more you suffer, the more you seek salvation.

Bertrand Russell is absolutely right that if man is given total natural freedom—freedom from this so-called conscience and morality—and if man is helped to become an integrated, natural being, intelligent, understanding, living

his life according to his own light, not according to somebody else's advice—the so-called religions will disappear
from the world.

I perfectly agree with him: the so-called religions will
certainly disappear from the world if people are not in
suffering; they won't seek salvation. But Bertrand Russell
goes on and he says religion itself will disappear from the
earth. There I don't agree with him. The so-called religions
will disappear, and because the so-called religions will disappear there will be for the first time in the world an opportunity for religion to exist. Christians will not be there,
Hindus will not be there, Mohammedans will not be there—
only then will a new kind of religiousness spread over the
earth. People will be living according to their own consciousness. There will be no guilt, no repentance, because these
things never change people. People remain the same; they
just go on changing their outer garb, their form. Substan-
tially, nothing changes through guilt, through fear, through
heaven, through hell. All these ideas have utterly failed.

Now, it is time to recognize that all the old religions
have failed. Yes, they have created a few beautiful people—
a Buddha here and a Jesus there—but out of millions and
millions of human beings, once in a while somebody has
bloomed. It is an exception, it cannot be counted. It should
not be taken into account. Buddhas can be counted on the
fingers.

If a gardener plants ten thousand trees and only one tree
blooms in spring, will you call him a gardener? What about
the other nine thousand nine hundred and ninety-nine trees?
If this tree has bloomed, it must have bloomed in spite of the
gardener. The credit cannot go to him—he must have somehow missed it.

We have lived in a very wrong kind of world; we have created a wrong kind of situation. People only go on changing superficially: the Hindu becomes a Christian, the Christian becomes a Hindu, and nothing ever changes. All remains the same.

The reformed prostitute is giving testimony with the Salvation Army on a street-corner on a Saturday night, punctuating her discourse by beating on a big brass drum. "I used to be a sinner!" she shouts (boom!) "Used to be a bad woman (boom!) I used to drink! (boom!) Gamble! (boom!) Whore! (boom! boom!) Used to go out Saturday nights and raise hell! (boom! boom! boom!) Now what do I do Saturday nights? I stand on this street corner, beating on this mother-fucking drum!"

Who shall conquer this world
And the world of death with all its gods?
Who shall discover
The shining way of the law?

You shall, even as the man
Who seeks flowers
Finds the most beautiful,
The rarest.

Understand that the body
Is merely the foam of a wave,
The shadow of a shadow.
Snap the flower arrows of desire
And then, unseen,
Escape the king of death.

And travel on.

Death overtakes the man
Who gathers flowers
When with distracted mind and thirsty senses
He searches vainly for happiness
In the pleasures of the world.
Death fetches him away
As a flood carries off a sleeping village.

Death overcomes him
When with distracted mind and thirsty senses
He gathers flowers.
He will never have his fill
Of the pleasures of the world.

The bee gathers nectar from the flower
Without marring its beauty or perfume.
So let the master settle, and wander.

Look to your own faults,
What you have done or left undone.
Overlook the faults of others.

Like a lovely flower,
Bright but scentless,
Are the fine but empty words
Of the man who does not mean what he says.

Like a lovely flower,
Bright and fragrant,
Are the fine and truthful words
Of the man who means what he says.

Like garlands woven from a heap of flowers,
Fashion from your life as many good deeds.

July 3

And Travel On

GOD IS NOT REALLY THE CENTER OF religious enquiry but death. Without death there would have been no religion at all. It is death that makes man seek and search for the beyond, the deathless.

Death surrounds us like an ocean surrounding a small island. The island can be flooded any moment. The next moment may never come, tomorrow may never arrive. Animals are not religious for the simple reason that they are not aware of death. They cannot conceive themselves dying, although they see other animals dying; but it is a quantum leap from seeing somebody else dying to concluding that "I am also going to die." Animals are not so alert, aware, to come to such a conclusion.

And the majority of human beings are also subhuman. A man is really a mature man when he has come to this conclusion: "If death is happening to everybody else, then I cannot be an exception." Once *this* conclusion sinks deep into your heart, your life can never be the same again. You cannot remain attached to life in the old way. If it is going to be taken away, what is the point of being so possessive? If it is going to disappear one day, why cling and suffer? If it is not going to remain for ever, then why be in such misery, anguish, worry? If it is going to go, it is going to go—it does not matter when it goes. The time is not that important—today, tomorrow, the day after tomorrow. But life is going to slip out of your hands.

The day you become aware that *you are going to die*, that your death is an absolute certainty…in fact the only certainty in life is death. Nothing else is so absolutely certain. But somehow we go on avoiding this question: this question of death. We go on keeping ourselves occupied in other matters. Sometimes we talk about great things—God, heaven and hell—just to avoid the *real* question. The real question is not God, cannot be, because what acquaintance have you got with God? What do you know about God? How can you enquire about something which is absolutely unknown to you? It will be an empty enquiry. It will be at the most curiosity, it will be juvenile, childish, stupid.

Stupid people ask about God, the intelligent person asks about death. And the people who go on asking about God never find God, and the person who asks about death is *bound* to find God—because it is death that transforms you, your vision. Your consciousness is sharpened because you have raised a real question, an authentic question, the most important question of life. You have created such a great challenge that you can't remain asleep for long; you will have to be awake, you will have to be alert enough to encounter the reality of death.

That's how Buddha's enquiry began:

The day Buddha was born…he was the son of a great king, and the only son, and he was born when the king was getting old, very old. Hence there was great rejoicing in the kingdom. The people had waited long. The king was very much loved by the people; he had served them, he had been kind and compassionate, he had been very loving and very sharing. He had made his kingdom one of the richest, loveliest kingdoms of those days.

People were praying that their king should have a son because there was nobody to inherit. And then Buddha was born in the king's very old age—unexpected was his birth. Great celebration, great rejoicing! All the astrologers of the kingdom gathered to predict about Buddha. His name was 'Siddhartha'—he was given this name, Siddhartha, because it means fulfillment. The king was fulfilled, his desire was fulfilled, his deepest longing was fulfilled—he wanted a son, he had wanted a son his whole life, hence the name Siddhartha. It simply means fulfillment of the deepest desire.

This son made the king's life meaningful, significant. The astrologers, great astrologers, predicted—they were all agreeing except one young astrologer. His name was Kodanna. The king asked, "What is going to happen in the life of my son?" And all the astrologers raised two fingers, except Kodanna who raised only one finger.

The king asked, "Please don't talk in symbols—I am a simple man, I don't know anything about astrology. Tell me, what do you mean by two fingers?"

And they all said, "Either he is going to become a *Chakra-vartin*—a world ruler—or he will renounce the world and will become a Buddha, an enlightened person. These two alternatives are there, hence we raise two fingers."

The king was worried about the second alternative, that he will renounce the world. "So again the problem: who will inherit my kingdom if he renounces the world?" And then he asked Kodanna, "Why do you raise only one finger?"

Kodanna said, "I am absolutely certain that he will renounce the world—he will become a Buddha, an enlightened one, an awakened one."

The king was not happy with Kodanna. Truth is very difficult to accept. He ignored Kodanna; Kodanna was not rewarded at all—truth is not rewarded in this world. On the contrary, truth is punished in a thousand and one ways. In fact, Kodanna's prestige fell after that day. Because he was not rewarded by the king, the rumour spread that he was a fool. When all the astrologers were agreeing, he was the only one who was not agreeing.

The king asked the other astrologers, "What do you suggest? What should I do so that he does not renounce the world? I would not want him to be a beggar, I would not like to see him a sannyasin. I would like him to become a Chakravartin—a ruler of all the six continents." The ambition of all the parents. Who would like his son or daughter to renounce the world and to move into the mountains, to go into one's own interiority, to seek and search for the self?

Our desires are extrovert. The king was an ordinary man, just like everybody else—with the same desires and the same ambitions. The astrologers said, "It can be arranged: give him as much pleasure as possible, keep him in as much comfort and luxury as is humanly possible. Don't allow him to know about illness, old age, and particularly death. Don't let him come to know about death and he will never renounce."

They were right in a way, because death is the central question. Once it arises in your heart, your lifestyle is bound to change. You cannot go on living in the old foolish way. If this life is going to end in death, then this life cannot be real life; then this life must be an illusion. Truth has to be eternal if it is true—only lies are momentary. If life is momentary, then it must be an illusion, a lie, a misconception, a misunderstanding; then life must be rooted somewhere in ignorance. We must be living it in such a way that it comes to an end.

We can live in a different way so that we can become part of the eternal flow of existence. Only death can give you that radical shift.

So the astrologers said, "Please don't let him know anything about death." And the king made all the arrangements. He made three palaces for Siddhartha for different seasons in different places, so that he never came to know the discomfort of the season. When it was hot he had a palace in a certain place in the hills where it was always cool. When it was too cold he had another palace by the side of a river where it was always warm. He made all the arrangements so he never felt any discomfort.

No old man or woman was allowed to enter the palaces where he lived—only young people. He gathered all the beautiful young women of the kingdom around him so he would remain allured, fascinated, so he would remain in dreams, desires. A sweet dreamworld was created for him. The gardeners were told that dead leaves had to be removed in the night; fading, withering flowers had to be removed in the night—because who knows?—seeing a dead leaf he might start asking about what has happened to this leaf, and the question of death may arise. Seeing a withering rose, petals falling, he might ask, "What has happened to this rose?" and he might start brooding, meditating, about death.

He was kept absolutely unaware of death for twenty-nine years. But how long can you avoid? Death is such an important phenomenon—how long can you deceive? Sooner or later he had to enter into the world. Now the king was getting very old and the son had to know the ways of the world, so slowly slowly he was allowed, but whenever he would pass through any street of the capital, old men, old women, would be removed, beggars would be removed; no sannyasin was allowed to cross while he was passing, because seeing a sannyasin he might ask "What type of man is this? Why is he in orange? What has happened to him? Why does he look different, detached, distant? His eyes are different, his flavour is different, his presence has a different quality to it. What has happened to this man?" And then the question of renunciation, and fundamentally, the question of death . . . .

But one day, it *had* to happen. It can't be avoided. We are also doing the same. If somebody dies and the death procession is passing by, the mother pulls the child inside the house and closes the door.

The story is very significant, symbolic, typical. No parents want that the children should know about death, because they will immediately start asking uncomfortable questions. That's why we build the cemeteries outside the town, so that nobody need go there. Death is a central fact; the cemetery should be exactly in the middle of the city so everybody has to pass it many times in the day—going to the office, coming to the home, going to the school, college, coming to the home, going to the factory . . . so that one is reminded again and again about death. But we make the cemetery outside the town, and we make the cemetery very beautiful: flowers, trees. We try to hide death; particularly in the West, death is a taboo! Just as once sex was a taboo, now death is the taboo. Death is the last taboo.

Someone like Sigmund Freud is needed—a Sigmund Freud who can bring death back into the world, who can expose people to the phenomenon of death. When a person dies in the West, his body is decorated, bathed, perfumed, painted. Now there are experts who do this whole job. And if you see a dead man or a dead woman, you will be surprised —he looks far more alive than he ever looked when he was alive! Painted, his cheeks are red, his face bright; he seems to be fast asleep in a calm and quiet space.

We are deceiving ourselves! We are not deceiving him; he is no more there. There is nobody, just a dead body, a corpse. But we are deceiving ourselves by painting his face, by garlanding his body, putting beautiful clothes on him, carrying his body in a costly car, and a great procession and much appreciation for the person who has died. He was never appreciated when he was alive, but now nobody criticizes him, everybody praises him.

We are trying to deceive ourselves; we are making death as beautiful as we can so that the question does not arise. And we go on living in the illusion that it is always the other who dies—obviously, you will not see your own death, you will always see others dying. A logical conclusion that it is always the other who dies, so why be bothered? You seem to be the exceptional one; God has made a different rule for you.

Remember: nobody is an exception. *Ais dhammo sanantano*—only one law rules all, one eternal law. Whatsoever happens to the ant is going to happen to the elephant too, and whatsoever happens to the beggar is going to happen to the emperor too. Poor or rich, ignorant or knowledgeable, sinner or saint, the law makes no distinction—the law is very just.

And death is very communist: it equalizes people. It takes no notice of who you are. It never looks in the pages of the books published like *Who's Who*. It simply never bothers whether you are a pauper or Alexander the Great.

One day Siddhartha *had* to become aware, and he became aware. He was going to participate in a youth festival; he was going to inaugurate it. The prince, of course, was supposed to inaugurate the yearly youth festival. It was a beautiful evening; the youth of the kingdom had gathered to dance and sing and rejoice the whole night. The first day of the year—a night-long celebration. And Siddhartha was going to open it.

On the way he met what his father had been afraid of him ever seeing—he came across those things. First he saw an ill man, his first experience of illness. He asked, "What has happened?"

The story is very beautiful. It says the charioteer was going to lie, but a disembodied soul took possession of the charioteer, forced him to speak the truth. He had to say, in spite of himself, "This man is ill."

And Buddha immediately asked the intelligent question, "Then can I also be ill?"

The charioteer was again going to lie, but the soul of a god, an enlightened soul, a disembodied soul, forced him to say, "Yes." The charioteer was puzzled that he wanted to say no, but what came out of his mouth was "Yes, you are also going to be ill."

Then they came across an old man—and the same questioning. And then they came across a dead body being carried to the burning *ghat*, and the same question...and when Buddha saw the dead body and he asked, "Am I also going to die one day?" the charioteer said, "Yes, sir. Nobody is an exception. Sorry to say so, but nobody is an exception—even you are going to die."

Buddha said, "Then turn the chariot back. Then there is no point in going to a youth festival. I have already become ill, I have already become old, I am already on the verge of death. If one day I am going to die, then what is the point of all this nonsense?—living and waiting for death. Before it comes I would like to know something which never dies. Now I will devote my whole life to the search for something deathless—if there is something deathless, then the only significant thing in life can be the search for it."

And while he was saying this, they saw the fourth sight— a sannyasin, a monk, in orange, walking very meditatively. And Buddha said, "What has happened to this man?" And the charioteer said, "Sir, this is what you are thinking to do —this man has seen death happening and he has gone in search of the deathless."

The same night, Buddha renounced the world, he left his home in search of the deathless, in search of truth.

Death is the most important question in life. And those who accept the challenge of death, they are immensely rewarded.

The sutras—Buddha says:

> *Who shall conquer this world*
> *And the world of death with all its gods?*
> *Who shall discover*
> *The shining way of the law?*

He is throwing a challenge to you. He is raising a question in your heart.

He is asking:

76

Who shall conquer this world
And the world of death with all its gods?

THIS WORLD IS THE WORLD OF DEATH, AND THE gods that you have created out of your imagination are part of this world—they *are* going to die. You, your world, your gods, they are *all* going to die. Because this world is created by your desire, and the gods are also created by your desire and imagination. You don't know who you are—how can you know the real God? And how can you know the real world? Whatsoever you know is a projection, is a kind of dream. Yes, when a dream is there, it appears real. Every night you dream, and you know that while in the dream you never suspect it, you never doubt it, you never raise a question.

Gurdjieff used to say to his disciples, "Every night when you are going to sleep, when you are just on the verge and the curtain of sleep is falling on you, a little bit you remember still, not yet drowned in the darkness of sleep, a little bit of awareness and sleep is coming...those moments, those intervals between waking and sleep," Gurdjieff used to say, "those are very significant. Raise a question in your mind and go on repeating it while you are falling asleep. A simple question: Is it real? Is it for real? Go on repeating the question while you are falling asleep, so that one day in dream you can ask: Is it real?"

That day brings a great benediction. If you can ask in a dream: Is it real?—the dream immediately disappears. Here you ask, and there the dream is no more. Suddenly a great awakening happens inside. In sleep you become alert. The sleep continues, hence the tremendous beauty of its experience. The sleep continues, the body remains asleep, the mind remains asleep, but something beyond

77

body and mind becomes alert, a witness arises in you. Is it real?—if you ask it in your dream...very difficult to remember because when you are dreaming you have completely forgotten yourself. Hence the device: while falling asleep, go on repeating this question—Is it real? Is it real? Fall asleep repeating this question.

Somewhere between three and nine months, one day it happens—in dream suddenly the question arises: Is it real? And you have one of the most profound experiences of your life. The *moment* the question is raised, the dream immediately disappears, and there is utter emptiness and silence. Sleep is there and yet a small light of awareness has happened.

And then only will you be aware of this life and its illusoriness; then you will be able to see the world of desires, jealousies, ambitions, is just a dream seen with open eyes. And if you can see that this world is also a dream, you are on the verge of enlightenment.

But remember: belief won't help. You can believe this world is illusory—in India millions of people believe and repeat continuously, parrotlike: This world is *maya*, illusion—this and that. And what they are saying is all rubbish, nonsense, because it is not their authentic experience. They have heard people say it, and they are repeating. They don't *know* on their own, they are not witnesses to it. Hence it never changes their lives. They go on repeating, "This world is unreal," and they go on living in this world as much as those who think it is real—there is no difference, no qualitative difference.

What is the difference between the materialist and the so-called religious person? What difference? Because he goes to the church every Sunday? or because he goes to the temple once in a while? That is the only difference; otherwise, in actual life, you will find them exactly the same. Sometimes the irreligious person may be more honest, more authentic, more sincere, more truthful, than the religious— because the religious person is already dishonest in being religious without any experience of his own. His religiousness is based on dishonesty; he has committed the greatest dishonesty a man can commit: he believes in God and he knows nothing of God; he believes in eternal life and he has no taste of it. He has not seen *anything*, and yet he goes on pretending. His religiousness is basically dishonest, hence it is not a wonder, not a surprise that in so-called religious countries like India, you will find the people more dishonest than in the so-called materialist countries of the West.

The Western materialist is more sincere. The Indian religious person is very mean, dishonest, deceptive, because if you can even deceive God, whom are you going to leave out? If your religion is pseudo, your whole life is going to be pseudo. The person who has the guts to say, "Unless *I* know God I am not going to believe," is tacitly sincere, honest. This is my observation: that atheists have more possibility of knowing God than the so-called theists.

> *Who shall conquer this world*
> *And the world of death with all its gods?*
> *Who shall discover*
> *The shining way of the law?*

Ais dhammo sanantano—who is going to discover the eternal, inexhaustible law? *Ais maggo visuddhia*—who is going to find the path of eternal purity? of eternal innocence? Who? Buddha throws you a challenge and then says:

> *You shall, even as the man*
> *Who seeks flowers*
> *Finds the most beautiful,*
> *The rarest.*

Yes, you can conquer this world of death—because at the deepest core of your being you are part of eternity, you are not part of time. You exist in time, but you belong to eternity. You are a penetration of eternity into the world of time. You are deathless living in a body of death. Your consciousness knows no death, no birth. It is only your body that is born and dies. But you are not aware of your consciousness; you are not conscious of your consciousness. And that is the whole art of meditation: becoming conscious of consciousness itself. The moment you know who is residing in the body, who you are, in that very revelation you have transcended death and the world of death. You have transcended all that is momentary.

> *You shall, just as the man*
> *Who seeks flowers*
> *Finds the most beautiful,*
> *The rarest.*

Jesus says: Seek and ye shall find, ask and it shall be given to you, knock and the door shall be opened unto you.

A great enquiry is needed, a great seeking is needed. Just as science enquires into the objective world, religion is an enquiry into the subjective. Science enquires into that which you see, and religion enquires into the seer itself. Religion, of course, is the science of the sciences.

Science can never be more important than religion; it is impossible that science can be more important than religion, because science after all is a human endeavour. It is what you do—but who is the doer inside you? The doer can never be less than his doing. The painter can never be less than his painting, and the poet can never be less than his poetry. The scientist knows about the world but knows nothing about the scientist himself.

Albert Einstein in his last days used to say, "Sometimes I suspect my life has been a wastage. I enquired into the farthest of stars and forgot completely to enquire into myself—and I was the closest star!"

Just because we are conscious, we take it for granted—the meditator never takes it for granted. He goes in, he knocks at the door of his own inner being, he seeks and searches inside, he leaves not a single stone unturned. He enters into his own being. And great is his fulfillment, the greatest, because he finds the rarest. Yes, there are many flowers, but there is no flower like the flower of your consciousness. It is the rarest—it is the one-thousand-petalled lotus, it is a golden lotus. Unless one knows it, one knows nothing. Unless one finds it, all riches are useless, all power is futile.

> *Understand that the body*
> *Is merely the foam of a wave,*
> *The shadow of a shadow.*
> *Snap the flower arrows of desire*
> *And then, unseen,*
> *Escape the king of death.*

THE BODY IS A MOMENTARY PHENOMENON. ONE day it was not, one day it will not be again. It exists only for the time being—it is like foam. Looks so beautiful from the shore, the foam, the white foam of a wave. And if the sun has risen, around the foam can be created a rainbow. Looks so beautiful, looks like diamonds, looks so white and so pure. But if you take it in your hands, it starts disappearing. Only your hands are left wet, that's all. So is the case with the body. It looks beautiful, but death is growing in it, death is hiding in it, old age is waiting there. It is only a question of time.

It is not that at a certain date you die. In fact, the reality is that the day you are born, you start dying. The child who is one day old has died a little bit, he has died one day. He will go on dying day by day. What you call your birthday is not really your birthday—you should call it your deathday. The man who is celebrating his fiftieth birthday is really celebrating his fiftieth deathday. The death has come closer. Now, if he is going to live seventy years, only twenty years are left. Fifty years he has already died!

We are continuously dying as far as the body is concerned ...it is foam disappearing. Don't be deceived by seventy years because seventy years mean nothing in the expanse of eternity—what is the meaning of seventy years? It *is* foam, it is momentary.

> *Understand that the body*
> *Is merely the foam of a wave,*
> *The shadow of a shadow.*

It is not even the shadow, but the shadow of the shadow. Buddha wants to emphasize the unreality of it. It is the echo of the echo, very very far removed from reality. God is the real—call it truth. Buddha would like to call it *dhamma* —the law. God is the ultimate reality, then the soul is his shadow and the body is the shadow of the shadow. Move from the body to the soul and from the soul to *dhamma*— to God, to the eternal law.

Unless you achieve the eternal law, don't rest, because nobody knows—today you are here, tomorrow you may not be. Don't waste these precious days hankering, longing for futile things.

People go on collecting junk, and then one day they are gone. And then all the junk that they collected their whole lives is left behind; they cannot take a single thing with them.

It is said that when Alexander the Great died, he asked his ministers that when his casket was being carried to the grave, his hands should be left hanging outside the casket.

"Why?" the ministers asked. "Nobody has ever heard of such a thing! It is never done! It is not traditional. Why this strange eccentric idea? Why should your hands be left hanging outside the casket?"

Alexander said, "I would like to let people know that even I, Alexander the Great, am going empty-handed. I am not taking anything with me. My whole life has been a sheer wastage. I worked hard"—and he really worked hard, he struggled hard, he was a really ambitious person, mad after power, wanted to become the ruler of the world, and had more or less succeeded, had more or less become the ruler of the then known world, but even he says, "I am dying and I cannot take anything with me. Hence the whole effort has been just an exercise in futility. Let the people know, let them become aware, let them understand my foolishness, my idiocy. It may help them to understand their own life patterns, their lifestyles."

> *Snap the flower arrows of desire*
> *And then, unseen,*
> *Escape the king of death.*

If you can become desireless, then death cannot have any sway over you. It is the desiring mind that's caught in the net of death—and we are all full of desires. Desire for money, for power, for prestige, respectability—a thousand and one desires. And desires create greed and greed creates competition, and competition creates jealousy, and one thing leads to another, and we go on falling into the mess, into the turmoil of the world. It is a mad mad world, but the root cause of madness is desire.

Once you sow the seeds of desire...desire means to have more. You have a certain quantity of money, you would like to have double that; desire means the longing for more. And nobody thinks twice that any quantitative change is not going to satisfy you. If you cannot be satisfied by ten thousand rupees, how can you be satisfied by twenty thousand rupees? The rupees will be doubled. But if ten thousand rupees cannot give you any satisfaction, your satisfaction cannot be doubled; there has been no satisfaction in the first place. In fact, when you have ten thousand rupees you have a certain quantity of anxiety, fear—those anxieties will be doubled when you have twenty thousand rupees, trebled when you have thirty thousand rupees, and so on and so forth. You can go on multiplying....

And whatsoever you have, somebody will always be having more than that; it is a *big* world. Hence jealousy, and jealousy is the fever of the soul. Except meditation there is no medicine for it. The physician can help you if your body is suffering from a fever, but only a Master can help you, a Buddha can help you, if you are suffering from the fever of the soul. And very few people are suffering from the physical fever, and almost everybody is suffering from the spiritual fever—jealousy.

Jealousy means somebody else has more than you have. And it is impossible to be the first in everything. You may have the largest amount of money in the world, but you may not have a beautiful face. And a beggar may make you jealous—his body, his face, his eyes, and you are jealous. A beggar can make an emperor jealous.

Napoleon was not very tall—he was only five feet five inches. I don't see anything wrong in it; it's perfectly alright —I am five feet five inches and I have never suffered because of it, because whether you are six feet or five feet your feet reach to the earth all the same! So where is the problem? If the five foot person was hanging one foot above the earth, then there would have been a problem! But Napoleon suffered very much; he was continuously conscious of the fact that he was not tall. And, of course, he was amongst very tall people. The soldiers, the generals, they were all tall people and he was very short.

He used to stand on something higher... exactly the same was the case with the first prime minister of India, Jawaharlal Nehru. He was also five five—this five five is something! And the last viceroy of India, Lord Mountbatten, was very tall—Lady Mountbatten even taller. Now when Lord Mountbatten gave him the oath of the first prime minister you can see in the picture, those pictures are available everywhere—Nehru is standing on a step and Mountbatten is standing on the floor, just to look at least equal if not taller than Mountbatten. Then too he is not taller than Mountbatten, even standing on a step. A deep sense of inferiority.

Napoleon was continuously self-conscious. One day he was fixing a clock and his hand was not reaching; the clock was high on the wall. His bodyguard—and bodyguards are bound to be taller people, strong people—his bodyguard said, "Wait, I am higher than you, I will fix it."

Napoleon was very angry and he said, "Stupid! Apologize! You are not higher than me, you are simply taller. Change your word. Higher? What do you mean?"

Very much offended. And the poor bodyguard was not meaning anything insulting to him—he was not even aware that saying 'higher' is offensive. Now, Napoleon had everything, but the height was the problem.

It is very difficult to have everything of the world and be the first in everything. It is impossible! Then the jealousy persists, it continues. Somebody has more money than you, somebody has more health than you, somebody has more beauty than you, somebody has more intelligence than you . . . and you are constantly comparing. The desiring mind continues to compare.

Goldstein and Weinberg were in business together and having a bad time. One day, Goldstein, while taking a stroll through the woods, was all of a sudden surprised by a real fairy godmother who said to him, "I grant you three wishes, but remember, whatever you wish for, Weinberg will get double."

On his way back Goldstein pondered, "I would not mind a spacious mansion." And before he realized what was happening, there it was—his mansion. But at the same time he saw Weinberg across the road proudly viewing his two villas. Goldstein repressed his jealousy and went in to see his new home. As he walked into the bedroom, a second desire struck him: "I would not mind a woman like Sophia Loren." And sure enough, there she was—a gorgeous piece looking just like Sophia Loren. But as he looked out of the bedroom window, he saw Weinberg on his balcony with two gorgeous women.

"Well," he sighed as he thought of the fairy godmother, "you can cut off one of my balls!"

Jealousy is jealousy. . . . If you cannot have all, at least you can stop anybody else having it. Jealousy becomes destructive, jealousy becomes violence. And jealousy is the shadow of desire. Desire always compares. And, because of comparison, suffers. And people waste their lives in desiring, in being jealous, in comparing. And the precious time is simply lost. Even if God gives you three wishes, you will do the same as Goldstein—because the Jew exists in everybody. Only a Buddha is not a Jew, otherwise everybody else is.

The nature of desire is Jewish, it wants more, it is mad for more. And those who live in desire are bound to be victims of death. Only the person who understands the foolishness of desiring, of greed, of constantly longing for more, of jealousy, of comparison, one who becomes aware of all this nonsense, and drops it, goes beyond death. He becomes unseen. Buddha uses a beautiful word.

He says:

And then, unseen,
Escape the king of death.

Death can only see a person who lives in the garments of desire. Death can only see desire. If desire is dropped, you become invisible to death; death cannot touch you, because without desire you are simply pure consciousness and nothing else. You are no more identified with the body or the mind. You simply know one thing, that you are a witness. Death cannot see you: you can see death.

Ordinarily, death can see you, you cannot see death—because desire is gross, can be seen by death. Consciousness is invisible, it is not matter—it is pure energy, it is light. *You* can see death, but death cannot see you. And to see death is again a great experience, a hilarious experience. One starts laughing when one sees death—death is so impotent.

Its power is not its own: its power is in your desiring mind. *You* give power to it.

The more you desire, the more you are afraid of death. The more greedy you are, the more afraid you are. The more you have, naturally the more anxious you are: death will be coming and everything will be taken away.

> *Snap the flower arrows of desire*
> *And then, unseen,*
> *Escape the king of death.*

> *And travel on.*

Remember this sentence:

> *And travel on.*

THEN THE REAL JOURNEY, THE PILGRIMAGE, begins. Before that you were just moving in circles, the same desires: more money, more money, more power, more power...vicious circles. Not going anywhere. Once you have dropped all desiring, your consciousness is freed from the grossness of desire, now *travel on*—now you can go into the infinite existence, you can move into the eternity of existence. Now, mysteries upon mysteries go on opening in front of you. Now the whole existence is available to you—in its totality it is yours...now travel on.

> *Death overtakes the man*
> *Who gathers flowers*
> *When with distracted mind and thirsty senses*
> *He searches vainly for happiness*
> *In the pleasures of the world.*
> *Death fetches him away*
> *As a flood carries off a sleeping village.*

If you are too much distracted by desires, pleasures, grati-
fications, and if you are too thirsty in your senses for titil-
lation, if you are searching foolishly for happiness in the
outer world, then death comes and fetches you away like
a flood which carries off a sleeping village.

The man who is searching for happiness in the outside
world is a man fast asleep; he is not aware of what he is
doing, because happiness has never been found in the outside. And whatsoever appears as happiness proves ultimately
to be the source of unhappiness and nothing else. The outer
world promises only, but never delivers the goods. When
you are far away, things appear very beautiful; the closer
you come, the more they start disappearing. When you
have got them after long and arduous effort, you are simply
at a loss. You can't believe what happened—it was a mirage.

Things are beautiful only from the distance. When you
have them, they have nothing in them. Money is significant
only for those who don't have it. Those who have it, they
know the futility of it. Fame is significant only for those
who don't have it; those who have it, ask them—they are
tired of being famous, they are utterly tired of being famous.
They want to be anonymous, they want to be nobodies.

Voltaire has written in his memoirs that when he was
not famous his only desire was to be famous; he was ready
to sacrifice everything for fame. And if you go on searching for a certain thing, you are bound to get it, remember.
One day he became famous. And then he wrote, "I was
so tired of my fame, because all privacy in my life disappeared, all intimate relationship disappeared—I was so
famous that I always was crowded by people, everywhere,
wherever I would go. . . . If I went for a stroll in the garden,
then a crowd would follow. I was almost like a showpiece,
a kind of walking circus."

His fame reached such peaks that it became dangerous for his life. Once when he was coming from the station to his house after a journey, he reached home almost naked, scratched all over the body, blood oozing from many places—because in France in those days this was the superstition, that if you can get a piece of the cloth of a famous man you can also become famous. So people tore his clothes, and in tearing his clothes, they scratched his body.

He cried and wept that day, and said, "How foolish I was that I wanted to be famous. How beautiful it was when nobody knew me and I was a free man. Now I am no more a free man."

Then he wanted to be a nobody. And it happened too that the fame disappeared. In this life nothing is permanent: one day you are famous, another day you are nobody. The day he died, only four people followed him to his grave, and out of those four one was his dog—so only three really. People had completely forgotten about him. They had forgotten that he was alive; they came to know only when the newspapers published the report that Voltaire had died— then people became aware and started asking each other, "Was he still alive?"

If you have fame, you get tired of it; if you have money, you will not know what to do with it; if you are respected by people, you become a slave, because then you have to go on fulfilling their expectations, otherwise your respectability will disappear. Only when you are not famous do you think it is something significant. When you are not respected, you long for it; when you are respected, you have to pay for respectability. The more people respect you, the more closely they watch you—whether you are fulfilling their expectations or not. All your freedom is gone.

But this is how people are living.

Buddha says it is like a sleeping village—the flood comes and takes over the whole village, the flood of death comes.

> *Death overcomes him*
> *When with distracted mind and thirsty senses*
> *He gathers flowers.*
> *He will never have his fill*
> *Of the pleasures of the world.*

AND NOBODY CAN EVER BE CONTENTED IN THE world—that's impossible. You can become more and more discontented, that's all. Because contentment happens only when you go inwards; contentment is your innermost nature. Contentment does not belong to things. You can be comfortable with things—a beautiful house, a beautiful garden, no worries about money—yes, you can be comfortable. But you remain the same! Comfortably discontented. In fact, when you have all the comforts and you have nothing to do to earn money, twenty-four hours a day you are aware of your discontent, because no other occupation is left.

That's why rich people are more discontented than the poor people. It should not be so; logically it should not be so, but that's how life is. Life does not follow Aristotle and his logic. Rich people coming from the West become very puzzled when they see poor Indian people with faces of contentment. They cannot believe their eyes. These people don't have anything—why do they look contented? And the Indian so-called saints and mahatmas and political leaders, they go on bragging to the world that "Our country is spiritual—look! people are so contented even though they are poor, because they are inwardly rich." This is all nonsense.

They are not inwardly rich. The contentment that you see on poor Indian faces is not that of inward realization. It is simply because they are so preoccupied with money, bread and butter, that they can't afford any time to be discontented, they can't afford to sit and brood about their miseries. They are so miserable that they have no time to *feel* miserable! They are so miserable and they have never known any pleasure, so they cannot have any comparison.

When a society becomes rich, it has time to think, "Now what next...." And there seems to be nothing left. When all outward things are available you start thinking, "What am I doing here? All things are there, but I am as empty as ever." One starts turning inwards.

Beggars look contented because they don't have any taste of richness. But a rich person becomes very discontented; because of his richness he becomes aware of the futility of all riches.

> Death overcomes him
> When with distracted mind and thirsty senses
> He gathers flowers.
> He will never have his fill
> Of the pleasures of the world.

You cannot have your fill. It is impossible. You cannot be satisfied with things; the mind will go on asking for more. The more you have, the more troubles you will create for yourself—because you can afford troubles, you have time. In fact, you have so much time on your hands you don't know what to do with it. You will start fooling around; you will create more miseries, more anxieties for yourself. And finding no satisfaction outside, you can become so dissatisfied that you may start thinking of committing suicide.

Many more people commit suicide in rich countries than in poor countries. Or you may become so dissatisfied that you may go mad, you may go nuts. Many more people go mad in rich countries than in poor countries.

To be rich is in a way very dangerous: it can drive you towards suicide, it can drive you towards some kind of madness—but it is also very significant because it can drive you towards religion, towards your inwardness, interiority, it can become an inward revolution. It depends on you. Alternatives are open. A rich person either has to become neurotic, suicidal, or he has to become a meditator; there is no third alternative available for him.

The poor man cannot be suicidal, cannot be neurotic; he has not even enough bread, what to say of the mind? He is so tired by the evening, he cannot think, no energy to think. Falls asleep...in the morning again the old rut of earning bread. Every day he has to earn, somehow to remain alive, to survive. He cannot afford the luxuries of neurosis, he cannot afford the luxuries of psychoanalysis—these are luxuries only rich people can afford! And he cannot be really a meditator either. He will go to the temple, but he will ask for something worldly. His wife is ill; his children are not getting admission into school, he is unemployed. He goes to the temple to ask these things. The quality of the religion of the poor is very poor.

There are two kinds of religiousness in the world: the religiousness of the poor—it is very worldly, it is very materialistic—and the religiousness of the rich—it is very spiritual, very non-materialistic. When a rich man prays his prayer cannot be for money. If he is still praying for money, he is not yet rich enough.

There was a Sufi saint, Farid. Once the villagers asked him, "Farid, the great king, Akbar, comes to you so many times—why don't you ask him to open a school for poor people in our village. We don't have a school."

Farid said, "Good, so why should I wait for him to come? I will go."

He went to Delhi, he was received—everybody knew that Akbar respected him tremendously. Akbar was praying in his private mosque; Farid was allowed in. He went in, he saw Akbar praying; he was standing behind Akbar. He could hear what he was saying. With hands spread, Akbar was just finishing his prayer, his *namaj*, and he was saying to God, "Almighty Compassionate One, shower more riches on me! Give me a greater kingdom!"

Farid immediately turned away. It was just the end of the prayer, so Akbar became aware that somebody had been and had turned away; he looked back, saw Farid going down the steps, ran, touched the feet of Farid and asked, "Why have you come?"—because for the first time he had come—"and why are you going away?"

Farid said, "I had come with the idea that you are rich, but listening to your prayer I realized that you are still poor. And if you are still asking for money, for more power, then it is not good for me to ask for money, because I had come to ask for a little money to open a school in my village. No, I cannot ask from a poor man. You yourself need more. I will collect some from the village and give it to you! And as far as the school is concerned: if you are asking from God, I can ask from God directly—why should I use you as a mediator?"

The story is reported by Akbar himself in his autobiography. He says, "For the first time I became aware that, yes, I am not yet rich enough, I am not yet dissatisfied with all this money. And it has not given me anything and I go on asking for more, almost completely unconsciously! It is time for me to be finished with it. Life has flown and I am still asking for rubbish. And I have accumulated much—it has not given me anything."

But almost mechanically one goes on asking. Remember, the religion that arises when you have lived in the world and known the world and the futility of it has a totally different flavour to it from the religion which arises in you because your physical needs are not fulfilled.

The poor man's religion is poor: the rich man's religion *is* rich. And I would like a rich religion in the world. Hence I am not against technology, against industrialization; I am not against creating an affluent society—I am all for it. Because this is *my* observation: that religion reaches its climax only when people are utterly frustrated with the worldly riches. And the only way to make them utterly frustrated is to let them experience them.

> *The bee gathers nectar from the flower*
> *Without marring its beauty or perfume.*
> *So let the master settle, and wander.*

BUDDHA HAS CALLED HIS MONKS 'BEGGING', *madhukari*. *Madhukari* means collecting honey like a bee. The *bhikkhu*, the Buddhist sannyasin, goes from house to house; he never asks from just one house because that may be too much of a burden. So he asks from many houses, just a little bit from one house, a little bit from another, so he is not a burden on anybody. And he never goes to the same house again. This is called *madhukari*—like a honey bee. The bee goes from one flower to another, and goes on moving from flower to flower—it is non-possessive.

> *The bee gathers nectar from the flower*
> *Without marring its beauty or perfume.*

It only takes so little from one flower that the beauty is not marred, the perfume is not destroyed; the flower simply never becomes aware of the bee—it comes so silently and goes so silently.

Buddha says: The man of awareness lives in this world like a bee. He never mars the beauty of this world, he never destroys the perfume of this world. He lives silently, moves silently. He asks only that much which is needed. His life is simple, it is not complex. He does not gather for tomorrow —the bee never gathers for tomorrow, the today is enough unto itself.

> *So let the master settle, and wander.*

A very strange statement:....*settle* and *wander*. Settle inside, be centered inside, and outside be a wanderer. Inside utterly rooted, and outside not staying long in any one place, not staying with one person for a long time, because attachments arise, possessiveness arises, so be just like a bee.

Just the other night I was reading a poet's memoirs. He says: "I have found one thing very strange—when I fall in love with a really beautiful person, I cannot possess him or her. And if I possess, I immediately see that I am destroying the beauty of the person. If I become attached, in some way I am wounding the other person, his freedom."

The poets are sensitive people; they can become aware of many things ordinary people never become aware of. But it is a beautiful insight, of profound depth: if you are really in love with a beautiful person you would not like to possess, because to possess is to destroy. You will be like a bee; you will enjoy the company, you will enjoy the friendship, you will share the love, but you will not possess. To possess is to reduce the person to a thing. It is to destroy his spirit, it is to make him a commodity. And this can be done only if you don't love. This can be done only if your love is nothing but hate masquerading as love.

Buddha says: Just like a bee, move in the life—enjoying, celebrating, dancing, singing, but like a bee—from one flower to another flower. Have all the experiences, because it is only through experiences that you become mature. But don't be possessive, don't get stuck anywhere. Remain flowing like a river—don't become stagnant. Settle inside, certainly, become crystallized inside, but on the outside remain a wanderer.

> *Look to your own faults,*
> *What you have done or left undone.*
> *Overlook the faults of others.*

The ordinary way of human beings is to overlook one's own faults and to emphasize, magnify others' faults—this is the way of the ego. The ego feels very good when it sees, "Everybody has so many faults and I have none." And the trick is: overlook your faults, magnify others' faults, so certainly everybody looks like a monster and you look like a saint.

Buddha says: Reverse the process. If you really want to be transformed, overlook others' faults—that is none of your business. You are nobody, you are not asked to interfere, you have no right, so why bother? But don't overlook your own faults, because they have to be changed, over-come.

When Buddha says:

Look to your own faults,
What you have done or left undone...

he does not mean repent if you have done something wrong; he does not mean brag, pat your own back if you have done something good. No. He simply means to look so that you can remember in future that no wrong should be repeated, so that you can remember in future that the good should be enlarged, enhanced, and the evil should be reduced—not for repentance but for remembrance.

That is the difference between the Christian attitude and the Buddhist attitude. The Christian remembers them to repent. Hence Christianity creates great guilt; Buddhism never creates any guilt. It is not for repentance: it is for remembrance. The past is past, it is gone and gone for ever—no need to worry about it. Just remember not to repeat the same mistakes again. Be more mindful.

Like a lovely flower,
Bright but scentless,
Are the fine but empty words
Of the man who does not mean what he says.

Those who go on repeating scriptures mechanically, their words are fine but empty. They are like flowers, lovely, bright, but with no perfume. They are like paper flowers or plastic flowers—they can't have perfume, they can't have aliveness. The aliveness, the perfume is possible only when you speak on your own, not on the authority of the scriptures—when you speak on your own authority, when you speak as a witness to truth, not as a learned scholar, not as a pundit, but when you speak as one who is awakened.

> *Like a lovely flower,*
> *Bright and fragrant,*
> *Are the fine and truthful words*
> *Of the man who means what he says.*

Remember not to repeat others' words. Experience, and only say that which *you* have experienced, and your words will have substance, weight, and your words will have a radiance, your words will have perfume. Your words will attract people; not only attract—influence. Your words will be pregnant with great meaning, and those who are ready to hear them will be transformed through them. Your words will be breathing, alive; there will be a heartbeat in them.

> *Like garlands woven from a heap of flowers,*
> *Fashion from your life as many good deeds.*

Let your life become a garland—a garland of good deeds. But good deeds, according to Buddha, arise only if you become more mindful, more alert, more aware. Good deeds are not to be cultivated as character; good deeds have to be by-products of your being more conscious.

Buddhism does not emphasize character but consciousness—that's its greatest contribution to humanity and humanity's evolution.

am I getting conned?

*I don't believe a word
about this mystery!*

*why doesn't this realization in my
head reach to my innermost core?*

are sex and money connected?

July 4

Spread
the Rumour!

The first question

Bhagwan,
Everything appears to be very paradoxical: having to
be total and yet having to remain a witness, a watcher;
having to be drowned in love and yet to be alone. It
sounds very mysterious, and I feel utterly lost and
confused. Am I getting conned?

Prem Urja,

LIFE IS BEAUTIFUL BECAUSE IT IS PARADOXI-
cal. It has salt because it is paradoxical—it is
not just sweet, it has salt in it too. If it was
just sweet, it would become too sugary, saccharine.

Life has tremendous mystery in it because it is based on
paradox. You are feeling confused because you have a certain
fixed idea about how life should be—you don't allow life
to be as it is. You want to impose a certain concept on it,
a certain logic on it. The confusion is of your own creation.

Try to impose some logical pattern on life and you will become very much confused, because life has no obligation to fulfill your logic. Life is as it is. You have to listen to it. It has all the colours, the whole spectrum—it is a rainbow. But you have a certain idea that it should be only blue or it should be only green or it should be only red—but it is *all* the seven colours. Then what are you going to do about the six other colours which are not part of your conception? Either you have to ignore them, block them, so that you don't become aware of them; repress them, simply deny them.... But whatsoever you do, life is not going to drop its colours; they will be there—denied, rejected, repressed, they will be there, waiting for the right moment to explode into your consciousness.

And whenever they explode you will be confused. The confusion is your responsibility. Life is not confusing at all. Life is mysterious but never confusing. Because you don't want it to be mysterious, you want it to be mathematical, you want it very clear-cut so that you can calculate and measure—hence the difficulty. It is not created by life. Drop your conceptions and then look.... Then you will find the storm that comes brings a silence with it—which is illogical! The silence that is felt after the storm is the deepest, the profoundest. If there is no storm, the silence remains superficial, the silence remains dull; it has no depth. After the storm...the greater the storm, the deeper the silence. Now, it is paradoxical.

It is paradoxical only because you want to impose a certain logic. The storm, and creating silence? It does not fit with your idea—that is true—then you become confused. But why should it fit with your idea? Life has to be perceived not conceived. See what is the case; don't have ready-made answers. Don't go through life with prejudices, with a prejudiced mind; don't have any *a priori* conceptions. Go innocent, naked; go ignorant. Function from the state of not knowing. And then...then life is not confusing. It is a tremendous joy, it is ecstasy. Then what appears today as confusing, you will feel thankful for it, grateful for it, that it is so, that it is not logical.

Life would have been utterly boring if God had followed Aristotle. It is a great relief that he is not an Aristotelian; it is a great relief that God knows nothing of Aristotle, that he has not read his books, that he does not believe in logic, that he believes in dialectics. Hence these paradoxes.

One can be in deep love and yet be alone. In fact, one can be alone only when one is in deep love. The depth of love creates an ocean around you, a deep ocean, and you become an island, utterly alone. Yes, the ocean goes on throwing its waves on your shore, but the more the ocean crashes with its waves on your shore, the more integrated you are, the more rooted, the more centered you are.

Love has value only because it gives you aloneness. It gives you space enough to be on your own.

But you have an idea of love; that idea is creating trouble —not love itself, but the idea. The idea is that in love lovers disappear into each other, dissolve into each other. Yes, there are moments of dissolution—but this is the beauty of life and all that is existential, that when lovers dissolve into each other, the same are the moments when they become very conscious, very alert, that dissolution is not a kind of drunkenness, that dissolution is not unconscious. It brings great consciousness, it releases great awareness. On the one hand they are dissolved, on the other hand for the first time they see their utter beauty in being alone. The other defines them, their aloneness; they define the other. And they are grateful to each other: it is because of the other that they have been able to see their own selves; the other has become a mirror in which they are reflected. Lovers are mirrors to each other. Love makes you aware of your original face.

Hence, it looks very contradictory, paradoxical, when stated in such a way: "Love brings aloneness." You were thinking all along that love brings togetherness. I am not saying that it does not bring togetherness, but unless you are alone you cannot be together. Who is going to be together? Two persons are needed to be together, two independent persons are needed to be together. A togetherness will be rich, infinitely rich, if both the persons are utterly independent. If they are dependent on each other, it is not a togetherness—it is a slavery, it is a bondage.

If they are dependent on each other, clinging, possessive, if they don't allow each other to be alone, if they don't allow each other space enough to grow, they are enemies, not lovers; they are destructive to each other, they are not helping each other to find their souls, their beings. What kind of love is this? It may be just fear of being alone, hence they are clinging to each other. But real love knows no fear. Real love is capable of being alone, utterly alone. And out of that aloneness grows a togetherness.

Kahlil Gibran says: Two lovers are like two pillars of a temple—they support the same roof, but they stand separate. Together as far as supporting the same roof is concerned, but utterly separate as far as their own being is concerned. Be pillars of a temple, supporting the same temple of love, the same roof of love, yet rooted in your own being, not distracted from there. And then you will know both the beauty, the purity, the cleanliness, the health, the wholeness of aloneness, and you will also know the joy, the dance, the music of being together.

There is a beauty when somebody is playing a solo instrument—a solo flute player—there is tremendous beauty in that. And there is also beauty in an orchestra. And love knows both together: it knows how to be a solo flute player and it also knows how to be in rhythm, harmony with the other.

There is *no* contradiction in reality—the contradiction appears only because you have a certain idea. Drop the idea and then where is confusion? Confusion comes only out of conclusions. If you have a conclusion already and then life appears as something else, you are confused. Rather than trying to fix life, drop your conclusions.

Never function out of conclusions!—that's what I go on repeating every day to you: don't function from the state of knowledge. Knowledge means conclusions, and all conclusions are borrowed. Life is so vast that it cannot be condensed into a conclusion. All conclusions are partial. And whenever the part claims to be the whole, it creates a kind of fanaticism, orthodoxy; it creates a dull and stupid mind.

> Urja, you say:
> *Having to be total and yet having to remain a witness,*
> *a watcher...seems to be very paradoxical.*

It only seems, the paradox is only apparent. Otherwise, to be total is to be a watcher. Whenever you are totally into something, a great awareness is released in you—you become a witness. Suddenly! Not that you practise witnessing. If you are totally in it...one day, dance totally and see what I am saying.

These are not logical conclusions that I am giving to you: these are existential indications, hints. Dance totally!—and then you will be surprised. Something new will be felt.

When the dance becomes total, and the dancer is almost completely dissolved in the dancing, there will be a new kind of awareness arising in you. You will be totally lost into the dance; the dancer gone, only dance remains. And yet you are not unconscious, not at all—just the opposite. You are very conscious, more conscious than you have ever been before.

But if you start thinking about it, then the paradox will come. Then you will not be able to manage, and you will become very confused.

Experience it. Whatsoever is being said here is to help you to experience. I am not handing over to you any knowledge, any information—just a few hints to taste the multidimensional qualities of life.

> You say:
> *It seems paradoxical . . . having to be drowned in love and yet be alone.*

It is not—it only appears. But you seem to be too much attached to your conclusions; hence the idea arises:

> *Am I getting conned?*

In a way, yes: you are being conned out of all your prejudices, out of all your conclusions, out of all your knowledge. I am trying to take you into the world of innocence again. I am trying to give you a new birth, so that you can become a child again—full of awe and wonder.

The child never sees any paradox anywhere—and that is the beauty of the child. The child can be in tremendous love with you and can say, "I cannot live without you even for a single moment," and the next moment he is angry and says, "I will never see your face again." And he is total in both his statements. And after a few moments he is again sitting in your lap with great joy—and that too is total.

The child is total each moment, and the child never sees any contradiction. When he is angry, he is really anger; and when he is loving he is really love. He moves from one moment to another moment without creating any confusion for himself. He is never confused. He never brings this paradox, because he has not yet arrived at conclusions. He does not know how one should be. He simply allows himself to be whatsoever is the case—he flows with life.

Urja, you have become stagnant somewhere. You have too much knowledge, and that is functioning as a barrier. It won't allow you to flow with me, and it won't allow you to flow with my people. It won't allow you to flow with life, it won't allow you to flow with God.

God is both day and night, summer and winter, birth and death...and you have to be capable of absorbing all these so-called paradoxes. If you can absorb all these so-called paradoxes, without becoming confused, enlightenment is not far away.

Enlightenment is the state when all paradoxes have disappeared. One simply takes note of the life as it is. One has no conclusions to compare with, no ideas to judge with. Then how can you be confused? You cannot confuse me—it is impossible! because I have no conclusions. Without conclusions, without knowledge, just taste life as it is. It is a mystery, not a paradox.

The second question

Bhagwan,
I don't believe a word about this mystery. Nothing
like that exists! My guess is that you are only adver-
tising your new commune because the press office is
too lazy, and not as clever as you can be.

Sarjano,

IT IS NOT A QUESTION OF BELIEVING OR NOT
believing—it is so. The question of belief arises only because
you are not aware of it. Belief is significant, and disbelief
too—when you are not aware of the reality. Then either
you believe or you disbelieve.

I am not saying believe in the mystery I am talking about.
I am not saying disbelieve either—I am saying: Come with
me! It is so! Let me wake you up...it is so.

You say:
I don't believe a word about this mystery.

It is very good. Please, don't believe a word, because if you
start believing you will not be able to experience. I am not
interested in believers: I am interested in enquirers. But
please don't start guessing either, because a guess is a guess.
A guess is not going to help. It will become a belief—if you
go on guessing for a long time, and if you go on repeating
the same guess again and again, it becomes a belief. You
create your own belief then, and that will become a barrier.

And beliefs are such subtle barriers, and disbeliefs too;
remember, whenever I say belief I always include disbelief
in it—because that is the other side of the coin. Belief and
disbelief, both are barriers. Once you have created a belief

system around yourself...either borrowed from others or guessed by yourself, either borrowed from the Bible, *Mein Kampf*, *Das Kapital*, Bhagavad Gita, or guessed by yourself, home-made. It does not matter—a belief becomes a barrier, an invisible barrier. And once it settles, it won't allow you to see anything else that goes against it.

Just the other day I was reading about an experiment. Sarjano, meditate over it:

A certain naturalist made the following experiment: a glass jar was divided into two halves by a perfectly transparent glass partition. On the one side of the partition he placed a pike, on the other a number of small fishes such as form the prey of the pike.

The pike did not notice the partition, and hurled itself on its prey with, of course, the result of only a bruised nose. The same happened many times, and always the same result. At last, seeing all its efforts ended so painfully, the pike abandoned the hunt; so that in a few days, when the partition had been removed, it continued to swim about among the small fry without daring to attack them.... Does not the same happen with us?

Now the partition is no more there, it has been removed, but a belief system has arisen in the pike's mind. Now he believes that there is a transparent partition; now the belief is enough: he never goes beyond that partition which is no more there. Now he can go! Now there is nothing to debar him, but his belief...he has created a belief. And, of course, out of his experience, Sarjano, not even guesswork—it was his experience, a repeated experience. He tried again and again and again, and each time a bruised nose and pain: of course, a belief has arisen. You have to forgive him—a poor pike has come to conclude that it is futile: "There is a barrier, transparent, so I cannot go..." and he never tries again. He will never try again his whole life. Now he can go and eat the fishes, they are available, but he will go only up to a certain line and from that line he will come back.

This is the situation of human beings too. A Hindu has a barrier around himself, a Mohammedan another, a Jaina still another—all people live hidden behind transparent barriers. And because of those barriers they cannot see beyond.

Life is a mystery, Sarjano. And my commune is going to be just an experiment in total living—an experiment in moving into life beyond all barriers—barriers of belief, barriers of ideologies, barriers of Catholicism, and communism...going beyond words.

Man is not what he appears to be: he is far more. Neither are flowers only what they appear to be...it depends on you. When a scientist goes to a flower, he only sees a part of it, the scientific part of it—he has a barrier, a transparent barrier. He never goes beyond that. He will see the scientific part, the material part of the flower. The rose is no more beautiful, because beauty is not his concept. He will weigh, measure, he will look into the constituents of the flower, how much colour, how much water, how much earth, et cetera...but he will never think of the beauty.

When the poet goes, he never bothers about the weight, measurement, earth, water, and other elements that constitute the rose. For him, the rose is constituted of pure beauty; it is something from the beyond which has descended to the earth. He has a different kind of vision, far bigger than the scientist's, far more significant than the scientist's.

But when a mystic goes to the same flower, he dances—

he dances in tremendous joy, because a rose is nothing but God. A rose contains the whole universe for him—all the stars and all the suns and all the moons, all the possible worlds and impossible worlds are contained in the small roseflower. It is equivalent to God—neither less nor more, exactly equivalent to God. He may pray, he may bow down.

The scientist will laugh, the poet will feel a little puzzled. . . . The scientist will laugh at the stupidity of the mystic: "What is he doing?—praying to a rose! praying to a tree or praying to a river or praying to a mountain!? All nonsense, superstition!" He rejects it. He simply denies the world of the mystic.

The poet will feel a little puzzled. Enjoying the beauty of the rose he *can* understand, but praying to the rose? bowing down to the rose? shouting 'hallelujah!' to the rose? That he cannot understand. That is beyond his perspective. He will feel puzzled. He will think this mystic a little mad.

The scientist will think him superstitious, ignorant. The poet will think him a little eccentric, a little mad—because he is going beyond his barrier, the mystic is going beyond the barrier of the poet. The mystic is going beyond *all* barriers—that's why he is called the mystic, because he lives in the mysterious.

Sarjano, what I am saying about the new commune is absolutely true. And I am not saying much about it, because it is dangerous to say much about it. I don't want to attract the wrong kind of people to it. So just a few hints only for those who will be able to understand the hints. I am speaking in a special code which can be understood only by those who are searching for the mysterious and the miraculous. Others will be debarred—not by me, by their own prejudice, by their own transparent barrier.

You can see it happening here! People are coming from all over the world; who is debarring the Poonaites? They are welcome, but they won't come on their own—their transparent barriers are enough. And it is good that they are not coming, because they will be only a nuisance here. Only a few people from amongst them are coming who are capable of understanding the beyond, the incomprehensible, who are capable of comprehending something of the incomprehensible.

But whether you believe in it or not, listen to this anecdote:

Two homosexuals are talking. First homosexual: "Have you heard of the latest scientific discovery? Normal intercourse causes cancer."

Second homosexual: "Is that so?"

First homosexual: "No, of course not! But spread the rumour."

Sarjano, whether you believe in it or not, please spread the rumour. The rumour has to reach to the farthest corners of the earth. Let it be a rumour! Don't be worried. It is up to me to make it a truth or not. If I find the right people—and I am finding them—it is going to materialize.

This mystery that I am talking about is going to materialize. But it will be materialized only for those who are ready to risk all their prejudices, who are ready to sacrifice all their conclusions.

Sarjano is one of those people. I trust in him. He has not asked this question for himself; he has asked it for others—because I know he is perfectly mad. He is not only a poet, but just on the verge of becoming a mystic. He has asked this question for others; it is not his own heart's question. His heart agrees totally with me.

You cannot hide your hearts from me. The moment you come close to me, the only thing that I am interested in is your heart. I talk to your head and I go on looking into your heart. Even in the first encounter with me, I know what is possible with you and what is impossible with you.

I have loved Sarjano from the very first moment. In his head he may have many theories and much knowledge and information—that is not my concern at all. My concern is that he has a beautiful heart—the heart that can be transformed into the heart of a mystic.

The third question

Bhagwan,
My understanding about myself is that all my doing arises out of a desire to communicate. Even the subtlest thought is a conversation, an attempt to have others experience and verify my existence.
With the realization that I am the only one who can experience my experiences and give them validity, all of this unnecessary doing should disappear. It is so simple and obvious. Why does not this realization reach to my innermost core?

Prem Steven,

IT IS NOT YET A REALIZATION—IT IS STILL information, it is still guesswork, it is still thinking. On the right track, certainly, in the right direction, true, but it is not a realization yet.

'Realization' is a great word. One should use that word

very cautiously. You can think great thoughts, but they don't become your realization by thinking. You can think about God and you can come to the conclusion that God is, and you can feel that now there is no doubt in your mind about God's existence—still it is not a realization.

Realization means precisely realization—it should become a reality to you! not just an idea. Even if a good idea is there, it is still an idea. And the idea can't transform you, and the idea can't reach to the very core of your being. It remains on the circumference.

All ideas are peripheral—just as all waves remain on the surface. The wave cannot go deep into the ocean; there is no way for it to go. At the deepest core there are no waves. On the surface a storm may be raging, but at the deepest core, the ocean is calm and quiet—and always so. Only the surface can get disturbed.

All thinking is a disturbance on the circumference of your being. Bad ideas, good ideas, all are peripheral. People have this belief that bad ideas are peripheral and good ideas are central—that's not so. Good or bad, it makes no difference. An idea is an idea and the idea remains peripheral.

Only witnessing can be at the center.

So the first thing is to realize that you have not realized yet. Once something is realized it is bound to transform you —instantly it transforms you. Then the question cannot arise:

> It is so simple and obvious. Why does not this realization reach to my innermost core?

This 'why?' is not possible then. If you realize something, your character immediately changes. Your character is a shadow of your consciousness. Once the consciousness is new, the whole character becomes new.

114

If you ask why, if you ask how to change, then the realization is only an idea—and don't trust in ideas. They deceive you; they are great deceivers, they are false coins. You can go on accumulating them believing that you are becoming rich, but one day you will be shattered. And the repentance will be great, and the misery will be great, because all that time you were accumulating those false coins is simply wasted. And it cannot be reclaimed—it is gone for ever.

> The second thing—you say, Steven:
> *My understanding about myself is that all my doing arises out of a desire to communicate. Even the subtlest thought is a conversation, an attempt to have others experience and verify my existence.*

Why? Why should you want others to verify your existence? to give validity to your existence? Because you are suspicious about it, you are doubtful about your existence. You really don't know that you are. You know you are only when others say you are. You depend on others' opinions.

If they say you are beautiful, you think you are beautiful. If they say you are intelligent, you think you are intelligent. Hence, you want to impress people—with your intelligence, with your beauty, with all kinds of things you want to impress people. Because if you can see something in their eyes, that becomes a validity for you.

That's why it is so enraging when somebody insults you, so damaging to the image when somebody calls you an idiot. Otherwise, why should you be bothered? It is none of your business. If he calls you an idiot, that is *his* problem. Just by his calling you an idiot, you don't become an idiot. But you become, because you depend on others' opinions.

That's how we live in the society. We are continuously

trying to impress each other. That's why we live as slaves, because if you want to impress other people you have to follow *their* ideas; only then are they impressed. You have to be good the way they want you to be good. If they are vegetarians, you have to be vegetarian, then they will be impressed; they will say you are a saint. If they are living a certain kind of lifestyle, you have to live that; then only will they recognize you.

You can gain respectability only if you follow people's ideas. It is a mutual understanding that you support their ideas—so they feel good that their ideas are right hence they are right—and then they support you and they give you respect: because you are following right ideas, you are a right person. They appreciate you, they shower you with honours, they call you a saint, a sage.... It feels very gratifying to you. It is gratifying to them because you pay respect to their ideology, and they pay respect to your personality. This is a mutual arrangement. And you are both in illusion. You are supporting their illusion, they are supporting your illusion. You are partners in the same business of hallucination.

Why should one want to be verified, validated by others? If you know on your own, if you have experienced your being and its beauty and its joy and its grandeur and its glory, who cares what others say?

BUDDHA WAS PASSING THROUGH A VILLAGE, AND the people of that village were very much against Buddha. Why were they against Buddha? Because Buddha was born in that village, he had lived in that village for many years, and the villagers could not believe that a man who was born amongst them had become enlightened. It was offensive to their egos!

That's why Jesus says: "A prophet is not respected, is not loved, by his own people." Jesus himself was thrown out of his birthplace. He went only once; after he became enlightened he went only once. And the people were so enraged by his assertion, "I have become realized, I am the son of God," that they took him to the hills to throw him from the mountains. They wanted to kill him. He had to escape somehow from their clutches, from their hands. And he never went back there.

Buddha was passing through the village in which he was born, just somewhere on the border of India and Nepal, and the people gathered and started insulting him, abusing him, calling him names. And he listened silently, for half an hour, and then he said, "It is getting hot and I have to reach the other village, and the people will be waiting for me. More time I cannot give you this time. If you have any more things to say to me, please wait. When I am coming back, then I will have a little more time. You can gather, and you can communicate whatsoever you want to communicate. But this time, excuse me. I have to go."

So cool, so calm, and they were really calling him dirty names. They could not believe their eyes. They said, "We are not saying something to you—we are insulting you, we are abusing you! Can't you understand what we are saying?"

Buddha said, "I can hear, I can understand everything that you are saying—but that is not my problem! If you are angry, that is your problem. It is none of my business to interfere in your life. If you want to be angry, if you are enjoying it, enjoy! But I am not going to take any nonsense from you.

"In fact, you have come a little late. If you really wanted me to be disturbed, you should have come ten years ago. Then I would have been really angry with you. I would have reacted, I would have hit you! But now, a great realization has happened that my being does not depend on other people's opinions. What you think about me only shows something about you, not about me! I *know* myself; hence I don't depend on anybody's opinions about me. People who are ignorant of their own selves, they have to depend on others."

Steven, this whole mind of communicating with people in an attempt to be verified by them simply shows a deep darkness inside. Otherwise, there is no need. And I am not saying that when a man becomes full of light, he stops communication, no. Only *he* can communicate, because he *has* something to communicate. What have you got to communicate? What is there that you can share with people? You are a beggar. You are begging.

When you want to be verified, validated, certified, you are begging. You are telling them, "Please say something good to me, something nice, so I can feel nice about myself. I am feeling very down, I am feeling very worthless—give me some worth! Make me feel significant." You are begging: it is not communication. Communication is possible only when a song has burst forth in your being, when a joy has arisen, when a bliss has been experienced—then you can share. Then not only communication, not only verbal communication, but on a far deeper level, communion also starts happening. But then you are not a beggar: you are an emperor.

Only Buddhas can commune and communicate. Others have nothing to say, nothing to give. In fact, what you are doing while you are talking with people...and people are continuously talking, chattering, if not actually, then in their minds, just as you say that deep in your mind also you are always talking with somebody, some imaginary person. You are saying something from your side, and you are also answering from the other side. A continuous chattering, a dialogue inside you.

This is a state of *un*sanity. I will not call it a state of insanity but unsanity. The whole of humanity exists in the state of unsanity. The insane person has gone beyond the normal boundary. The unsane person is also insane but within boundaries. He remains insane inside, but on the outside he goes on behaving in a sane way. So for him I have this word 'unsanity'.

Sanity happens only when you become so totally silent that all inner chattering disappears. When the mind is no more, you are sane. Mind is either unsane—that is normally insane—or insane—that means abnormally insane. No-mind is sanity. And in no-mind you understand, you realize, not only your own being but the being, the very being of existence. Then you have something to share, to communicate, to commune, to dance, to celebrate.

Before that, it is a desperate effort to somehow collect an image of yourself from others' opinions. And your image will remain a mess, because you will be collecting opinions from so many sources, they will remain contradictory.

One person thinks you are ugly, hates you, dislikes you; another person thinks you are so beautiful, so graceful, that there is nobody who can be compared to you—you are incomparable. Now what are you going to do with these two opinions? You don't know who you are; now these two opinions are there—how can you judge which is right? You would like the opinion to be right which says you are beautiful. You don't like the opinion which says that you are ugly, but it is not a question of liking or disliking. You cannot be deaf to the other opinion; that too is there. You can repress it in the unconscious, but it will remain there.

And you will be collecting opinions from your parents, from your family, from your neighbourhood, from the people you work with, from the teachers, from the priests... thousands of opinions clamouring inside you. And this is how you are going to create an image of yourself? It will be a mess. It will not have any face, any form; it will be a chaos. That's how everybody is: a chaos. No order is possible, because the very center is missing which can create the order.

That center I call awareness, meditation—*ais dhammo sanantano*—this is the inexhaustible law, the ultimate law, that only those who become aware know who they are. And when they know, then nobody can shake their knowing. Nobody can! The whole world may say one thing, but if you *know*, if you have realized yourself, it doesn't matter.

The whole world was saying that Jesus was mad. The day he was crucified, there was not a single person...thousands had gathered—not a single person who was in favour of him. All were thinking he was mad.

It was the custom in those days that on particular holidays one criminal could be forgiven. That day was a holiday and three persons were being crucified: two thieves and Jesus. Pontius Pilate asked the people, "We can forgive one person out of the three. Which one would you like to be forgiven?" He was thinking that they would ask for Jesus to be forgiven, but they didn't ask for Jesus. They asked for a thief to be forgiven—not Jesus but a thief, a well-known thief; the whole city knew about him. But they could not forgive the innocent man Jesus. Why?

But Jesus is not shaken. The whole world may be against him—he knows God is with him. He dies with a calm and quiet mind, undistracted, with a prayer on his lips—a prayer which is unique. The last words of Jesus are: "Father, forgive them, because they know not what they are doing. Amen.... Forgive them, for they know not what they are doing." They are crucifying him, but his heart is full of compassion for all those people.

When you know, you know so absolutely; when realization happens, it is so ultimate, that even if the whole world is against it, it makes no difference at all. You don't need any validity from anybody else.

The fourth question

Bhagwan,
Why do I always feel that sex and money are some-how deeply connected with each other?

Nirmal,

THEY ARE CONNECTED. MONEY IS POWER. Hence it can be used in many ways. It can purchase sex, and down the ages that has been the case. Kings have been keeping thousands of wives. Just in this century, the twentieth century, just thirty years ago, forty years ago, the Nizam of Hyderabad had five hundred wives.

It is said that Krishna had sixteen thousand wives. I used to think that this was too much, but when I came to know that the Nizam of Hyderabad had five hundred wives, just forty years ago, then it doesn't seem too much—only thirty-two times more! It seems humanly possible. If you can manage five hundred, why not sixteen thousand?

All the kings of the world were doing that. Women were used like cattle. In the great kings' palaces the women were numbered. It was difficult to remember names, so the king could say to his servants, "Bring number four hundred and one"—because how to remember five hundred names? Numbers...just as soldiers are numbered; they don't have names but only numbers. And it makes a lot of difference.

Numbers are absolutely mathematical. Numbers don't breathe, they don't have any heart. Numbers don't have any soul. When a soldier dies in the war, on the noticeboard you simply read, "No. 15 died." Now "No. 15 died" is one thing; if you say exactly the name of the person, that is totally different. Then he was a husband and the wife will be a widow now; and he was a father and the children will be orphans now; and he was the only support of his old parents, now there will be no support. A family is deserted; the light of a family has disappeared. But when number fifteen dies, number fifteen has no wife, remember; number fifteen doesn't have any children, number fifteen doesn't have any old parents. Number fifteen is just number fifteen!

And number fifteen is replaceable—another person will come and will become number fifteen. But *no* individual human being is replaceable. It is a trick, a psychological trick, to give numbers to soldiers. It helps...nobody takes any note of numbers disappearing; new numbers go on coming and replacing the old numbers.

Wives were numbered, and it depended on how much money you had. In fact, in the old days, that was the only way to know how rich a man was; it was a kind of measurement: How many wives has he?

Now, Hindus, particularly Arya Samajis, criticize Hajrat Mohammed very much for having nine wives—and they don't think of Krishna who had sixteen thousand wives. And he is not an exception: he is the rule. In this country, as in other countries, down the ages, the woman has been exploited—and the way to exploit is money! The whole world has suffered through prostitution. It degrades human beings. But what is a prostitute? She has been reduced to a mechanism, and you can purchase her with money. But remember perfectly well that your wives are not very different either. A prostitute is like a taxi, and your wife is like your own car; it is a permanent arrangement. Poor people cannot make permanent arrangements; they have to use taxis. Rich people can make permanent arrangements—they can have their own cars. And the richer they are, the more cars they can have.

I know one person who had three hundred and sixty-five cars—one car for every day. And he had one car made in solid gold....

Money is power, and power can purchase anything. So, Nirmal, you are not wrong that there is some connection between sex and money. One thing more has to be understood.

The person who represses sex becomes more money-minded, because money becomes a substitute for sex. Money becomes his love. See the greedy person, the money maniac: the way he touches hundred rupee notes—he touches them as if he is caressing his beloved; the way he looks at gold, look at his eyes—so romantic. Even great poets will feel inferior. Money has become his love, his goddess.

In India, people even worship money. There is a particular day to worship money—actual money: notes and coins, rupees, they worship. Intelligent people doing such stupid things.

Sex can be diverted in many ways. It can become anger if repressed. Hence the soldier has to be deprived of sex, so that the sex energy becomes his anger, his irritation, his destructiveness; so he can be more violent than he ever was. Sex can be diverted into ambition. Repress sex...once sex is repressed, you have energy available, you can channel it into any direction. It can become a search for political power, it can become a search for more money, it can become a search for fame, name, respectability, asceticism, etc., etc.

Man has only one energy—that energy is sex. There are not many energies with you. And only the one energy has been used for all kinds of drives. It is a tremendously potential energy.

And people are after money in the hope that when they have more money, they can have more sex, they can have far more beautiful women or men, they can have far more variety. Money gives them freedom of choice.

The person who is free of sexuality, whose sexuality has become a transformed phenomenon, is also free of money, is also free of ambition, is also free of the desire to be famous. Immediately all these things disappear from his life. The moment sex energy starts rising upwards, the moment sex energy starts becoming love, prayer, meditation, then all lower manifestations disappear.

But sex and money are deeply associated. Your idea, Nirmal, has some truth in it.

A wizened little client in a fancy whorehouse is heard

shouting from the upper floor: "No! Not that way! I want it *my* way, the way we do it in Brooklyn. So quit it! Do it *my* way, or forget it!"

The madam climbs the stairs and erupts into the girl's room. "What is the matter with you, Zelda?" she says. "Give it to him *his* way."

She leaves, the girl lies down, and the man makes love to her in perfectly routine fashion. She sits up, puts on her dressing gown, lights a cigarette and says, "That's your way, Hymie, huh?"

"That's it," he says proudly from the bed.

"That's how you do it in Brooklyn?"

"Right you are!"

"So what is so different about it?"

"In Brooklyn I get it for nothing."

People can be so much obsessed with money, as much as they are obsessed with sex. The obsession can be shifted towards money. But money gives you purchasing power and you can purchase anything. You cannot purchase love, of course, but you can purchase sex. Sex is a commodity, love is not.

You cannot purchase prayer, but you can purchase priests. Priests are commodities—prayer is not a commodity. And that which can be purchased is ordinary, mundane. That which cannot be purchased is sacred. Remember it: the sacred is beyond money, the mundane is always within money's power.

And sex is the most mundane thing in the world.

A man enters a modern Chicago whorehouse-nightclub run by the gangland syndicate which is now planning to streamline its image. The whorehouse takes up various floors of a skyscraper hotel, and he is received by a lovely young receptionist in a sexy uniform, who sits him at a teakwood interview desk and asks how much money he wants to spend. She explains that prices range from $5 up to $1000, depending on the quality and number of girls wanted. Everything is shown on the television intercom. The higher prices are for the lower floors, which have higher ceilings, mirrors over the beds, three and four girls in bed with you at one time, etc. Lower prices are for lesser delights, ending with $5 for a 'coalblack nigger mammy with big nostrils', as the lovely young receptionist explains.

The client thinks it over. "Haven't you anything cheaper than $5?" he asks at last.

"Of course," says the receptionist. "Seventh floor—roofgarden. One dollar a shot. Self-service."

Money is certainly associated with sex, because sex can be purchased. And anything that can be purchased is part of the world of money.

Remember one thing: your life will remain empty if you know only things which can be purchased, if you know only things which can be sold. Your life will remain utterly futile if your acquaintance is only with commodities.

Become acquainted with things which cannot be purchased and cannot be sold—then for the first time you start growing wings, for the first time you start soaring high.

ONE GREAT KING, BIMBISAR, REACHED Mahavira. He had heard that Mahavira had attained *dhyana* —meditation, samadhi. In Jaina terminology, it is called *samayik*—the ultimate state of prayer or meditation. Bimbisar had everything of this world. He became worried: "What is this *samayik*? What is this samadhi?" He could not rest at ease, because now for the first time he was aware that there was one thing he had not got—and he was not a man to remain contented without getting anything that took his fancy.

He travelled to the mountains, found Mahavira, and said, "How much do you want for your *samayik*? I have come to purchase it. I can give you anything you desire, but give me this *samayik*, this samadhi, this meditation—what is this? Where is it? First let me look at it!"

Mahavira was surprised at the whole stupidity of the king, but he was a very polite man, soft, graceful. He said, "You need not have travelled so far. In your own capital I have a follower who has attained to the same state, and he is so poor that he may be willing to sell it. I am not willing, because I don't need any money. You can see I am naked, I don't need any clothes. I am utterly satisfied—I don't have any needs, so what will I do with your money? Even if you give me your whole kingdom I am not going to accept it. I had my own kingdom—that I have renounced. I had all that you have got!"

And Bimbisar knew it, that Mahavira had had all and had renounced, so it was difficult to persuade this man to sell. Certainly, money meant nothing to him. So he said, "Okay, who is this man? Give me his address."

And Mahavira told him, "He is very poor, lives in the poorest part of your city. You may never have visited that part. This is the address...you go and ask him. And he is your subject, he can sell it to you. And he is in much need. He has a wife and children and a big family and is really poor."

It was a joke. Bimbisar returned happy, went directly to the poor parts of his capital where he had never been.

People could not believe their eyes—his golden chariot and thousands of soldiers following him.

They stopped in front of the poor man's hut. The poor man came, touched the feet of the king, and said, "What can I do? Just order me."

The king said, "I have come to purchase the thing called samadhi, meditation, and I am ready to pay any price you ask."

The poor man started crying, tears rolled down his cheeks, and he said, "I am sorry. I can give you my life, I can die for you, right now, I can cut my head—but how can I give you my samadhi? It is not sellable, it is not purchasable—it is not a commodity at all. It is a state of consciousness. Mahavira must have played a joke on you."

Unless you know something which cannot be sold and cannot be purchased, unless you know something which is beyond money, you have not known real life. Sex is not beyond money, love is. Transform your sex into love, and transform your love into prayer—so one day even kings like Bimbisar may feel jealous of you. Become a Mahavira, a Buddha, become a Christ, a Zarathustra, a Lao Tzu. Only then have you lived, only then have you known the mysteries of life!

Money and sex are the *lowest*, and people are living only in the world of money and sex—and they think they are living. They are not living: they are only vegetating, they are only dying. This is not life. Life has many more kingdoms to be revealed, an infinite treasure which is not of this world. Neither sex can give it to you, nor money. But you can attain to it.

You can use your sex energy to attain it, and you can use your money power to attain it. Of course, it cannot be attained by money or by sex, but you can use your sex energy, your money power, in such an artful way that you can create a space in which the beyond can descend.

I am not against sex, and I am not against money, remember it. Always remember! But I am certainly for helping you go beyond them—I am certainly for going beyond.

Use everything as a step. Don't deny anything. If you have money, you can meditate more easily than the poor person. You can have more time to yourself. You can have a small temple in your house; you can have a garden, rose-bushes, where meditation will be easier. You can allow yourself a few holidays in the mountains; you can go into isolation and live without worry. If you have money, use it for something which money cannot purchase, but for which money can create a space.

Sexual energy is a wastage if it only remains confined to sex, but it becomes a great blessing if it starts transforming its quality. Sex not for sex' sake: use sex as a communion of love. Use sex as a meeting of two souls, not only of two bodies. Use sex as a meditative dance of two persons' energies. And the dance is far richer when man and woman are dancing together—and sex is the ultimate in dance: two energies meeting, merging, dancing, rejoicing.

But use it a stepping-stone, as a jumping-board. And when you reach the climax of your sex orgasm, become aware of what is happening, and you will be surprised: time has disappeared, mind has disappeared, ego has disappeared. For a moment there is utter silence. This silence is the *real* thing!

And this silence can be attained through other means too, and with less wastage of energy. This silence, this mindless-ness, this timelessness, can be attained through meditation.

In fact, if a person consciously goes into his sex experience, he is bound to become a meditator sooner or later. His consciousness of the sex experience is bound to make him aware that the same can happen without any sexuality involved in it. The same can happen just sitting silently by yourself, doing nothing. The mind can be dropped, time can be dropped. And the moment you drop mind and time and the ego, you *are* orgasmic.

The sexual orgasm is very momentary, and whatsoever is momentary brings frustration in its wake, brings misery and unhappiness and sadness and repentance. But the quality of being orgasmic can become a continuity in you, a continuum—it can become your very flavour. But it is possible only through meditation, not through sex alone.

Use sex, use money, use the body, use the world, but we have to reach God. Let God remain always the goal.

The perfume of sandalwood,
Rosebay or jasmine
Cannot travel against the wind.

But the fragrance of virtue
Travels even against the wind,
As far as the ends of the world.

How much finer
Is the fragrance of virtue
Than of sandalwood, rosebay,
Of the blue lotus or jasmine!

The fragrance of sandalwood and rosebay
Does not travel far.
But the fragrance of virtue
Rises to the heavens.

Desire never crosses the path
Of virtuous and wakeful men.
Their brightness sets them free.

How sweetly the lotus grows
In the litter of the wayside.
Its pure fragrance delights the heart.

Follow the awakened
And from among the blind
The light of your wisdom
Will shine out, purely.

July 5

In the Litter
of the Wayside

MAN IS NOT A BEING BUT ONLY A becoming. Man is a process, a growth, a possibility, a potentiality. Man is not yet actual. Man has to be, he has yet to arrive. Man is born not as an essence but only as an existence...a great space where much can happen, or nothing may happen—it all depends on you.

Man has to create himself. He is not ready-made, he is not given. And the creation has to be a self-creation—nobody else can make you. You are not a thing, a commodity; you cannot be produced or manufactured. You have to self-create yourself, you have to become awakened on your own; nobody can wake you up.

This is man's grandeur, his glory, that he is the only being on the earth who is not a being but a freedom to be. All other beings are already fixed, patterned. They bring a blueprint, and they simply follow the blueprint. The parrot will become a parrot, the dog will become a dog, the lion a lion...there is no question of the lion being somebody else. But with man it is relevant to ask whether he is really a man.

Each lion is really a lion, and each elephant is an elephant too, but man is a question mark. A man may be a man, may not be. A man can fall below the animals, and a man can rise above the gods. That ultimate state above the gods is buddhahood—the awakening, the ultimate awakening, the realization of your potential in its totality.

The Buddha is above gods. This was one of the reasons Hindus could not forgive Gautam the Buddha, because he said the Buddha is above the gods. Gods are also asleep; of course, their dreams are nice; their dreams are not nightmares, they live in heaven. Their lives are only of pleasure. Heaven is nothing but pure hedonism; the very idea is hedonistic. Hell is just the opposite. Hell is pain, heaven is pleasure; hell is a nightmare, heaven a sweet dream. But dreams *are* dreams, sweet or bitter, it does not matter.

The gods are also asleep and dreaming beautiful dreams. The Buddha is awakened, he is no longer dreaming. The Buddhist scriptures say: The day Siddhartha Gautam became a Buddha gods came from the sky to worship him, to wash his feet. Hindus could not forgive this idea, because for them the gods in heaven—Indra and other gods—are the suprememost. And look at the arrogance of the Buddhists who say gods came from heaven to wash the feet of a human being.

Buddhism raised humanity to its highest pinnacle. No other religion has done that. Man becomes the center of existence. God is not the center of existence according to Buddha, but the man who has become awakened. The periphery consists of those who are asleep and blind, and the center consists of those who have eyes, who are awakened.

Gods are simply dropped; they are no more relevant. What Nietzsche did after two thousand years, Buddha had done already.

A great poet, Chandidas, was very much impressed by Gautam Buddha—and who will not be impressed by this man?—he has said: *Sabar upar manush satya, tahar upar nahin* —the truth of man is the highest truth, there is no other truth higher than that. But let me remind you again: when Buddha talks about man, he talks about the realized man, not about you—you are only on the way, you are only in the process. You are a seed.

The seed can have four possibilities. The seed may remain a seed forever, closed, windowless, not in communion with existence, dead, because life means communion with existence. The seed *is* dead, it has not yet communicated with the earth, with the sky, with the air, with the wind, with the sun, with the stars. It has not yet made any attempt to have a dialogue with all that exists. It is utterly lonely, enclosed, encapsulated into itself, surrounded by a China Wall. The seed lives in its own grave.

The first possibility is that the seed may remain a seed. That is very unfortunate—a man may remain simply a seed. With all the potential at your disposal, with all the blessings ready to shower on you, you may never open your doors.

The second possibility is that the seed may be courageous enough, may dive deep into the soil, may die as an ego, may drop its armour, may start a communion with existence, may become one with the earth. Great courage is needed, because who knows?—this death may be ultimate, there may be no birth following it. What is the guarantee? There is no guarantee; it is a gamble. Only a few men gather courage enough to gamble, to risk.

To be a sannyasin is the beginning of the gamble. You are risking your life, you are risking your ego. You are risking because you are dropping all your securities, all your safety arrangements. You are opening windows...

who knows who is to come in—the friend or the enemy? Who knows? You are becoming vulnerable. That's what sannyas is all about. That's what Buddha was teaching his whole life. Forty-two years continuously, transforming seeds into plants—that was his work—transforming ordinary human beings into sannyasins.

A sannyasin is a plant, a sprout—soft, delicate. The seed is never in danger, remember. What danger can there be for the seed? It is absolutely protected. But the plant is always in danger; the plant is very soft. The seed is like a stone, hard, hidden behind a hard crust. But the plant has to pass through a thousand and one hazards. That is the second stage: the seed dissolving into the soil, the man disappearing as an ego, disappearing as a personality, becoming a plant.

The third possibility...which is even more rare, because not all plants are going to attain to that height where they can bloom into flowers, a thousand and one flowers. Very few human beings attain to the second stage, and very few of those who attain the second stage attain the third, the stage of the flower. Why can't they attain the third stage, the stage of the flower? Because of greed, because of miserliness; they are not ready to share. Because of a state of unlovingness.

Courage is needed to become a plant, and love is needed to become a flower. A flower means the tree is opening up its heart, releasing its perfume, giving its soul, pouring its being into existence. The seed can become a plant although it is difficult to drop the armour, but in one way it is simple. The seed will only be gathering more and more, accumulating more and more; the seed only takes from the soil. The tree only takes from the water, from the air, from the sun— the greed is not disturbed; on the contrary, their ambitions are fulfilled. They go on becoming bigger and bigger. But a moment comes when you have taken so much that now you have to share. You have been benefitted so much, now you have to serve. God has given you so much, now you have to thank, be grateful—and the only way to be grateful is to shower your treasures, give them back to existence, be *as* unmiserly as existence has been with you. Then the tree grows into flowers, it blossoms.

And the fourth stage is that of fragrance. The flower is still gross, it is still material, but the fragrance is subtle, it is almost something non-material. You cannot see it; it is invisible. You can only smell it, you cannot grab it, you cannot grasp it. A very sensitive understanding is needed to have a dialogue with the fragrance.

And beyond fragrance there is nothing. The fragrance disappears into the universe, becomes one with it.

These are the four stages of the seed, and these are the four stages of man too. Don't remain a seed—gather courage. Courage to drop the ego, courage to drop the securities, courage to drop the safeties, courage to be vulnerable. But then don't remain a tree, because a tree without flowers is poor. A tree without flowers is empty, a tree without flowers is missing something very essential. It has no beauty—without love there is no beauty. And it is only through flowers that the tree shows its love. It has taken so much from the sun and the moon and from the earth; now it is time to give!

Life has to attain a balance always. You have taken so much, now give it. Become a flower! Only when you become a flower is there a possibility of disappearing as a fragrance. But then too, remember, don't remain a closed flower, don't remain a bud; otherwise your fragrance will not be released. And unless your fragrance is released, you are not free, you are in a bondage.

This bondage Buddha calls *samsara*—the world. And he calls the freedom, the freedom of the fragrance, *nirvana*—total cessation, disappearance, dissolution. The part disappears into the whole, the dewdrop slips into the ocean and becomes the ocean. The day you disappear and become the ocean is the day when in one sense you are no more, and in another sense you are for the first time—you have attained beinghood.

This beinghood is real godhood. This beinghood, this crystallized, oceanic experience, is liberation, salvation, *moksha, kaivalya, nirvana*—you can use any word that you want to use but they all mean the same: absolute freedom of the soul, with no boundaries, with no limitations.

The sutras:

The perfume of sandalwood,
Rosebay or jasmine
Cannot travel against the wind.

OBVIOUSLY! THE FRAGRANCE OF SANDALWOOD, rosebay or jasmine is part of the material world. It can travel only with the wind, not against the wind. It has to follow the laws of matter. It *is* matter. Because it has to follow the laws of matter it is not really free—free only in a relative sense. The fragrance is more free than the flower, the flower is more free than the tree, the tree is more free than the seed. But these freedoms are only relative, not absolute.

And Buddha says, remember: the target is absolute freedom, transcendence of all laws. It is only in transcending all laws that you will become part of the ultimate law: *ais dhammo sanantano*. It is only by transcending all limitations of gross matter that you will be able to become as infinite as the sky.

And unless you become universal you have not attained to your potential. You are meant to become universal, and you have become small persons, confined, almost as if you are living in a prison cell, dark and dismal, no door, no window, an ugly existence, surrounded by all kinds of pathologies—ego, greed, anger, lust, jealousy, possessiveness. These are your companions. What fragrance have you experienced in life?

You have not yet known love without lust. You have not known yet any state where no limitation exists. You are bound to certain very gross laws. You are part of the gravitation; you have not yet known anything of grace. You go on and on downwards, because those laws of gravitation go on pulling you downwards. You don't know how to rise, soar upwards. You don't know anything about levitation.

In science, they don't talk about levitation, they only talk about gravitation, the downward pull. But this is such a simple phenomenon to understand, that in nature everything is balanced by its polar opposite. If there is a downward pull, gravitation, then there must be an upward pull to balance it—that is levitation. In a more poetic language it is called grace.

There are two laws: the law of gravitation, the earthly law, gross, material; and the law of grace, the divine law, what Buddha calls the divine law—*ais dhammo sanantano*— the eternal, inexhaustible law, the divine law, which pulls you upwards.

The perfume of sandalwood,
Rosebay or jasmine
Cannot travel against the wind.

It has certain absolute limitations. It can only ride on the wind; it cannot have its own will. It is not really free. Unless you can exist in total freedom, something is missing. If you have to follow the laws, then you are a prisoner. The laws may give you enough rope, but still you are a prisoner.

That's how things are: if enough rope is given to you, you forget about the prison. For example, these so-called nations—India, Pakistan, Japan, Germany—these are all great prisons, but they are so great that you cannot see the boundaries of your prison. Cross the boundaries of your nation and you will see that you were a prisoner. But the prison is big enough; you can move in the prison anywhere you want. But move out of the prison, try to enter another prison, and then you will see the limitation.

These are man-made prisons; big enough so they can give you a false feeling of freedom, but there is no freedom. Unless all nations disappear from the world, the earth will remain a slave, humanity will remain in prisons, small and big. But it makes no difference whether the prison is very big and you cannot see the wall surrounding it.... The walls may be very subtle—of passports and visas—the walls may be *very* subtle, you may not see them, but they are there. You are not free to move.

Almost all the constitutions of the world say that the freedom of movement is the birthright of every human being, but it is only written in the books, it is not true. You cannot move freely. If you want to go to Russia, impossible; if you want to enter into China, impossible.

Nations have become such great prisons, and your presidents and your so-called prime ministers are all nothing but jailors. Those who talk about freedom are nothing but policemen. They say they are guarding you for your own safety, but in fact they are prison wardens watching so that you cannot escape.

I have heard:

An old Russian was dying, and he heard a knock on the door. He asked, "Who is there?" And some very ghostly voice said, "Death." The old Russian said, "Thank God, I was thinking it is the secret police."

And there are prisons within prisons like Chinese boxes—boxes within boxes.... India is a big prison; then there are Hindus and Mohammedans and Christians and Sikhs and Jainas and Buddhists—now these are small prisons. The Christian can go to the church, he cannot go to the temple; the Hindu can go to the temple, he cannot go to the church. He has been taught and conditioned that the church is not a religious place; the Christian has been told that the church is the only right place to go—all other religions are false, and all other religions lead you astray. Unless you are a Christian you cannot be saved. And then within Christianity there are Catholics and Protestants, and then among Protestants and Catholics there are smaller and smaller sub-sects. And prisons become smaller and smaller.

Then there are political prisons: somebody is a communist and somebody is a socialist, and somebody is a capitalist... and so on and so forth. And you are not satisfied even with these: then you make Rotary Clubs and Lions Clubs.... Your thirst to be a prisoner is such that you can't simply be a human being. You have to be a Rotarian and you proudly declare, "I am a Rotarian," "I am a Lion." You are not satisfied with being simply a human being, you have to be a Lion. And then there are smaller and smaller confinements.

Rather than getting out of these prison cells, we go on decorating them, we go on making them more and more comfortable. We are living under the law of gravitation, we are living as prisoners, we cannot go against the wind, our life is gross. Buddha says: Be aware of it—what are you doing with your life? Reconsider, meditate over it, what you have made of yourself.

> But the fragrance of virtue
> Travels even against the wind,
> As far as the ends of the world.

BUDDHA SAYS: BUT THERE IS A FLOWERING OF your inner being, which is far more beautiful than sandal-wood, rosebay or jasmine. Its beauty is its absolute freedom. It can go against the wind. The really virtuous man lives in freedom; he follows no commandments, he follows no scriptures, he follows nobody else but his own inner light. He lives according to his heart—he is a rebel.

But Buddha is talking about the fragrance of real virtue; he is not talking about the so-called righteous, he is not talking about the so-called 'people of character'. Your so-called saints and mahatmas, he is not talking about them. They are not free people. In fact, the fragrance of sandal-wood, rosebay and jasmine is far more free than your so-called saints. They live according to man-made laws. The fragrance of rosewood, the fragrance of sandalwood, the fragrance of other flowers, at least follow the laws of nature. But your saints, your so-called virtuous people, they follow laws which are man-made—laws made by blind people, laws made by ignorant people, laws made by people who are not yet awakened, who know nothing of awareness.

Who makes your laws? Who makes your constitutions? Who is responsible for running the society and arranging and managing the society? Just people as blind as you, maybe more learned, maybe more informed. But it makes no difference whether a blind man is more informed about light or less informed about light—a blind man is a blind man. Just watch your saints, and you will be surprised!—they live in far deeper bondage than ordinary people.

A Jaina monk wanted to come to see me. He sent a message that he had been longing to see me for many years, and now he was in the town and he wanted to see me, but his followers didn't allow him. The Jainas don't allow him to come to this commune. Now what kind of saint is this man whose followers decide where he should go and where he should not go? But there is a mutual arrangement: the followers call him a saint, they worship him, now he has to concede, compromise—he has to follow the followers.

Your so-called saints and leaders are followers of their own followers. It is such a stupid world, so ridiculous, the whole situation. On the surface it seems the saint is the decisive factor; he gives people advice to follow him. But if you look deep down, you will be surprised—the saint is following his own followers. In fact, they decide. And they have decisive power because they can worship you and they can insult you. They can worship you if you follow them, if you go according to the ideas, prejudices, that they carry in their minds; otherwise you are no more a saint. They can degrade you—they have the power to raise you to sainthood or to degrade you to being a sinner. If you want to be a saint you have to follow all kinds of stupidities. You may know deep down that this is stupid.

I sent him a message saying, "This is stupid, ridiculous! Why should you ask your followers? Who is the follower, you or they? Why should you ask them?"

He said, "You are right, but I have to depend on them. At my age, I cannot leave them because I have never worked in my life. I depend for my food, for my clothes, for everything, on them."

Now you see the arrangement. This is called spirituality, and the arrangement is financial!

A really virtuous man is certainly free, and is so free that he can go against the wind, he can go against the whole society, he can go against the whole past, he can go against all conventions. In fact, he does—because in going against all the conventions and the dead past he asserts his freedom.

It is because of this that I am being condemned all over this country and now, slowly slowly, all over the world. The only reason is that they wanted me to go with the wind, they wanted me to be conventional, orthodox. They were ready to worship me, they had come many times to me saying that if I could simply follow the traditional religion they would worship me as a saint. I said, "I am not interested in being worshipped or in being a saint. I want just simply to be myself. And I am not going to compromise with anybody, whoever he is. Compromise is not my way."

Because I am going against the wind they are very much offended. But if you are virtuous...and what is virtue? It is not some character cultivated from the outside. Virtue is the fragrance of meditativeness; virtue is the fragrance of the flower of meditation. Hence, I say it is not righteousness, it is not moralistic.

I have heard:

The town whore in Jerusalem is being stoned. When Jesus says, "Let whoever is without sin among you cast the first stone," an old lady struggles over with an enormous rock, drops it on the town whore's head, and polishes the bitch off. Jesus looks down and says, "You know, mother, sometimes you really piss me off."

The righteous, the moralistic, the puritan, is always ready . . .in fact his whole joy is how to condemn, how to send more and more people to hell, how to crucify people, how to kill and destroy. He is ready to suffer, he is ready to be a masochist, he is ready to go through all kinds of foolish austerities, just to enjoy the feeling of superiority, the feeling of holier-than-thou, the feeling that "You are all sinners and I am a saint."

The real saint has a totally different quality. He is not moralistic; he knows how to forgive, because he knows God has forgiven him so much; he knows human limitations, because he himself has suffered through those human limitations. He can forgive. He is understanding.

The moralist is never understanding, he is never forgiving, he cannot forgive because he has been so hard with himself. He has attained to his so-called character with such difficulty that the only joy, the only pleasure that he can get is that of holier-than-thou—how can he forgive? If he forgives then he cannot enjoy the egoistic trip that he has been on.

The ascetic is the most egoistic person in the world. The virtuous person is not an ascetic.

The story is told about Buddha himself:

For six years when he left his palace he lived through great austerities—that was the traditional way of seeking

146

and searching for the truth. He tortured his body, he fasted, he fasted so much that it is said that he became absolutely thin, just bones; you could have counted his ribs. He became so thin that his stomach was touching his back; there was nothing left between the stomach and the back. He became so weak that he could not cross a small river, the Niranjana. I had been to the place just to see. The Niranjana is such a small river, and it was not the rainy season, but he could not cross, he could not swim the river. He must have been utterly weak.

That day, a great revelation happened to him: "I have been doing unnecessary violence to myself." He had five followers; they were all ascetics and they had become followers of Buddha because he was far ahead of them. They could only do so much, but he was doing many times more, hence they were followers. That evening Buddha decided, "It is stupid to torture the body and how can you attain to the soul by torturing the body? There seems to be no logical relationship." And he saw, "If I cannot even cross the river, the poor river Niranjana, how am I going to cross this huge ocean of the world? The body needs food, the body needs nourishment, the body needs strength, so that I can meditate, so that I can contemplate, so that I can enquire, with zest, enthusiasm, energy."

He decided to drop all austerities. His five disciples immediately left him. They said, "Gautam has fallen from his holy state, he is no more a saint." They left him immediately; they were not with *him*. They were only with him because of his masochistic lifestyle; they must have been masochists themselves.

And Gautam Buddha became enlightened the next day. Dropping all austerities, dropping all that unnecessary inner conflict, that civil war, he became so quiet, so silent, that the next morning he could see, he became perceptive. In his silence, all turmoil, all chattering, were dissolved. In the early morning as the sun was rising, he started rising within his being. He was awakened, he became a Buddha.

Virtue came out of silence, out of meditativeness, out of relaxation—not out of effort, not out of tension, not out of struggle.

He went in search of his five old followers to give them the message: "Don't torture yourselves any more. This has nothing to do with holiness. This has nothing to do with religion."

Meditation has to happen first, then character comes as a shadow to it. And if meditation does not happen, then your character is just a hypocrisy and nothing else. Your saints are great hypocrites; they say one thing, they think another, maybe just the opposite. They do one thing, but they want to do something exactly the opposite. On the surface they show one thing, but deep down they are just its contrary.

A girl confesses that she let her boyfriend put his hand on her knee. "And is that *all* he did?" asks the priest.

"No. He slid his finger under the elastic of my panties too."

"And then what?"

"And then he spread open my fuzz and began to tickle my doo-funny."

"And then? And then?"

"And then my mother walked in."

"Oh shit!" says the priest.

These priests, these saints, they are far more ugly than you are, far more ugly than you ever can be, because they are far more split, divided. They are so much repressed that their conscious and unconscious have fallen apart. They preach one thing, they practise another. At their front door you will find one person, at the back door you will find a totally different person. You will not even be able to recognize them—they wear masks.

These are not virtuous people; Buddha is not talking about such virtue. He is talking about the virtue that arises out of the flowering of meditation. Buddha is insistent on *dhyana*—meditation. That is his basic contribution to the world. His most fundamental approach is that first you have to become awakened at the center, then your circumference will be full of light—of its own accord, not vice versa.

You have been told by the priest to first practise character, and then your center will change. That is nonsense. The center can never follow the circumference, because the center is far more important, far more basic—it is the center, it *cannot* follow the circumference. But the circumference always follows the center. Transform the center first, and don't be worried about the circumference.

That's my insistence too; there I absolutely agree with Buddha. Meditation first, and then all else shall follow of its own accord.

Jesus says: Seek ye first the kingdom of God, and all else shall be added unto you.

What Jesus says with 'kingdom of God' Buddha says with 'meditation'. Buddha's words are far more scientific than Jesus'. Jesus is more a poet than Buddha; Jesus talks more in parables than Buddha. Buddha talks in a clear-cut, logical, mathematical way. He is a man who does not want to say anything in any way which can be interpreted in many ways; he does not want to use poetry, because poetry is vague, can have many interpretations. He talks as a mathematician, he talks as a logician, so that each word has a fixed meaning and a fixed connotation.

> *The fragrance of virtue*
> *Travels even against the wind,*
> *As far as the ends of the world.*
>
> *How much finer*
> *Is the fragrance of virtue*
> *Than of sandalwood, rosebay,*
> *Of the blue lotus or jasmine!*

THE FRAGRANCE OF A BLUE LOTUS OR JASMINE or sandalwood is fine, subtle, but compared to the fragrance of virtue it is very gross. Virtue really has a fragrance, and it travels to the farthest corners of the world.

How have you come here to me? From different corners of the world you have travelled, sometimes not even exactly clear as to why; but something has been pulling you, some unknown force has moved your heart, something has been felt by the deepest core of your being. Sometimes you have come even against yourself. Your mind was saying, "Don't go! There is no need to go anywhere." Still you have come. You must have smelled a perfume—a perfume which has nothing to do with the visible. It is an invisible phenomenon.

Many many more people will be coming soon. The fragrance is reaching them, is bound to reach. Anybody anywhere who is really in search of truth is bound to come. It is irresistible, it *has* to happen. That's how it has been happening all along, down the ages. Thousands of people travelled to Buddha, thousands of people travelled to Mahavira, to Lao Tzu, to Zarathustra—for *no* reason at all, because whatsoever they were saying was available in the scriptures.

What I am saying here you can read in the Bhagavad Gita, in the Bible, in the Koran, in the Dhammapada, what I am saying you can find easily in the Upanishads, in the Tao Te Ching—but you will not find the fragrance. Those are flowers—old, dead, dried up. You can keep a roseflower in your Bible; soon it will be dry, the fragrance will be gone, it will be only a corpse, a remembrance of the real flower. So are the scriptures. They have to be made alive again by another Buddha, otherwise they cannot breathe.

That's why I am speaking on the Dhammapada, on the Gita, on the Bible—to let them breathe again. I can breathe life into them. I can share my fragrance with them, I can pour my fragrance into them. Hence, the Christian who is really a Christian, not just by social conditioning but because of a great love for Christ, he will find Christ alive again in my words. Or if somebody is a Buddhist he will find in my words Buddha speaking again—in twentieth century language, with twentieth century people.

> *How much finer*
> *Is the fragrance of virtue*
> *Than of sandalwood, rosebay,*
> *Of the blue lotus or jasmine!*

It is so fine it can travel against the wind, it can travel against all the laws. It can go against gravitation, it can rise upwards; it can reach the highest skies.

> *The fragrance of sandalwood and rosebay*
> *Does not travel far.*
> *But the fragrance of virtue*
> *Rises to the heavens.*

The fragrance of the flowers cannot travel far—it is momentary, it is finite; it can go only so far and then it disappears. But the fragrance of Buddhahood can travel to the very ends of the world because it is infinite, *and* it is something beyond time, beyond space. In fact, even when the body of a Buddha is gone, the fragrance continues to travel.

Those who are really perceptive, sensitive, can catch hold of it even when a Buddha has been gone for centuries. It is possible to be a contemporary of Buddha even now, to have a communion with Jesus even now. The flower is no more, but the fragrance has become part of the universe— the trees have it, the winds have it, the clouds have it. Now Jesus is not in the physical body, but Jesus has become universal. If you know how to drink out of the universal, if you know how to contact the universal, you will be surprised: all the Buddhas become alive because they are all contemporary, time makes no difference.

That's my whole effort here: to make you contemporaries of Jesus, of Buddha, of Zarathustra, of Lao Tzu. If you can be contemporaries of these awakened souls, what is the point of remaining contemporaries to your ordinary world and its ordinary citizens, the so-called human beings, who have nothing of humanity in them, who have not yet become beings, who are just hollow, empty, meaningless? What is the point of living in the neighbourhood of empty cells when you can be a neighbour of Gautam the Buddha?

Yes, that is possible—it is possible by transcending time and space. And in meditation you transcend both. In meditation you don't know where you are, you don't know the time, you don't know the space. In meditation, time and space both disappear—you simply are.

That moment, when you simply are, Buddha is just by your side; you are surrounded by Buddhas of all the ages.

You will be living for the first time, a life worth living, a life of significance: when you can hold hands with Buddhas and Krishnas, when you can dance with Krishna and sing with Meera and sit with Kabir. It is possible! Because only the flowers have disappeared, but the fragrance is eternal—it cannot disappear.

And then all the scriptures become alive for you. Then reading the Bible, you are not just reading a book—then Moses speaks to you, Abraham speaks to you, Jesus speaks to you, *face to face!*

> *Desire never crosses the path*
> *Of virtuous and wakeful men.*
> *Their brightness sets them free.*

DESIRE MEANS GREED FOR MORE AND MORE. Desire means discontent—discontent with what is, discontent with the present. Hence you seek contentment in your hopes for the future. Today is empty, you can live only by the hope of tomorrow. The tomorrow will bring something...although many tomorrows have come and gone and that something never happens, but you go on hoping against hope. Only death will come.

Desires are never fulfilled. In the very nature of things they cannot be fulfilled. The wakeful person looks into the desiring mind and laughs—the desiring mind is the most stupid mind, because it is desiring something which cannot be fulfilled in the very nature of things. Just as you cannot get oil through the sand—you can go on and on working on the sand, but you will not get oil out of it—it does not exist in the sand. It is impossible! Exactly like that, desire is just a deception.

It keeps you occupied—obviously, that's its whole purpose —it keeps you occupied, it keeps you hoping, it keeps promising you. Desire is a politician: it goes on promising you, "Just wait—five years more and everything is going to be absolutely right. Just five years more and the world is going to become a paradise." And the politicians have been saying that for thousands of years, and look at the unintelligent humanity: it still goes on believing in the politicians. It changes politicians; when it becomes tired of one, it starts listening to another. But that is not a change at all. One politician is replaced by another.

Hence democracies live as two-party systems. One party remains in power for five years; according to the promises you go on hoping, then you are frustrated—nothing happens. Things get worse than they were before. But by this time, the other party that is not in power starts promising you. And the stupidity is such that you start believing the other party. You bring the other party into power; for five years it will deceive you. By that time the first party that has deceived you before has again become creditable, again has attained credit; again it has criticized the ruling party and again it has gained respect in your eyes. And *again* it has stirred your hoping mind. And people's memories are very short, hence politicians go on deceiving.

Desire is a politician. One desire keeps you occupied for many years, then, frustration in your hands, you are tired of it, weary of it, you drop out of it—but immediately you enter into another desire. Another politician is waiting for you. You were after money, then tired, you forget all about it and you start rushing for power or for fame.

Desire is so cunning that it can even take the form of religion, it can become religious. It is ready to have any mask. It can start thinking of heaven and heavenly pleasures.

It can give you the idea that this life it is not possible, but next life you are going to be in paradise, and in paradise all kinds of fulfillments... wish-fulfilling trees. You just sit underneath the tree, you wish, and it is fulfilled. What are you going to wish for? Your wishes will be stupid because they will come out of your mind. What pleasures are you going to seek in heaven? Just one day think that you have reached heaven: now what do you want? You will start asking for a hotel, for a moviehouse, for a woman, for a man... what else? The same things! And the same frustrations will follow.

> *Desire never crosses the path*
> *Of virtuous and wakeful men.*

Buddha says: I call that man virtuous who has become utterly aware of the deceptiveness of desire and hence desire never crosses his mind. His mind remains desireless. The only way to be desireless is to be wakeful, watchful. Watchfulness creates a light in you, and in that light the darkness of desire cannot enter.

> *Their brightness sets them free*

AND WHEN YOU ARE WATCHFUL THERE IS A luminosity in your being; a great intelligence arises in you. Ordinary man lives in stupidity; the ordinary man lives in a very foolish way. The moment you become attuned to your inner music, you become attuned to meditativeness, great intelligence is released. In that intelligence it is impossible for you to be deceived by desire. In that intelligence for the first time you start understanding things as they are, you stop *mis*understanding.

Ordinarily all your understanding is nothing but mis-understanding. You may think that you are very intelligent, but only stupid people think that they are intelligent. Intelligence itself is very unselfconscious. It functions—functions perfectly, but it creates no self-consciousness, it brings no idea of the ego, no superiority. It is very humble, it is very simple.

But as ordinary man exists, he goes on misunderstanding. You read the Bible and you misunderstand. Even those closest disciples of Jesus never understood him. I say again and again that Jesus is one of the most unfortunate Masters who has ever walked on the earth—not only because he was crucified and had only three years time to work, but because he had a very stupid lot of followers.

The day Jesus is going to be caught, and it has become absolutely certain that he has been betrayed by one of his disciples, Judas, he asks his other eleven apostles, "Have you something to ask me?"

And do you know what they asked? They asked such foolish things. Jesus must have cried. He may have prayed deep down in his heart, as he did later on again on the cross: "Father, forgive them, for they know not what they are asking."

What were they asking? They were asking, "Master, now that you are leaving, a few things have to be made clear. In the world of God, in the kingdom of God, that you have talked about so much again and again, you will certainly be on the right hand of God, then who will be on your right hand? Amongst us who is going to be second to you and who is going to be third and the fourth? What will the hierarchy be?"

See the question! The Master is going to be crucified tomorrow, and these foolish people are worried about hierarchy, who will be the highest. They are ready to concede to Jesus, "Okay, that much we accept, that you will be second to God, but who will be third and the fourth and the fifth? Let it be decided clearly, because now you are leaving and we may not meet again soon, so everything has to be certain!"

The desirous mind, the ambitious mind—they have not understood Jesus at all. And it is said Jesus fell on his knees and prayed and tears rolled down his cheeks. Nobody knows what he prayed, but he must have been praying: "Forgive these people, they know not what they are asking." And he must have been crying because this was his whole life's work, these people. And he has been telling them not to desire, not to be ambitious; he has been telling them, "Those who are the first in this world will be the last in my kingdom of God, and those who are the last will be the first." But they have not understood that he is telling them not to be ambitious.

Just the other day, Premgeet sent me a small anecdote on misinterpretation:

The frantic nurse ran after a screaming patient down the corridor of the ward, carrying a bowl. She was stopped by the surgeon who said, "Nurse! Nurse! I told you to prick his boil!"

You get it? She was boiling his prick! But this is exactly what goes on happening—the mob mind cannot understand. Misunderstanding is inevitable, because the mass mind is deaf. While you are talking to people they are not really listening, they are only pretending to listen. A thousand and one thoughts are crossing through their minds; they are not really there, they are never present to any situation, they

157

are always absent. They are not where they are, they are always somewhere else. When they are in Poona, they are in Peking; when they are in Peking, they are in Poona. Strange people! Wherever they are you can be certain that there at least they are not; anywhere else in the world they can be. How can they understand?

And they listen only to words, they never listen to the meaning—because the meaning can be listened to only by the heart. The words can be listened to by the head. Now, they don't know how to listen through the heart. Listening through the heart is the meaning of being a disciple; listening through the heart means listening in love, in trust, in deep sympathy, and finally in deep empathy. Listening through the heart means listening as if you have become one with what is being told to you—when the disciple becomes so attuned to the Master that even before the words are uttered he hears them, and not only the words but the meaning, the fragrance that is carried by the words. But it is very invisible. The head is gross. The invisible can be caught only in the net of the heart.

People even follow, but then too they follow out of misunderstanding. Just by becoming a follower it does not change anything in your life. It is not a question of following somebody: it is a question of understanding somebody who is awakened. Hence, I don't call you my followers but only my friends. If you can be my friends, if you can be in deep love and trust here in my presence, if you can be present to my presence, if we can face each other and mirror each other, tremendously important things will start happening of their own accord—because your heart will understand, and when the heart understands, *immediately* transformations happen.

When the head understands, then it asks, "How? Yes

it is right. Now how can it be done?" Remember this difference: in the head, knowledge and action are two different things; in the heart, knowledge *is* action.

Socrates says: "Knowledge is virtue." And he has not been understood down the ages. Not even his own disciples, Plato and Aristotle, have understood him rightly. When he says, "Knowledge is virtue," he means there is a way of listening and understanding in which the moment you understand a thing you can't do otherwise. When you see that this is the door, then you cannot try to get out through the wall, you will get out through the door. Seeing means acting. Seeing brings action.

If I tell you, "This is the door. Whenever you want to get out, please get out through this door, because enough you have hurt your head by trying to get out through the wall," you say, "Yes, sir, I understand perfectly well, but how to get out through the door?" your question will show that the heart has not listened, only the head. The head always asks "How?"

The head always asks questions which seems to be very pertinent on the surface but are absolutely ridiculous. The heart never asks—it listens and acts. Listening and action are one in the heart; love knows and acts accordingly. It never asks "How?" The heart has an intelligence of its own. The head is intellectual, the heart is intelligence.

> *How sweetly the lotus grows*
> *In the litter of the wayside.*
> *Its pure fragrance delights the heart.*

REMEMBER IT AGAIN AND AGAIN BECAUSE YOU will forget again and again, that it is a question of the heart. If the heart delights in something, then you can be certain your life is growing, expanding; your consciousness is becoming clearer, your intelligence is being released from its bondage.

> *How sweetly the lotus grows*
> *In the litter of the wayside.*

The word for lotus that Buddha uses is *pankaj;* it is one of the most beautiful words. *Pankaj* means that which is born out of the mud, out of dirty mud. The lotus is one of the most miraculous phenomena in existence, hence in the East it has become the symbol of spiritual transformation. Buddha is seated on a lotus, Vishnu is standing on a lotus—why a lotus? Because the lotus has one very symbolic significance: it grows out of dirty mud. It is a transformation symbol, it is a metamorphosis. The mud is dirty, maybe stinking, and the lotus is fragrant, and it has come out of the stinking mud.

Buddha is saying: Exactly in the same way, life ordinarily is just stinking mud—but the possibility of becoming a lotus is hidden there. The mud can be transformed, you can become a lotus. Sex can be transformed and it can become samadhi. Anger can be transformed and it can become compassion. And hate can be transformed and it can become love. Everything that you have that looks negative right now, mudlike, can be transformed. Your noisy mind can be emptied and transformed, and it becomes the celestial music.

> *Follow the awakened*
> *And from among the blind*
> *The light of your wisdom*
> *Will shine out, purely.*

But the only possible way out of this mess is being in tune

160

with somebody who is already awakened. You are asleep; only somebody who is awake can shake you out of your sleep, can help you to come out of it.

Gurdjieff used to say: If you are in a jail, only somebody who is out of jail can manage it, can arrange it so that you can escape from the jail. Otherwise it is impossible. And you are not only in a jail—you have been hypnotized and told that this is not a jail, this is your home. And you are not only in a jail—you have believed it to be your home and you are decorating it. Your whole life is nothing but decorating the jail. And you are competing with other prisoners who are decorating their dark cells.

Only somebody who is free, who has been in the jail once and is no more in the jail, can manage to wake you, to make you aware of the reality. He can manage to dehypnotize you; he can help you to be unconditioned. And he can devise methods and means so that you can escape from the jail. He can bribe the warden, the jailor; he can bring a ladder close to the wall, he can throw a rope inside. He can make a hole in the wall from the outside...a thousand and one possibilities.

But the only hope for you is to be in deep contact with somebody who is awakened. The awakened one is called the Master—*sadguru*. If you can find a Master, don't miss the opportunity, surrender, relax into his being, imbibe his awareness, let his fragrance surround you. And the day is not far away when you will also be awakened, you will also be a Buddha.

Keep on reminding yourself that unless you are a Buddha, your life is a wastage. Only by being a Buddha does one's life have grace, beauty, intelligence, significance, benediction.

is it as easy to hate as it is to love?

what is?

what is your opinion of scientology?

can't psychoanalysis solve
man's problems?

I don't find sex tiring...?

what will be your last words
to the world?

July 6

This is It

The first question

Bhagwan,
You have always pointed out that most things and
states are two extremes of one state, polar opposites.
Then hate is the other end of love. Does this mean
it is as easy to hate as it is to love? Love is so beauti-
ful. Hate is so ugly, and yet it happens too.

Zareen,

LOVE IS A NATURAL STATE OF CONSCIOUS-
ness. It is neither easy nor difficult. Those
words don't apply to it at all. It is not an
effort; hence, it can't be easy and it can't be difficult either.
It is like breathing! It is like your heartbeat, it is like blood
circulating in your body.

Love is your very being...but that love has become
almost impossible. The society does not allow it. The society
conditions you in such a way that love becomes impossible

163

and hate becomes the only possible thing. Then hate is easy, and love is not only difficult but impossible.

Man has been distorted. Man cannot be reduced to slavery if he is not distorted first. The politician and the priest have been in a deep conspiracy down the ages. They have been reducing humanity to a crowd of slaves. They are destroying every possibility of rebellion in man—and love *is* rebellion, because love listens only to the heart and does not care a bit about anything else.

Love is dangerous because it makes you an individual, and the state and the church, they don't want individuals, not at all. They don't want human beings—they want sheep. They want people who only look like human beings, but whose souls have been crushed so utterly, damaged so deeply, that it seems almost irreparable.

And the best way to destroy man is to destroy his spontaneity of love. If man has love, there can't be nations; nations exist on hate. The Indians hate the Pakistanis, and the Pakistanis hate the Indians—only then can these two countries exist. If love appears, boundaries will disappear. If love appears, then who will be a Christian and then who will be a Jew? If love appears, religions will disappear.

If love appears, who is going to go to the temple? For what? It is because love is missing that you are searching for God. God is nothing but a substitute for your missing love. Because you are not blissful, because you are not peaceful, because you are not ecstatic, hence you are searching for God—otherwise, who bothers? who cares? If your life is a dance, God has been attained already. The loving heart is full of God...there is no need for any search, there is no need for any prayer, there is *no* need to go to any temple, to any priest.

Hence, the priest and the politician, these two are the

enemies of humanity. And they are in a conspiracy, because the politician wants to rule your body and the priest wants to rule your soul. And the secret is the same: destroy love. And then a man is nothing but a hollowness, an emptiness, a meaningless existence. Then you can do whatsoever you want with humanity and nobody will rebel, nobody will have courage enough to rebel.

Love gives courage! Love takes all fear away! And the oppressors depend on your fear. They create fear in you, a thousand and one kinds of fear. You are surrounded by fears. Your whole psychology is full of fears. Deep down you are trembling. Only on the surface do you keep a certain façade; otherwise, inside there are layers and layers of fear.

And a man full of fear can only hate—hate is a natural outcome of fear. And a man full of fear is also full of anger. And a man full of fear is more against life than for life. Death seems to be a restful state to the fear-filled man. The fearful man is suicidal, he is life-negative. Life seems to be dangerous to him, because to live means you will have to love—how can you live? Just as the body needs breathing to live, the soul needs love to live. And love is utterly poisoned.

By poisoning your love energy they have created a split in you, they have made an enemy within you, they have divided you in two. They have created a civil war, and you are always in conflict. And in conflict your energy is dissipated. Hence your life does not have zestfulness, cheerfulness. It is not overflowing with energy; it is dull, insipid. It is unintelligent.

Love sharpens intelligence: fear dulls it. Who wants you to be intelligent? Not those who are in power. How can they want you to be intelligent? Because if you are intelligent, you will start seeing the whole strategy, their games. They want you to be stupid and mediocre. They certainly want you to be efficient as far as work is concerned, but not intelligent.

Hence, humanity lives at the lowest, at the minimum of its potential. The scientific researchers say that the ordinary man uses only five percent of his potential intelligence in his whole life. The ordinary man, only five percent—what about the extraordinary? What about an Albert Einstein, a Mozart, a Beethoven? The researchers say that even those who are very talented, they don't use more than ten percent. And those whom we call geniuses, they use only fifteen percent.

Think of a world where everybody is using one hundred percent of his potential...then the gods will be jealous of earth, then gods would like to be born on earth. Then the earth will be a paradise, a super-paradise. Right now it is a hell.

Zareen, you say that it should be easier to love than to hate. If man is left alone, unpoisoned, then love will be simple, very simple. There will be no problem. It will be just like water flowing downwards, or vapour rising upwards, trees blossoming, birds singing. It will be so natural and so spontaneous!

But man is not left alone. As the child is born the oppressors are ready to jump on him, to crush his energies, to distort them to such an extent, to distort them so deeply, that the person will never become aware that he is living a false life, a pseudo life, that he is not living as he was meant to live, as he was born to live; that he is living something synthetic, plastic, that this is not his real soul.

That's why millions of people are in such misery—because they feel somewhere that they have been distracted, that they are not their own selves, that something has gone basically wrong....

Love is simple if the child is allowed to grow, helped to grow, in natural ways—in the way of Dhamma. If the child is helped to be in harmony with nature and in harmony with himself, if the child is in every way supported, nourished, encouraged to be natural *and* to be himself, a light unto himself, then love is simple. One will be simply loving!

Hate will be almost impossible, because before you can hate somebody else first you have to create the poison within yourself. You can give something to somebody only if you have it. You can hate only if you are full of hate. And to be full of hate is to suffer hell. To be full of hate is to be in fire. To be full of hate means you are wounding yourself first. Before you can wound somebody else, you have to wound yourself. The other may not be wounded; it will depend on the other. But one thing is absolutely certain: that before you can hate, you have to go through long suffering and misery. The other may not accept your hatred, may reject it. The other may be a Buddha, he may simply laugh at it. He may forgive you, he may not react. You may not be able to wound him if he is not ready to react. If you cannot disturb him, what can you do? You will feel impotent before him.

So it is not necessarily so that the other is going to be wounded. But one thing is absolutely certain, that if you hate somebody, first you have to wound your own soul in so many ways, you have to be so full of poison that you can throw poison on others.

Hate is unnatural. Love is a state of health. Hate is a state of illness, just as illness is unnatural—it happens only when you lose track of nature, when you are no more in harmony with existence, no more in harmony with your being, with your innermost core, then you are ill, psychologically, spiritually ill. Hatred is only a symbol of illness, and love one of health and wholeness and holiness.

ZAREEN, LOVE SHOULD BE ONE OF THE MOST natural things, but it is not. On the contrary, it has become the *most* difficult thing—almost the impossible thing. Hate has become easy; you are trained, you are prepared for hate. To be a Hindu is to be full of hate for Mohammedans, for Christians, for Jews; to be a Christian is to be full of hate for other religions. To be a nationalist is to be full of hate for other nations.

You know only one way of love: that is, hate others. You can show your love for your country only by hating other countries, and you can show your love for your church only by hating other churches. You are in a mess!

And these so-called religions go on talking about love, and all that they do in the world is create more and more hate. Christians talk about love and they have been creating wars, crusades. Mohammedans talk about love and they have been creating *jehads*—religious wars. Hindus talk about love, but you can look into their scriptures—they are full of hate, hate for other religions.

You can study Dayananda's so-called great book, *Sathiarth Prakash*, and you will find hate on each page, in each sentence. And these books are thought to be spiritual books.

And we accept all this nonsense! And we accept it without any resistance, because we have been conditioned to accept these things, we have been taught that this is how things are. And then you go on denying your own nature.

Just the other day I was reading a joke:

A woman was confessing—she was a nun—she was confessing to the mother superior, crying, tears rolling down her cheeks, tremendously disturbed she looked. And she was saying, "I have committed a sin—something unforgivable. This man entered into my room last night, and I was alone. And at the point of a revolver he made love to me. He gave me only two alternatives: 'Either die or make love to me.' I am ruined!" she was saying. "My whole life is ruined!"

The mother superior said, "Don't get so disturbed, don't get so worried—God's compassion is infinite. And it is said in the old scriptures that a man is allowed to do anything if it is a question of survival—except spitting on the Bible. A man is allowed to do *anything* if it is a question of survival, and it was a question of survival for you. So *don't* be worried! You *are* forgiven!"

But the woman remained disturbed and started crying again and said, "No. It won't help!"

The mother superior said, "Why won't it help?"

And the nun looked up and she said, "Because I liked it."

You can deny nature but you cannot destroy it. It remains somewhere in the deepest recesses of your being, alive. And that's the only hope.

Love has been poisoned, but not destroyed. The poison can be thrown out, out of your system; you can be cleansed. You can vomit all that the society has enforced upon you, you can drop all your beliefs and all your conditions—you can be free. The society cannot keep you a slave forever if you decide to be free.

That's what sannyas is all about.

Zareen, it is time—now become a sannyasin. It is time to drop out of all old patterns and start a new way of life, a natural way of life, a non-repressive way of life. A life not of renunciation but of rejoicing.

Ordinarily, if you look at human beings, love is impossible, only hate is possible. But the space that I am creating here is totally different: here love is the only possibility. Hate will become more and more impossible. Hate is the polar opposite of love—in the sense that illness is the polar opposite of health. But you need not choose illness.

Illness has a few advantages which health cannot have; don't become attached to those advantages. Hate also has a few advantages which love cannot have. And you have to be very watchful. The ill person gets sympathy from everybody else; nobody hurts him, everybody remains careful what they say to him, he is so ill. He remains the focus, the center, of everybody—the family, the friends—he becomes the central person. He becomes important. Now, if he becomes too much attached to this importance, to this ego-fulfillment, he will never want to be healthy again. He himself will cling to illness. And psychologists say there are many people who are clinging to illnesses, because of the advantages illnesses have. And they have invested in their illnesses so long that they have completely forgotten that they are clinging to those illnesses. They are afraid: if they become healthy, they will be nobody again.

You teach that too: when a small child becomes ill, the whole family is so attentive. This is absolutely unscientific. When the child is ill, take care of his body but don't pay too much attention. It is dangerous, because if illness and your attention become associated...which is bound to happen if it happens again and again. Whenever the child is ill he becomes the center of the whole family: daddy comes and sits by his side and enquires about his health, and the doctor comes, and the neighbours start coming, and friends enquire, and people bring presents for him.... Now he can become too much attached to all this; it can be so nourishing to his ego that he may not like to be well again.

And if this happens, then it is impossible to be healthy. No medicine can help now. The person has become decisively committed to illness. And that's what has happened to many people—the majority.

When you hate, your ego is fulfilled. The ego can exist only if it hates, because in hating you feel superior, in hating you become separate, in hating you become defined, in hating you attain a certain identity. In love the ego has to disappear. In love you are no more separate—love helps you to dissolve with others. It is a meeting and a merger.

If you are too much attached to the ego, then hate is easy and love is most difficult. Be alert, watchful: hate is the shadow of ego, and love needs great courage. It needs great courage because it needs the sacrifice of the ego. Only those who are ready to be nobodies are able to love. Only those who are ready to become nothing, utterly empty of themselves, are able to receive the gift of love from the beyond.

If you are watchful, Zareen, love will become very simple and hate will become impossible. And the day hate becomes impossible and love becomes natural, you have arrived home. Then there is nowhere to go...God has been achieved.

To be absolutely natural is all that is meant by finding God.

The second question

Bhagwan,
What is?

Prabhati,

THERE ARE TWO KINDS OF THINGS IN EXISTENCE: one, that which can be explained; and the other, that which can only be experienced. The things that can be explained are mundane, ordinary, have no intrinsic value in them. And the things that cannot be explained are really significant, have intrinsic value.

For example: sex can be explained, love cannot be explained. Hence, sex becomes a commodity; it can be sold, it can be purchased. Love is not a commodity; you cannot sell it, you cannot purchase it—there is no way. Sex can be explained because it is part of physiology. Love cannot be explained—it is part of your inner mystery.

Unless your sexuality rises and reaches to love it is mundane, it has nothing sacred about it. When your sex becomes love, then it is entering into a totally different dimension—the dimension of the mysterious and the miraculous. Now it is becoming religious, sacred, it is no more profane.

And there is an even higher stage of love—I call it prayer —which is absolutely unexplainable, which is absolutely ineffable. Nothing can be said about it.

When a disciple asked Jesus, "What is prayer?" Jesus fell on his knees and started praying. What else can you do? Prayer cannot be explained; nothing can be said about it. But it can be shown. What can you say about death, what can you say about life? Whatsoever you say will fall

172

short; it cannot soar to the heights of life and death. Those are experiences.

What can you say about beauty? Even if the lake is full of beautiful lotuses and it is a full-moon night, and all is benediction, somebody can ask, "What is beauty?" what can you say? You can show! You can say, "This is it!" But he will say, "I am asking for a definition."

Rabindranath, one of the greatest poets of this country, was living on a small houseboat. He used to live for months together on that houseboat; he loved living on the houseboat. It was a full-moon night and he was reading in his room, a small cabin, just by a small candlelight, and he was reading about aesthetics—what is beauty? And the full moon outside! and the cuckoo calling from the distant shore, and the moon reflecting all over the lake, and the whole lake was silver! And it was a tremendously silent night, nobody around, except that cuckoo calling. And once in a while, a bird would fly over the boat, or a fish would jump in the lake—and those sounds would deepen the silence even more. And he pondered over great books on aesthetics in search of the definition of what beauty is.

Tired, exhausted, in the middle of the night, he blew out the candle...and he was shocked, surprised. As he blew out the candle, the moonrays entered through the window, through the door, inside the cabin. That pale light of the candle had been keeping the moon out. Suddenly, he heard the cuckoo calling from the distant shore. Suddenly, he became aware of the tremendous silence, the depth of the silence surrounding the boat. And a fish jumped, and he came out.... He had never seen such a beautiful night. A few white clouds floating in the sky, and the moon and the lake and the cuckoo calling...he was transported into another world.

He wrote in his diary: "I am foolish! I have been searching in books for what beauty is, and beauty was standing outside my door, knocking on my door! I was looking for beauty, searching for beauty, with a small candle, and the small candlelight was keeping the moonlight outside."

He wrote in his diary: "It seems my small ego is keeping God out—the small ego, like a pale small candlelight, keeping the light of God outside. And he is waiting outside. All that I need to do is to close the books, blow out the candle of the ego and go out—*and see!*"

> Prabhati, you ask me:
> *What is?*

This...thisness...this moment you are surrounded by the is. It is within you and without you. The chirping of the birds...and this silence...and you ask me what is?

It is not a question that can be answered. It is a dangerous question too, dangerous in the sense that you may find some foolish person who answers it, and then you may cling to that answer. Somebody will say, "God is," and you will cling to that answer. And then another question will arise: "What is God?" And now you are ready to fall into an infinite regress.

A man who once did God a favour received as his reward the promise of an answer to one question, any question. But God warned him that some things can only be experienced and cannot be explained. As he pondered and then started to ask his one cosmic question, God warned him again about experience versus explanations.

The man could contain his question no longer, and

demanded to know, "What is after death?" and God slew him where he stood.

What else could God do? He slew him where he stood, immediately he killed him. Because if you want to know what is after death, you have to die! Be very careful. You can be given explanations about things which belong to the world, to the objective world. For that you should ask the scientist; he knows, it is his concern. Don't ask the mystic about things which can be explained; that is not his concern. His concern is with things which can be experienced.

Don't ask me any question which cannot be explained. Be in my presence, feel my presence, be open and vulnerable. We are here to experience something. All explanations about the mysteries of life are nothing but explaining away those things.

The basic, root meaning of the word 'explanation' is 'to flatten a thing'—but to flatten a thing is to destroy it. If anybody could answer "What is God?" "What is love?" "What is prayer?" "What is?" he would have flattened a beautiful, tremendously beautiful, incredible experience, into ugly words.

All words are inadequate.

Be and know! Be still and know! You are here not to learn more words; you are here to get deeper into silence. Use my words as hints towards a wordless existence.

This is it! What are you asking about? Feel this moment . . .in its totality, in all its dimensionality, and a great beauty will descend, a great beatitude, a great benediction will surround you, a grace, a very silent ecstasy will start rising in you. You will feel drunk with existence.

Be drunk with existence, that is the only way to know it.

THE BOOK OF THE BOOKS

The third question

Bhagwan,
What is your opinion of scientology?

Aida,

IT IS FANTASTIC...I MEAN BULLSHIT, UTTER
bullshit! Be aware of such stupid things. They move in the
world in the name of science because science has credit, so
any kind of stupidity can pretend to be scientific. And people
are very much impressed by words: 'scientology'. People
are very much impressed by shining gadgets, instruments....

Man is so unaware and unconscious of himself that he
falls a victim to anything! You just need to propagate it,
advertise it. And our century has the most efficient media
to advertise, to propagate things.

Scientology is nothing but a kind of hypnosis; it can
hypnotize you. And real religion is just the opposite: it is
de-hypnosis. You are already hypnotized; you don't need
any scientology any more. You need a process of de-
hypnosis, you need de-conditioning; you need to come
out of all kinds of ideologies. Scientology is an ideology. And
it talks in terms of science, and science has great appeal.
Science is the modern superstition.

The modern man is immediately impressed if you bring
science in. So anything and everything has to be proved
scientifically. And there are quacks who even go on proving
God scientifically, and who are trying to measure states of
meditation—as if meditation can be measured. Whatsoever
you can measure will be mind; no-mind cannot be measured.
All your alpha waves, etc., are not going to help. They can

176

only go to a certain extent *in* the mind. But meditation begins only where mind ends.

Mind is measurable, because mind *is* a machine. But no-mind is immeasurable; it has no limits. So all the nonsense that goes on in the name of measuring...and people are very much impressed. They are sitting before very shiny gadgets—it gives an impression of science—wires attached to the head, to the hands, just like a cardiogram. They are trying to figure out the inner silence. It is impossible! Whatsoever you come to record *is* mind. All waves are of the mind.

Meditation is wavelessness because it is thoughtlessness. Meditation cannot be recorded; there can be no cardiogram, there can be no machine which can record it. It is very elusive. It is very subjective; it cannot be reduced to an object. But because the Western mind is very objective, is trained in science, now there are quacks around who are cashing in on this attraction and this training.

Scientology is one of those pseudo religions. The real religion has no need of any such thing. And scientology is destroying many people's minds.

Modern man is in a special situation: the old religions have lost their grip, their credibility. And the new religion has not yet arrived—there is a gap. And man cannot live without religion; it is impossible. Religion is such a need. So if the true is not available, the false becomes prevalent, the false becomes a substitute.

Scientology is a false religion. And there are many like scientology.

Real religion consists of becoming utterly silent, unconditioned, unhypnotized. It is going beyond mind, beyond ideology; it is going beyond scripture and beyond know-ledge. It is simply falling into your own interiority, becom-ing utterly silent, not knowing a thing, and functioning from that state of not knowing, from that innocence.

When you function out of innocence, your actions have a beauty of their own. That's what virtue is—*ais dhammo sanantano*.

The fourth question

Bhagwan,
Cannot psychoanalysis solve man's problems? Is religion really needed at all?

Neelima,

PSYCHOANALYSIS IS A SUPERFICIAL THING— helpful but very superficial. It only analyses the surface rumblings of your mind. It is far better than scientology, certainly, because at least it analyses *actual* reality. It is con-cerned with the mind that you have got. It tries to penetrate into your unconscious, into the repressed part of your mind. It can help you, but it cannot solve all your problems, because its reach is very limited. Hence, Freud could not satisfy, he could only touch a part of your mind. Adler touched another part of your mind—he could not satisfy either. Jung touched still another part of your mind—he could not satisfy, because parts are parts and the problem belongs to the whole.

Assagioli goes a little deeper than all these three. He drops psychoanalysis and starts calling *his* endeavour 'psy-chosynthesis'. That is a little better; he synthesizes. Freud is a fanatic; he claims that whatsoever he is saying is the truth and the only truth and the whole truth. And anybody who is against it is against truth. There can be no other possibility—this is the only way. The fanatic always claims, "This is the only way." The fanatic does not allow life its richness, its variety.

And so is Adler. They were all basically disciples of Freud, although they rejected his knowledge. But they never could reject his basic fanaticism. They rejected what he said, but they never could reject the impression that he had left on their beings.

Jung was also a follower, a disciple, then rebelled against him. But even in his rebellion he remained, deep down, the same person—the same emphasis of claiming the whole, of knowing the whole.

Assagioli is far better, because he says all these three persons are talking sense but they are partial—they have to be synthesized. A synthetic approach is needed which combines all the endeavours. But Assagioli commits a mistake which is very fundamental. You can dissect a man's body to know what is inside; once you have dissected it you will not find any soul—that is not the way to find a soul. You will find hands and legs and head and eyes and heart and kidneys, and thousands of things you will find, and you can make a long list...but you will not find the soul. And naturally you will conclude there is no soul.

That's what was done by Freud, Adler and Jung. Then came Assagioli. He said, "This is not right. Dissection is not the way, analysis is not the way—I will try synthesis." So he puts all those parts together again, stitches them together; does a good job of stitching, but still the man is not alive, the soul is not there. Once the soul has left, just by putting the body together you cannot bring it back. So now it is a corpse—better than Freud, Adler and Jung, because they were only like the proverbial blind men, the five blind men, who had gone to see the elephant. Each was claiming, "My experience of the elephant *is* the elephant." The one who had touched the leg of the elephant was saying that the elephant is nothing but a pillar...and so on and so forth. Freud, Jung and Adler are all blind, feeling parts of the elephant. And the elephant of life is really huge, enormous.

Now what Assagioli has done is that he has collected the opinions of the five blind men and he has put all those opinions together, and he says, "This is the right thing. I have made the synthesis, this is the truth." This is not the way to find the truth. By putting five blind men's opinions together, you don't arrive at the real elephant.

The real elephant needs *eyes* to be seen. Psychoanalysis is blind and so is psychosynthesis—a little wiser but blind all the same.

They cannot solve man's problems because man's basic problem is not psychological but spiritual, not psychological but existential. Man is not only the body, otherwise the physiologist would have solved all his problems. And man is not only a psyche, otherwise the psychologist would have solved his problems. Man is far more: man is an organic unity—body, mind, soul—these three plus something mysterious: the fourth. The mystics in India have called it just the fourth—*turiya*. They don't give it any name because no name can be given to it. Body, mind, soul, these three are nameable.

The body is available for objective observation. The mind is available for both objective and subjective observation—you can observe it from the outside as behaviour and from the inside as ideas, thoughts, imagination, memory, instinct, feeling. so on and so forth. The soul is available only as a subjective experience. And beyond all these three is the fourth that keeps them all together: *turiya*—the fourth, unnameable. That fourth has been called 'God', the fourth has been called 'nirvana', the fourth has been called 'enlightenment'.

Man's problem is complex. If he were only the body, things would have been simple; science would have solved everything. If he were only the mind, psychology would have been enough. But he is a very complex phenomenon, four-dimensional. And unless you know the fourth, unless you enter the fourth, you don't know the man in his totality. And without knowing him in his totality, the problem cannot be solved.

Psychoanalysis can give you a philosophic approach, but not an existential transformation.

During the last days of a psychiatrists' convention, one of the doctors present at the closing lecture noticed an attractive female Ph.D. being pawed by the man seated next to her.

"Is he bothering you?" the gallant observer asked the woman.

"Why should I be bothered?" she replied. "It is *his* problem."

Psychoanalysis, psychiatry, psychology, can give you a philosophical approach towards life. They can give you the quality of being distant from life's problems, but they are not solved. And the psychiatrist has not even solved his own problems—how can he help others to solve theirs?

Even Sigmund Freud is not a Buddha, is full of problems —in fact more than the so-called human beings. He was very much afraid of death, too much afraid of death—so much so that even the word 'death' was not uttered in

181

front of him by his disciples, because once or twice just hearing the word 'death' he had fainted. Just the word 'death' was enough! He would faint, he would become unconscious, he would fall down from his chair.

Freud brought sex into the light; he did a great work. He destroyed one taboo—the taboo that had remained for centuries. Sex was a taboo subject, not to be talked about. He brought it into the light, he did a great pioneer work. He should be respected for it. But death was taboo to him; he could not even hear the word. There seems to be a connection.

This is *my* observation: that there have been two kinds of societies in the world—one society which makes sex taboo, then it is not afraid of death; and the other society which drops the taboo against sex, then it immediately becomes afraid of death. We have not yet been able to create a society in which neither sex nor death are taboos.

My sannyasin has to do that. Why does it happen so?

For example, in India, sex is taboo—you should not talk about it—but death is not taboo. You can talk about it; in fact, all the religious teachers talk about death. They make people so much afraid of death, talking again and again and again about it, they create so much fear in people that out of fear people start becoming religious. All Indian scriptures are full of the description of death. Death seems to be one of the most talked about subjects in India—not sex. Sex is taboo. Sex is life, and if you choose death you cannot choose sex—either/or.

Freud did a great service to humanity; he brought sex from the dark corners of the soul into the open world. But immediately death became taboo; he himself became afraid of death. Both are polar opposites, and the total man will be able to understand both.

And the total man, the whole man, is my definition of a holy man. He will be able to talk about sex, observe, analyse, dissect, go into it, meditate—and he will be able to do the same with death. Because you are neither sex nor death: you are the witness of both. You are neither life nor death: you are a witness to both. This witnessing will bring you to the fourth—the *turiya*. And only when you enter the fourth do all problems disappear, dissolve. Before that, problems remain.

You can become very very expert in analysing problems—that is not going to help.

A beautiful woman visits a psychoanalyst. "Take off your clothes," says the psychoanalyst as soon as she enters.

"But really I was...."

"I am telling you to take off your clothes," insists the shrink without giving her time to answer.

"But, doctor, I came because I have a problem and I thought...."

"Don't think. Take off your clothes and don't waste my time," insists the shrink even more rudely.

The astonished and embarrassed woman takes off her clothes and immediately the shrink jumps on her.

After half an hour, the shrink, zipping up his trousers, looks at the woman who still does not understand what is happening and more calmly says, "Well, now that I have solved my problem, let us see if I can solve yours."

Only a Buddha can help you to solve your problems—one who has no problems of his own.

Religion cannot be dropped, can never be dropped. Religion is not something superficial and accidental: it is an intrinsic need, it is absolutely needed.

Neelima, you ask me:
Cannot psychoanalysis solve man's problems?

No. It can help you to understand your problems a little
bit more. And by understanding your problems you can
control your life in a certain way, to a certain extent.
Psychoanalysis can help you to become a little more normal
than you are; it can reduce your heated, excited abnormality
to a little calmer and cooler space—that's all. It can bring
your temperature down a little, but it cannot solve. It can
only help, it can console.

I have heard about a man who used to smoke three cigarettes at one time—that was his obsession. Now, it was very
embarrassing; people would look at him, what he was
doing, and he would feel very shy and ashamed. But it
was impossible, he couldn't help it, he had to do it that way,
otherwise he would remain very dissatisfied.

He had tried every possible way, whatsoever was suggested to him. Nothing helped. Then somebody suggested,
"You go to a psychoanalyst."

After one year of psychoanalysis and thousands of dollars
wasted, a friend asked him, "Did psychoanalysis help you?"

He said, "Certainly!"

But the man could not believe it, because he saw he was
still smoking three cigarettes. So he asked, "But you are
still smoking three cigarettes, so I don't understand how
psychoanalysis has helped you?"

He said, "Now I am no more ashamed! My psychoanalyst
has helped me to understand that this is just normal. What is
wrong in it? A few people smoke one, I have heard of one
person who smokes two, I smoke three! The difference is
only of quantity—and what is wrong in smoking three

cigarettes?! For one year persistently my psychoanalyst has said that there is nothing wrong in it; now I don't feel ashamed. In fact, I am the only person in the world who smokes three cigarettes simultaneously! Now I feel very superior."

Psychoanalysis can give you many consolations. It can help you rationalize, it can help you normalize, it can help you not to feel ashamed—but it doesn't solve. It cannot. Problems are never solved if you remain at the same plane of existence. This is something very fundamental to be understood.

If you want to solve a problem you have to rise above the plane. It can't be solved on the same plane. The moment you reach a higher plane, the lower plane problems simply disappear. That is the way of religion: to help you go higher and higher and higher; the moment you have reached the fourth state, *turiya*, all problems disappear, dissolve, lose meaning. Not that you have found solutions, no, not at all. Religion is not interested in solutions. No solution can ever solve a problem; it may help you to solve one problem, but it will create another. The solution itself may become the problem. You may become so much attached and dependent on the solution....

It happens almost every day in your life: you are ill, you take a certain medicine, it helps, and then you become dependent on the medicine, then you are addicted, then you cannot leave the medicine. Now the medicine has its own side-effects—now they start torturing you. Now for them you will need other medicines...and so on and so forth. There is no end to it.

No solution can really become a solution. Religion has a totally different approach. It does not give you a solution:

it simply helps you to raise the level of your consciousness. Religion is consciousness-raising. It raises you higher than the problem; it gives you a bird's-eye view. Now you are standing on a hilltop looking at the valley...and the problems of the valley are simply meaningless. They don't have *any* significance for the man who is standing on the sunlit hilltop. They have simply lost all relevance.

The fifth question

Bhagwan,
I have been here nine months and am giving birth to my first question.
Today in lecture you said, 'Sex is tiring....' For me, sex is the sweetest explosion of music, colour, light, brimming and bursting every cell of my being. It is slipping the net of my skin, melting with love in God's arms, being exquisitely lost, out of time, out of mind—being God. And those words don't say it.
It is these experiences that led me to you. I don't even have a glimpse of the 'stupidity of sex'. Sex is my source of deepest relaxation and boundless energy, as well as highest bliss: the opposite of tiring.
Do men find sex more tiring than women or do I just have so far to go towards dropping it? or what? Please comment.

Apurna,

YOUR EXPERIENCE IS PERFECTLY VALID, BUT because it is such an ecstasy, such an excitement, how long can you go on repeating it? Sooner or later a moment arrives when it becomes repetitive, the same, and then it will start losing its joy. That moment it becomes tiring.

Your experience is perfectly valid, but very limited. Life is far more. It begins in sex, but it doesn't end in it. I am perfectly happy that you are enjoying your sex—enjoy it as much as possible while it lasts. And the more you enjoy it, the sooner you will be tired of it.

But no need to worry about that. I was answering somebody else's question, who is tired of it. He has lived all these joys, he has played with all these toys. You are giving big names to those toys—these are all teddy bears. You can call your teddy bear 'God', and nothing is wrong.... When a child is carrying his teddy bear and calling him 'God' and cannot go to sleep without it, it is very relaxing, and if you take the teddy bear he becomes very tense! Even dirty teddy bears and he will carry them. Even parents feel ashamed because if they are going on a holiday he is carrying his teddy bear—dirty, smelly...but the child cannot live without it. It is his very life. But one day, hopefully, he will be tired of it and he will throw it in a corner and will forget all about it forever.

It is really difficult to answer your questions, because one person's question is relevant only to him, and the answer that I give is relevant only to him. It may not be your experience.

On one day I said that homosexuality is a perversion. Immediately a few letters arrived—very angry, because there are a few homosexuals here. And they said, "What are you talking about? We have come here only because we thought that you accept all! That you don't reject, don't condemn anything." I have not condemned. But the question and the answer were for a particular person. You need not be worried about it; it may not be relevant to you.

To a homosexual, homosexuality is religion—his religion. He does not believe in heterosexuality; he thinks the heterosexuals are a little perverted, or at least very orthodox, out-of-date people, should not exist any more, are no more contemporaries—what nonsense are they talking about?!

To the heterosexual, the homosexual seems to be *very* perverted, animalistic, even below the animals. And to the homosexual, the heterosexual is animalistic, because homosexuality is the invention of man, the superior man. Animals are not homosexual—at least not in their wild state. In zoos sometimes, yes, but there they become affected by human beings, they learn from human beings. But in the wild they are not homosexuals.

So homosexuality is something special that man has discovered. It is a defining phenomenon. Just as Aristotle says man is a rational being, the homosexual says man is a homosexual being—only man has the capacity to rise to such heights. Heterosexuality is just ordinary: dogs do it and.... It is nothing special! One should not brag about it.

Two camels slowly approach each other in the desert, their riders identically dressed in excessively long Bermuda shorts and topi helmets. They pause, and the riders speak—in an exaggerated British accent:

"English?" "Of cawss."

"Foreign Office?" "Cinema photography."

"Oxford?" "Cambridge."

"Homosexual?" "Certainly not!"

"Pity!"

And the two camels continue their separate ways across the desert.

I have to talk to many kinds of people—camels are there. So if it is not your question, don't be bothered by my

answer, forget all about it. It concerns somebody else—
who is far more mature than you. . . .

The last question
Bhagwan,
What are your last words going to be to the world?

IT REMINDS ME OF A STORY GEORGE GURDJIEFF
used to tell his closest disciples:

The story is about a great past Master, a Buddha, who
had a self-appointed right-hand man who was a faithful
follower for year after year. And when the Master was in
his room on his deathbed, all of the followers silently
waited by the door not knowing what to do and incapable
of believing that their mystical Master was really dying.

Finally, through the sorrowful stillness, the Master's
voice was faintly heard to call the name of the right-hand
man, and all of the followers looked at him intently as he
made his way to the Master's door. As he reached for the
knob he glanced at the peering faces around him and imagined their envy and respect for him at being the only one
to be called to the Master's side during his final moments.
He already imagined how after the Master's death he would
slowly emerge from the room as the new head of the
System, a veritable Peter-of-the-Rock.

Quietly he entered the darkened room and slowly he
made his way and knelt by the bed. The old Master nodded
for him to come nearer, and he leaned over with his
awaiting ear by the old man's mouth, and the Master
whispered, ''Fuck you.''

How long the night to the watchman,
How long the road to the weary traveller,
How long the wandering of many lives
To the fool who misses the way.

If the traveller cannot find
Master or friend to go with him,
Let him travel on alone
Rather than with a fool for company.

"My children, my wealth!"
So the fool troubles himself.
But how has he children or wealth?
He is not even his own master.

The fool who knows he is a fool
Is that much wiser.
The fool who thinks he is wise
Is a fool indeed.

Does the spoon taste the soup?
A fool may live all his life
In the company of a Master
And still miss the way.

The tongue tastes the soup.
If you are awake in the presence of a Master
One moment will show you the way.

The fool is his own enemy.
The mischief he does is his undoing.
How bitterly he suffers!

Why do what you will regret?
Why bring tears upon yourself?
Do only what you do not regret,
And fill yourself with joy.

July 7

Does the Spoon Taste the Soup?

MAN IS A BRIDGE BETWEEN THE KNOWN and the unknown. To remain confined in the known is to be a fool. To go in search of the unknown is the beginning of wisdom. To become one with the unknown is to become the awakened one, the Buddha.

Remember again and again that man is not yet a being—he is on the way, a traveller, a pilgrim. He is not yet at home; he is in search of the home. One who thinks that he is at home is a fool, because then the search stops, then the seeking is no more there. And the moment you stop seeking and searching, you become a stagnant pool of energy, you start stinking. Then you only die, then you don't live at all.

Life is in flowing, life is in remaining a river—because only the river will reach the ocean. If you become a stagnant pool then you are going nowhere. Then you are not really alive. The fool does not live, he only pretends to live. He does not know, he only pretends to know. He does not love, he only pretends to love. The fool is a pretension.

The wise lives, loves; the wise enquires. The wise is ready, always ready, to go into the uncharted sea. The wise is adventurous.

The fool is afraid.

When Buddha uses the word 'fool' you have to remember all these meanings of the word. It is not the ordinary meaning that Buddha gives to the word 'fool'. For him, the fool means one who lives in the mind and knows nothing of the no-mind. One who lives in information, knowledge, and has not tasted anything of wisdom. One who lives a borrowed life, imitative, but knows nothing of *anything* that arises in his own being.

By 'the fool' Buddha means one who is well acquainted with the scriptures, but has not tasted a single moment of truth. He may be a great scholar, very learned—in fact, fools *are* scholars; they have to be because that is the only way to hide their foolishness. Fools are very learned people; they have to be, because it is only through learning words, theories, philosophies, that they can hide their inner ignorance, that they can hide their emptiness, that they can believe that they also know.

If you want to find the fools, go to the universities, go to the academies. There you will find them—in their utter ignorance, but pretending to know. They certainly know what others have said, but that is not real knowing. A blind man can collect all the information there is about light, but he will still remain blind. He can talk about light, he can write treatises on light; he may be very clever in guessing, in fabricating theories, but still he remains a blind man and he knows nothing of light. But the information that he collects may not only deceive others, it may deceive he himself too. He may start thinking that he knows, that he is no more blind.

When Buddha uses the word 'fool' he does not mean simply the ignorant, because if the ignorant person is aware that he is ignorant, he is not a fool. And it is more possible for the ignorant person to be aware that he is ignorant than it is for the so-called learned people. Their egos are so puffed up; it is very difficult for them to see. It goes against their investment. They have devoted their whole lives to knowledge, and now, to recognize the fact that all this knowledge is meaningless, futile, because they have not tasted truth themselves, is difficult, is hard.

The ignorant person can remember that he is ignorant— he has nothing to lose—but the learned, he cannot recognize that he is ignorant—he has much to lose. The knowledgeable person is the real fool. The ignorant person is innocent; he knows that he knows not, and because he knows that he knows not, because he is ignorant, he is just on the threshold of wisdom. Because he knows he knows not, he can enquire, and his enquiry will be pure, unprejudiced. He will enquire without any conclusions. He will enquire without being a Christian or a Mohammedan or a Hindu. He will simply enquire as an enquirer. His enquiry will not come out of ready-made answers: his enquiry will come out of his own heart. His enquiry will not be a by-product of knowledge: his enquiry will be existential. He enquires because it is a question of life and death to him. He enquires because he really wants to know. He knows that he knows not—that's why he enquires. His enquiry has a beauty of its own. He is not a fool, he is simply ignorant.

The real fool is one who thinks he knows without knowing at all.

Socrates was trying to do the same thing in Athens: he was trying to make these learned fools aware that all their learning was false, that they were really fools, pretenders, hypocrites. Naturally, all the professors and all the philosophers and all the so-called thinkers. . .and Athens was full of them. Athens was the capital of knowledge in those days. Just as today people look towards Oxford or Cambridge, people used to look towards Athens. It was full of the learned fools, and Socrates was trying to bring them down to the earth, was shattering their knowledge, was raising such questions—simple in a way, but difficult to be answered by those who have only acquired knowledge from others.

Athens became very angry with Socrates. They poisoned this man. Socrates is one of the greatest men who has ever walked on the earth; and what he did very few people have done. His method is a basic method. The Socratic method of enquiry is such that it exposes the fools as fools. To expose a fool as a fool is dangerous, of course, because he will take revenge. Socrates was poisoned, Jesus was crucified, Buddha was condemned.

The day Buddha died, Buddhism was thrown out of the country, expelled from the country. The scholars, the pundits, the Brahmins, could not allow it to remain. It was too uncomfortable for them. Its basic attack was on the Brahmins, the learned fools, and naturally they were offended. They could not face Buddha, they could not encounter him. They waited for their opportunity in a cunning way: when Buddha died, then they started fighting the followers. When the light was gone, then it was the time for the owls, the learned fools, to reign over the country again. And since that time they have reigned even up to now—they are still in power. The same fools!

The world has suffered much. Man could have become the glory of the earth, but because of these fools. . .and because they are powerful they can harm, and because they are powerful they can destroy any possibility, any opportunity for man to evolve. Man has been moving in circles, and these fools would not like man to become wise, because if man becomes wise, these fools will be nowhere. They won't be in power any more—religiously, politically, socially, financially, all their power will be gone. They can remain in power only if they can go on destroying all possibilities of wisdom for man.

My effort here is to create a Socratic enquiry again, to ask again the fundamental questions that Buddha raised.

IN THE NEW COMMUNE WE ARE GOING TO HAVE seven concentric circles of people. The first, the most superficial circle, will consist of those who come only out of childish curiosity, or out of already accumulated prejudices, who are deep down antagonistic—the journalists, et cetera.

They will be allowed only to see the superficial part of the commune—not that anything will be hidden, but just because of their approach they will not be able to see anything more than the most superficial. They will see only the garments.

Here also the same goes on happening. They come and they see only the superficial. Just the other day I was reading a journalist's report; he was here for five days. He writes 'for five days' as if it is a very long time to be here; five days as if he has been here for five lives. Because he has been here for five days he has become an authority. Now he knows what is happening here because he has watched people meditating. How can you watch people meditating? Either you can meditate or not, but you cannot watch people meditating. Yes, you can watch people's physical gestures, movements, dance, or their sitting silently under a tree, but you cannot *see* meditation! You can see the physical posture

196

of the meditator, but you cannot see his inner experience. For that, you have to meditate, you have to become a participant.

And the basic condition for being a participant is that you should drop this idea of being a watcher. Even if you participate, if you dance with the meditators, with this idea that you are participating only to watch what happens, then nothing will happen. And, of course, you will go with the conclusion that it is all nonsense—nothing happens. And you will feel perfectly right inside yourself that nothing happens, because you even participated and nothing happened.

That man writes that he was in darshan and much was happening to sannyasins—so much was happening that after a deep energy contact with me they were not even able to walk back to their places; they had to be carried away. And then he mentions, "But nothing happened to me." That is enough proof that all that was happening was either hypnosis, or people were pretending, just because the journalist was there, or it was just an arranged show, something managed—because nothing was happening to him.

There are things which can happen only when you are available, open, unprejudiced. There are things which can happen only when you put aside your mind.

The journalist writes again: "The people who go there, they leave their minds where they leave their shoes—but I could not do that. Of course," he says, "if I had left my mind behind, then I would have also been impressed." But he thinks the mind that he has is something so valuable— how can he leave it behind? He feels himself very clever because he didn't leave his mind behind.

Mind is the barrier not the bridge.

197

In the new commune, the first concentric circle will be for those who come like journalists—prejudiced people, who already know that they know. In short, for the fools.

The second concentric circle will be for those who are enquirers—unprejudiced, neither Hindus nor Mohammedans nor Christians, who come without any conclusion, who come with an open mind. They will be able to see a little deeper. Something of the mysterious will stir their hearts. They will cross the barrier of the mind. They will become aware that something of immense importance is happening—what exactly it is they will not be able to figure out immediately. But they will become aware vaguely that something of value *is* happening. They may not be courageous enough to participate in it; their enquiry may be more intellectual than existential, they may not be able to become part, but they will become aware—of course, in a very vague and confused way, but certainly aware—that something more is going on than is apparent.

The third circle will be for those who are sympathetic, who are in deep sympathy, who are ready to move with the commune a little bit, who are ready to dance and sing and participate, who are not only enquirers but are ready to change themselves *if* the enquiry requires it. They will become aware more clearly of deeper realms.

And the fourth will be the empathic. Sympathy means one is friendly, one is not antagonistic. Empathy means one is not only friendly—one feels a kind of unity, oneness. Empathy means one feels with the commune, with the people, with what is happening. One meets, merges, melts, becomes one.

The fifth circle will be of the initiates, the sannyasins—one who is not only feeling in his heart but who is ready to be committed, to be involved. One who is ready to risk.

One who is ready to commit, because he feels a great, mad love—mad, mad love—arising in him. The sannyasin, the initiate.

And the sixth will be of those who have started arriving—the adepts. Those whose journey is coming closer to the end, who are no more sannyasins only but are becoming siddhas, whose journey is coming to a full-point, is getting closer and closer to the conclusion. The home is not far away, a few steps more. In a way, they have already arrived.

And the seventh circle will consist of arhatas and bodhi-sattvas. The arhatas are those sannyasins who have arrived but are not interested in helping others to arrive. Buddhism has for them a special name: arhata—the lonely traveller who arrives and then disappears into the ultimate. And the bodhisattvas are those who have arrived but they feel a great compassion for those who have not yet arrived. The bodhisattva is an arhata with compassion. He holds on, goes on looking back and goes on calling forth those who are still stumbling in darkness. He is a helper, a servant of humanity.

There are two types of people. The one who is at ease only when he is alone; he feels a little uncomfortable in relationship; he feels a little disturbed, distracted, in rela-tionship. That type of person becomes an arhata. When he has arrived, he is finished with everything. Now he does not look back.

The bodhisattva is the second type of person: one who feels at ease in relationship, in fact far more comfortable when he is relating than when he is alone. He leans more towards love. The arhata leans more towards meditation. The path of the arhata is of pure meditation, and the path of the bodhisattva is that of pure love. The pure love contains meditation, and the pure meditation contains love—but the pure meditation contains love only as a flavour, a perfume; it is not the central force in it. And the pure love contains meditation as a perfume; it is not the center of it.

These two types exist in the world. The second type— the follower on the path of love—becomes a bodhisattva. The seventh circle will consist of arhatas and bodhisattvas.

Now, the seventh circle will be aware of all the six other circles, and the sixth circle will be aware of the other five circles—the higher will be aware of the lower, but the lower will not be aware of the higher. The first circle will not be aware of anything other than the first circle. He will see the buildings and the hotel and the swimming pool and the shopping center and weaving and pottery and carpentry. He will see the trees, the whole landscape . . . he will see all these things. He will see thousands of sannyasins, and he will shrug his shoulders: "What are these people doing here?" He will be a little puzzled, because he was not thinking that so many mad people can be found in one place: "All are hypnotized!" He will find explanations. He will go perfectly satisfied that he has known the commune. He will not be aware of the higher—the lower cannot be aware of the higher. That is one of the fundamental laws of life—*ais dhammo sanantano*— only the higher knows the lower, because he has passed from the lower.

When you are standing on the sunlit mountain peak, you know everything down in the valley. The valley people may not be aware of you at all; it is not possible for them. The valley has its own occupations, its own problems. The valley is preoccupied with its own darkness.

The fool can come to a Master but will remain unbene- fitted because he will see only the outer. He will not be able to see the essential, he will not be able to see the core. The fool comes here too, but he listens only to the words—*and* he goes on interpreting those words according to his own ideas. He goes perfectly satisfied that he knows what is happening.

There are many fools who don't come here—they don't feel the need. They simply depend on other fools' reports. That's enough. Just one fool can convince thousands of fools, because their language is the same, their prejudices are the same, their conceptions are the same...there is no problem! One fool has seen, and all the other fools are convinced. One fool reports in the newspaper and all the other fools read it early in the morning, and *are* convinced.

The sutras:

How long the night to the watchman,
How long the road to the weary traveller,
How long the wandering of many lives
To the fool who misses the way.

THE NIGHT IS VERY LONG TO THE WATCHMAN— why? He cannot relax, he has to keep himself somehow awake. It is a struggle. He has to keep himself awake *against* nature, because the night is meant for relaxing and resting and going to sleep. He is fighting against nature—so is the fool. The fool goes on fighting against nature. He tries to swim against the current; hence, his misery is long, unnecessarily long. He multiplies it a thousandfold because he cannot let go, he cannot relax.

The first indication of a foolish mind is that it cannot relax, it is always tense, it is always on guard, it is always afraid.

How long the night to the watchman...

It is not so long for those who are resting, relaxing, and have gone into deep sleep. It goes so fast! Just one moment you were awake, then you fall asleep...and the next moment you are awake, it is morning. You cannot believe the night has flown so fast. If you had been really restful... the more you rest, the faster the night flies. If your rest is total, time disappears. This is something to be understood.

Time is a psychological phenomenon. I am not talking about the time that you see on the clock, I am talking about the psychological time. When you are happy, relaxed, peaceful, time flies fast. When you are in pain, misery, anguish, time goes very slowly; it seems unending.

Have you sat by the side of a dying man in the night? It seems as if the morning will never come. The night seems so long...it is the *same* night. The same night you can sit with your beloved, and it flies so fast that you cannot believe it—because you were happy and you were relaxed and you were enjoying and you were moving with nature, not fighting. Love means surrender, love means relaxation.

Albert Einstein was asked again and again in his life, "What is the theory of relativity?" It is a complicated theory and it cannot be explained easily to people who are not aware of higher mathematics. In fact, it is said that only twelve persons on the whole of the earth understood exactly what Einstein meant by the theory of relativity. How to explain it to a layman?

So he had made this beautiful explanation. He would say, "Sit on a hot stove and then one second seems to be almost like eternity, non-ending—it is so hot, is it so painful. And then you hold the hand of your beloved and sit by her side on the bank of the river on a full-moon night, and *hours* go like moments." This, he used to say, is the theory of relativity.

Everything depends on you, on your psychological state. Time is not a physical, material phenomenon; it is psychological. Hence, in deep meditation time disappears totally. And this is not something new: the mystics have known it down the ages. They have said, all the mystics of all countries, that time stops when meditation really begins.

Jesus is asked by somebody, "You talk so much about the kingdom of God—what is going to be very special about it, something that we don't know at all? Tell us something about the kingdom of God which will be absolutely special."

And do you know what he said? A very strange answer— he said, "There shall be time no longer."

Yes, in the kingdom of God there can be time no longer, because time exists only in proportion to pain, anguish, anxiety. If all anxiety, all pain, all nightmares disappear, time disappears. Time is a mind phenomenon: if there is no mind, there is no time. And you also know about it. This relativity you have felt.

Vivek was saying just the other day, and many times she has said it, that time flies so fast here that she cannot believe that she has been here for seven years. It looks as if just seven days ago she had come here.

And still we are amidst the world! Once we have moved away from the world, once we have our own small world, once we drop all the bridges, time will start disappearing. My effort is to give you a taste of timelessness. Once you have tasted it, then you can go back into the world and it will remain with you. The most important thing is to taste it once at least—no-time—and suddenly you are transported into another world.

This world consists of time and space. That's how Albert Einstein defines it: spaciotime. He makes one word out of the two, because he says time is nothing but the fourth dimension of space. So this world consists of space and time, and in meditation you disappear from both, or both disappear from your being. You don't know where you are. *You are*, certainly, more than you have ever been. You are totally there but there is no space confining you and no time defining you. A pure existence. Once tasted, all foolishness disappears.

The fool lives in time: the wise man lives in timelessness. The fool lives in mind: the wise man lives in no-mind.

> *How long the night to the watchman,*
> *How long the road to the weary traveller...*

JUST LOOK AT PEOPLE'S FACES—HOW TIRED, weary, utterly frustrated they look. And they not only look it, they are. Their souls are tired, their very beings have become a kind of boredom. They are dragging themselves— no joy, no dance in their steps, no song in their hearts, no gratitude, no thankfulness that they are. On the contrary, so many complaints.

One of Dostoyevsky's characters in *The Brothers Karamazov* says, "I would like to return this life back to God if I meet him. I don't want to live any more. Life is such an anguish!" He wants to return the ticket back. How can he be thankful?

Just think: if you meet God some day, what are you going to say to him? It will be difficult even to say "Hi!" You will be so angry with him, so utterly annoyed, irritated, that this is the man who created you, this is the man who created the world! It is simply because of this that God goes on hiding, otherwise people are bound to kill him. They won't leave him alive; he has to hide, just to survive he has to hide.

How long the road to the weary traveller,
How long the wandering of many lives
To the fool who misses the way.

And the fool is bound to miss the way. Why? Because he thinks he already knows the way, because he thinks he *is* on the way. Everybody else is wrong, he is right. He believes that if everybody follows him, everything will be right in the world. He is a fanatic. He has the Bible, the Koran, the Vedas—what else is needed? He knows all the beautiful dogmas of all the religions—what more is needed? He knows the way!

But when Buddha uses the word 'way', he means *dhamma—ais dhammo sanantano*. He means the way that takes you out of your ego, the way that takes you out of your mind, the way that takes you out of your identities, the way that makes you an absolute nothingness...the way that helps you to dissolve into the whole.

He is not talking about religions, he is not talking about so-called techniques, devices, methods. When he uses the word 'way' he means exactly what Lao Tzu means by 'tao'. Tao exactly means 'the way'—the way to what? The way beyond yourself, the way that leads you out of your confined, imprisoned state, into the open.

How long the wandering of many lives...

And it is really a long long wandering—not of one day or of one life, but of many lives, of millions of lives. And if people are tired it is not surprising. If their eyes look full of dust, it is not surprising. If their souls are covered with layers of dust, it is not surprising. If they no more reflect, if their mirrors are lost, it is not an accident—it is understandable, although unforgivable. Because nobody else is responsible for this situation except you. And if you decide, you can drop all the layers of dust *this* very moment. And the moment you drop all the dust of your thoughts, you are on the way. *You are the way!*

Jesus says, "I am the way, I am the truth, I am the door." Christians go on interpreting it as if *Jesus* is the way—that is not true, that is falsifying Jesus utterly. When Jesus says, "I am the way," he is saying, "Whoever can say 'I am', there is the way." He is not talking about Jesus, the son of Joseph and Mary; he is talking about this 'I-amness'.

The moment in deep silent meditation you come across this I-amness, you are the way. It is not a question of being a Christian. It is not what Christians go on telling the whole world, "Unless you come to Jesus, you will not find the way to God." That is sheer nonsense! Because Buddha has found without being a Christian, and Mohammed has found without being a Christian, and Mahavira has found and Krishna has found and Lao Tzu has found...I have found without being a Christian. That is nonsense.

But what Jesus really means *is* true.

Moses asked God when he encountered him.. a beautiful story, remember, it is a story, not history. History is a very ordinary thing; history consists of Tamurlaine, and Genghis Khan and Adolf Hitler and Joseph Stalin and Mao Tse Tung—history is very ordinary. It consists of all that is ugly. It is not history, it is a parable, a metaphor, of tremendous poetry and beauty.

It says when Moses encountered God he asked, "Who are you?" And God is reported to have said, "I am that I am."

That's what Jesus means when he says, "I am the way."

If you can feel your own being, your own amness, you will find the way. The fool cannot find it. He goes on and on...living in the same desires, in the same stupid thoughts, in the same memories. The fool is repetitive; he only repeats what he knows—he never endeavours to go beyond his knowledge. And truth is unknown.

Just watch your mind and you will be able to understand what I am trying to convey to you. Your mind is repetitive! It says, "Yesterday the food was very good, let us go to the same hotel again." "Yesterday that man was very friendly, let us find him again." It wants to repeat the yesterdays, and it does not allow the today to have its own being. It does not allow even the tomorrow to have its own being; for tomorrows also it has plans to repeat just what it has known in the past. And what have you known in the past except misery? But you have become familiar with it and you go on repeating it.

The fool is repetitive: the wise lives every moment anew.

All the soldiers of an American regiment in Korea put up a dollar apiece and draw lots for which of them will take the resultant money and spend one night in the finest brothel in the Orient.

Hymie Kaplowitz, the terror of Brooklyn, naturally wins, and on his return from the legendary brothel describes to his assembled bunk-mates what happened: the hanging gold curtains, the sensuous oriental music, the exotic aphrodisiacal meal served by little naked twelve-year-old girls beforehand, etc. etc., ending every passage with "...nothing like Brooklyn!"

Finally he describes how the most beautiful woman he had ever seen comes slowly down the ornate staircase, wearing only a pagoda-headdress with trailing veils of white lace, and leads him up the stairs by the hand to her perfumed bed. "...nothing like Brooklyn!"

"And then?" all the other soldiers ask feverishly.

"And then?" answers Hymie. "Oh, then it was just like Brooklyn."

The fool's mind goes on repetitively doing the same thing again and again. The fool's mind is a vicious circle—it moves in circles. The wise man is not at all repetitive. He lives each moment anew, he is born anew each moment. He dies to the past every moment, and is born again.

The wise man's whole life is a process of rebirthing. The wise man is not born once, he is born every moment again and again. The old never takes hold of him. But the fool is born only once, and then he goes on repeating.

If you go on repeating you will miss the way, because your amness, your being, is absolutely fresh and always young. It is never old. The mind grows old, the body grows old, but the being knows nothing of time—how can it grow old? It is always young, it is always youthful. It is as fresh as dewdrops in the early morning sun, it is as fresh as lotus leaves in the lake.

> *If the traveller cannot find*
> *Master or friend to go with him,*
> *Let him travel on alone*
> *Rather than with a fool for company.*

THE BEST THING IS TO FIND A MASTER, BECAUSE the Master is the greatest friend possible. Hence Buddha says 'Master *or* friend'.

> *If the traveller cannot find*
> *Master or friend to go with him,*
> *Let him travel on alone*
> *Rather than with a fool for company.*

But avoid fools. And that's what you never do. You collect fools around yourself. There is some secret in it: when you are surrounded by fools, you appear superior. It is very ego-fulfilling. Hence nobody wants to live with somebody who is superior; people want to live with their inferiors, because your inferiors give you the idea that you are great.

To be with a Master you will have to drop that idea that you are great, you will have to drop all that rubbish, you will have to drop your whole ego, you will have to surrender. You will have to dissolve in the Master. Hence people avoid Masters. How many people went to Jesus? Very few, can be counted on the fingers. How many people went to Buddha? Very few.... This has been always so. But people are very happy going to the Rotary Club; it feels very good when you are surrounded by fools—it feels very good: all fools dressed up, and every fool feeling better than the others, and every fool bragging about himself, and every fool is being supported by other fools.

People love to be in the crowds, because in the crowds you can forget your inferiority. That's why people don't leave crowds. One crowd is that of Hindus, another is that of Mohammedans, the third is that of Christians and so on and so forth. Nobody wants to leave the crowd.

And even if sometimes people leave one crowd, they immediately join another. They escape somehow from one prison just to enter into another—they cannot live alone. Buddha says it is better to live alone than with fools. If you can find a Master or a friend, good; if you cannot, then it is better to be alone. Hard, of course, it will be to be alone, difficult it will be because the crowd will create so many difficulties for you. The crowd does not love individuals, it does not want anybody to be independent; it wants everybody to be dependent on the crowd. It will create trouble for you. But all those troubles are cleansing, all those troubles are challenges. They sharpen your intelligence; they will make you wise.

> *"My children, my wealth!"*
> *So the fool troubles himself.*
> *But how has he children or wealth?*
> *He is not even his own master.*

The fool lives around the idea of 'my' and 'mine': 'my nation', 'my religion', 'my race', 'my family', 'my wealth', 'my children', 'my parents'...he lives around 'my' and 'mine'. And he has come alone and he will go alone; nobody brings anything into the world and nobody takes anything from the world. Alone, empty-handed we come; alone, empty-handed we go. The wise knows it; hence the wise claims nothing as 'mine'. He uses things, but he does not possess them. Using is perfectly good—use all the things of the world, they *are* for you. The world is a gift from God— use it! but don't possess it. The moment you become a possessor, you cannot use things—the things start using you. The moment you become a possessor, in fact you are possessed by your things, you become a slave.

And the very idea of possessing is stupid. How can you possess anything? You don't even possess your own being. What else can you possess? You are not even a master of yourself.

Buddha says:

> *"My children! My wealth!"*
> *So the fool troubles himself.*

And how many anxieties arise out of this 'mine', 'my' business? Totally false! Basically false, but it can create many

many miseries. It is like when in the dark night you see a rope and you think that it is a snake. Now you are running, screaming, trembling, you may have a heart attack. And there was no snake at all—there was only a rope! But the heart attack will be real, remember: an unreal snake can create a real heart attack.

These are unreal problems. Claiming 'mine'—anything! country, church, children, wealth—anything when you claim "It is mine!" you are creating a great source of anxiety, anguish for yourself. You are creating a hell around yourself.

> *But how has he children or wealth?*
> Buddha asks.
> *He is not even his own master.*

A fool fell out of a sixth-storey window. He is lying on the ground with a big crowd around him. A cop walks over and says, "What happened?"
The fool says, "I don't know. I just got here."

What do you know about how you got here? What do you know about from where you come? What do you know about where you are bound to go? What do you know about who you are?

The most fundamental questions remain in darkness, and still you go on claiming, "This is my house...."

When Buddha became enlightened, he came back home. The father was very angry, obviously—this was his only child and he became a.drop-out. The father was getting old, and he had managed a big kingdom; he was very much worried: "Who is going to own it? Who is going to rule it? That fool, my son, has escaped."
Many efforts were made to persuade Buddha to come

back, but all efforts failed. When he became enlightened he came on his own—that encounter is one of the most beautiful encounters in human history.

Buddha's old father is very angry, so angry that out of anger tears start coming in his old eyes. He shouts, screams, abuses, and Buddha stands there, utterly calm and quiet, as if nothing is happening. Maybe for half an hour, or for one hour...then the father, the old man, is exhausted. And then he becomes aware that the son has not even uttered a single word, he has not reacted at all: "And he looks so calm and quiet! What is the matter? Is he deaf or something? Has he gone mad or something." He asks, "Why are you not answering me?"

Buddha says, "The man who had left you is no more. You are not talking to *me*—you are talking to your son, who is no more. Much water has gone down the Ganges since then. Twelve years have passed. I am a totally different person."

Buddha, of course, means metaphorically. He means, "I am no more the same consciousness, no more in the same mind. My attitudes have dropped, my prejudices gone. I am a totally fresh being. Now I know who I am. That time I was a fool. Now the light has come within my soul. That's why," he says, "I am no more the same."

Buddha's old father again becomes infuriated. He says, "What do you mean that you are not the same? Can't I recognize my son? Don't I know you? I have given birth to you, my blood flows in your veins; you are made of my blood and bones—and I don't know you?! You have some guts to say this!"

And Buddha again says, "Excuse me, but I say again that my body may be a part of your body—I am not. Now I know that I am not my body, not my mind. Now I know who I am. And you have nothing to do with my being, you have not created my being, you have not given birth to my being. I have been before my birth, and I will be after my death. Please try to understand me; don't get irritated, don't be annoyed. I have come only to share my joy that I have found."

But parents think the children are theirs; the children think the parents are theirs. In this world, your being is absolutely alone. Yes, share your joy with others, but never possess. Only the fool possesses; the wise man has no possessiveness.

> *The fool who knows he is a fool*
> *Is that much wiser.*
> *The fool who thinks he is wise*
> *Is a fool indeed.*

PONDER OVER IT . . . WHAT DO YOU THINK ABOUT yourself? It is going to be painful to see your foolishness. It is easy to see other people as fools—in fact, everybody knows that everybody else is a fool—but to see your own foolishness is a great step towards wisdom. To see your own foolishness is already transforming your being, your consciousness.

A man is visiting in France. Does a little wandering the first night. Makes love to the host's wife, his daughter, the cook, the second maid, etc. The host berates him in the morning.

"What is the big idea? Here you are my guest. I receive you as a friend. And what do you do? You make love to my wife, my daughter, and half the servants—and for me, nothing?"

The fool is always concerned with only one thing: his ego. Anything that is for him is good—anything. And he is ready to cling to it. The fool even clings to misery, because it is *his* misery. He goes on accumulating whatsoever he can get, because the fool has no idea of his inner kingdom, of his inner treasures. He goes on accumulating junk because he thinks this is all that can be possessed. Junk outside and junk inside, that's what people go on collecting—things they collect and thoughts they collect. Things are junk outside, thoughts are junk inside, and you are drowned in your junk.

Have a look, a dispassionate, detached look at your life, what you have been doing with it, and what you have got out of it. And don't try to befool yourself, because this is how mind goes on. It says, "Look how much you have got! So much money in the bank, so many people know you, respect you, honour you; you have such a great post, politically you are powerful...what else? What else can one hope for? Life has given all that one can hope for."

But money or power or prestige are nothing, because death will come and all your great citadels of wealth, power, prestige, respectability, will just start falling as if you have made them with playing cards. Just a blow of death and everything shatters.

Unless you have something that you can take beyond death, remember you don't have anything at all—your hands are empty. Unless you have something deathless, eternal, you are a fool. The Buddha calls that man wise who has attained some real treasure—of meditation, of compassion, of enlightenment.

Does the spoon taste the soup?
A fool may live all his life
In the company of a Master
And still miss the way.

THE SPOON CANNOT TASTE THE SOUP, THE spoon is dead—so is the fool. He only appears to be alive; otherwise, his heart is dead, almost dead—because his heart is not functioning. He lives only through the head and the head is only a spoon.

Through the head you cannot taste any joy of life. Can you see beauty through the head? You can see the flower, but you will miss the beauty; you will see the moon, but you will miss the beauty; you will see the sunset, but you will miss the beauty. Your head cannot know anything of beauty.

Your head can know something about sex but cannot know anything about love. Your head can understand the prose part of life, your head is a calculation machine—but it cannot know the poetry of existence. And the poetry of existence contains the truth. The music of existence contains the real benediction. It can be known only by the heart. Only the heart can experience it.

Remember, all that is meaningless, the head is efficient with it; and all that is significant, only the heart is capable of it. And we all are living in the head. Our schools, colleges, universities, exist only for a single purpose, for a single crime they exist, and that crime is: divert people's energies from the heart to the head so that they can all become cal-culating machines, efficient clerks and deputy collectors, station masters. . . . But the education system does not allow you to become a lover, a poet, a singer; it does not allow

215

you to know the *real* significance of life. It does not allow you to enter into the temple, it keeps you outside.

The head is superficial, the heart is at the center. And if the heart is not functioning, you are a spoon, a wooden spoon. You will not taste the soup.

> *A fool may live all his life*
> *In the company of a Master*
> *And still miss the way.*

To be in the company of a Master is the greatest blessing possible, because being in the company of one who is awakened the possibility opens up for you also to be awakened. One who is awake can make you awake, because awakening is contagious. He can shake you out of your dreams and nightmares. But the fool can live in the company of a Master his whole life and miss. How does he miss? Because with the Master also he is connected through the head—that is his way of missing the Master.

Now, there are a few people here who *are* missing and who will go on missing if they remain head-oriented. This is not a place to live in the head. Be headless! A true sannyasin will be headless. He will be heartful, because it is only through the heart that I can penetrate into you. It is only through the heart that there is any possibility of communion. Otherwise, you will listen to my words and you will collect my words, and you will become parrots and you will repeat my words—and that is all futile...unless you taste, unless you drink out of me.

> *The tongue tastes the soup.*

Please don't be spoons, be tongues. When you are around a Buddha, don't be spoons, be tongues—be alive, be sensitive, be heartful, be loving, be trusting.

216

> *The tongue tastes the soup.*
> *If you are awake in the presence of a Master*
> *One moment will show you the way.*

A *single* moment is enough! It is not a question of being with
the Master for a long time; time does not enter into it. It
is not a question of quantity, of how long you have lived
with the Master. The question is how deep you have loved
the Master, not how long you lived with the Master—how
intensely, passionately you have become involved with the
Master. Not the length of time, but the depth of your
feeling. Then a single moment of awareness, of heart wakefulness, a single moment of silence . . . and the transmission—
the transmission beyond all scriptures.

> *The fool is his own enemy.*
> *The mischief he does is his undoing.*
> *How bitterly he suffers!*

"The fool is his own enemy," says Buddha. Why? Because
it is simply of his own accord that he goes on missing all
that is significant in existence. Nobody is barring the way.
The poetry of life is available to all. The fool remains deaf;
he keeps his ears closed. Life is full of light, but the fool
keeps his eyes closed. Life is continuously showering divine
joy, flowers go on showering, but the fool remains completely oblivious. Even if sometimes in spite of himself he comes
across a flower, he does not believe in it. He says, "I must
be deceived."

It happens almost every day: people write to me that in
their meditation something strange is happening—they are
feeling very happy, it can't be true! Nobody ever writes
to me, "I am feeling unhappy—it can't be true!" But whenever happiness is felt, joy arises, they become afraid, they

can't believe it. They start suspecting. They start suspecting and they start theorizing that it must be the hypnosis of the place, it must be the many orange people around, that's why they are being affected. How can they be happy?! They have known only misery their whole lives, they have become accustomed to it, misery has become their being. Now ecstasy?! No, these flowers can't be true, something is wrong.

In almost all the languages of the world there are proverbs such as this one in English—you say, "It can't be true because it is so good." The good can't be true? Nobody believes in the good. "Too good to be true," you say. Nobody says, "Too bad to be true." No proverb like that exists in any language of the world: "Too bad to be true." The bad is accepted, the ugly is accepted, the mundane is accepted—and the sacred is denied.

And even if you accept the sacred, you only accept it formally. You go to the temple and the church as a social formality; you don't really believe in God, you don't really believe in the temple. It is good, it keeps things smooth; it is like a lubricant. If you go to the temple and the church, people think you are a good man, honest, religious; and if people think you are religious, honest and good, you can cheat them in a better way than you could otherwise. They will trust you, and you can cheat them and deceive them only if they trust you. It is a social formality, maybe a social strategy to cheat and deceive people. But you don't believe.

Whenever something immense, huge, bigger than you, descends on you, you simply shrink back, you close your eyes, you become an ostrich. You simply deny it! It can't be so. It is not that God has not come on your way—he has come many times, he has knocked on your doors many times—but you don't open the doors. On the contrary, you go on finding rationalizations. Sometimes you say, "It must be the wind, it must be the rain, it must be some neighbourhood child playing on the steps, knocking on the door." You go on explaining to yourself...but you never open the door and see who is there.

> *The fool is his own enemy.*
> *The mischief he does is his undoing.*
> *How bitterly he suffers!*
>
> *Why do what you will regret?*
> *Why bring tears upon yourself?*

Out of his great compassion he raises this question—he is talking to *you!*

> *Why do what you will regret?*
> *Why bring tears upon yourself?*
>
> *Do only what you do not regret,*
> *And fill yourself with joy.*

REMEMBER, LET THIS BE THE CRITERION: WHATsoever brings joy and bliss and benediction *is* true—because bliss is God's nature. Truth is another name for bliss. Untruth brings misery. If you live in lies, you will live in misery. And if you are living in misery, remember and find out on what lies you have based your life. Withdraw yourself from those lies. Don't waste time and don't postpone. Immediately withdraw! That withdrawal I call sannyas.

It is not withdrawing from the world: it is withdrawing from the lies that you have been living up to now. It is not renouncing the world: it is renouncing the lies that you have based your life upon. The moment you withdraw yourself from the lies, they start falling, start dying—because they depend on you, they nourish themselves on you: they cannot live without your support. Withdraw your cooperation, and all lies disappear. And when all lies disappear, what is left is truth.

Truth is your innermost nature. Truth has not to be found anywhere else. *Ais dhammo sanantano*—this is the ultimate law, the inexhaustible law, the ultimate truth, that it is within you. You need not go anywhere. You can find it within yourself if you can fulfill only one condition: withdraw the lies in which you have invested so much—withdraw from them. Renounce all that is untrue.

And the misery is an indication of untruth. And whenever some bliss happens, trust it, and go in that direction...and you will be moving towards God. Bliss is his fragrance. If you can follow bliss, you will never go astray. If you follow bliss, you will be following nature. And if you are natural, blissful, relaxed, wisdom arises.

Wisdom is a very relaxed state of being. Wisdom is not knowledge, not information; wisdom is your inner being awake, alert, watchful, witnessing, full of light. Be full of light—it is your birthright. If you miss, you are a fool. And you have missed many lives already—this time, please, be a little more compassionate towards yourself.

I was taught to strengthen the ego
—you say kill it. . . ?

what is your vision
for the new commune?

psychology has not changed my life
—what should I do now?

you seem to be the first enlightened
Master to tell jokes—why?

July 8

God Loves Laughter

The first question

In the West I was trained as a social worker. I was taught that it is important that a person respects and loves himself and feels worthwhile. I was taught that it is important to give support to help strengthen the ego.
You say kill the ego. I am confused.

Prem Aradhana,

THE EGO IS NEEDED BECAUSE THE TRUE self is not known. The ego is a substitute, it is a pseudo entity. Because you don't know yourself you have to create an artificial center, otherwise functioning in life will be impossible. Because you don't know your real face, you have to wear a mask. Not knowing the essential, you have to trust in the shadow.

There are only two ways of living the life. One is: either to live it from the very core of your being—that has been the way of the mystics.... Meditation is nothing but a device to make you aware of your real self—which is not created by you, which need not be created by you, which you already are. You are born with it. You *are* it! It needs to be discovered. If this is not possible, or if the society does not allow it to happen...and no society allows it to happen, because the real self is dangerous. Dangerous for the established church, dangerous for the state, dangerous for the crowd, dangerous for the tradition—because once a man knows his real self, he becomes an individual. He belongs no more to the mob psychology; he will not be superstitious, and he cannot be exploited, and he cannot be led like cattle, he cannot be ordered and commanded. He will live according to his light; he will live from his own inwardness. His life will have tremendous beauty, integrity. But that is the fear of the society.

Integrated persons become individuals, and the society wants you to be non-individuals. Instead of individuality, the society teaches you to be a personality. The word 'personality' has to be understood. It comes from a root, *persona*—*persona* means a mask. The society gives you a false idea of who you are; it gives you just a toy, and you go on clinging to the toy your whole life.

The one way is to live through meditation—then you live a life of rebellion, of adventure, of courage. Then you really live! The other way to live, or to fake living, is the way of the ego—strengthen the ego, nourish the ego, so that you need not look into the self, cling to the ego. The ego is an artefact created by the society to deceive you, to distract you.

The ego is man-made, manufactured by us. And because it is manufactured by the society, society has power over it. Because it is manufactured by the state and the church, and those who are in power, they can destroy it any moment. It depends on them, and you have to be constantly in fear, and you have to be constantly obeying them, conforming to them, so that your ego remains intact. The society gives you respect if you are not an individual. The society honours you if you are not a Jesus, not a Socrates, not a Buddha. It respects you only if you are a sheep, not a man.

The West has completely forgotten how to meditate— and Christianity has been the reason. Christianity has created a very false religion, which knows nothing of meditation. Christianity is very formal; it is a ritual. It is part of the society and the political structure of the society.

Karl Marx is perfectly right about it, that it is the opium of the people. Because of Christianity, the West has lost track of its own being. And one cannot live without *some* idea of one's self—and if you cannot discover, then create something. It will be false, but something is better than nothing.

Aradhana, what you have been told is utter nonsense. It does not matter who has been telling it—the universities, the politicians, the priests. Certainly, you will be feeling confused, because I am telling just the opposite: I am telling you to get rid of the ego. Because if you get rid of the ego, you get rid of the rock that is preventing the flow of your consciousness.

Your consciousness is there, just behind the rock; it has not to be brought from somewhere else. Remove the rock—real religion consists only of removing that which is unnecessary, and then the necessary starts flowing. That which is unessential has to be removed. And the essential is already there, is already the case! You remove the rock and you will be surprised: you need not create the real self—it reveals itself to you.

225

And the real has beauty, and the real is deathless. Because it is deathless it has no fear. The unreal is constantly trembling. The ego is always in danger; anybody can destroy it. Because it has been given to you by others, they can take it back. Today they respect you, tomorrow they may not respect you. If you don't follow *their* idea of life, if you don't confirm their style of being, they will withdraw their respect. And you will be flat on the ground...and you will not know who you are.

Borges writes:
"I dreamt that I was awakening from another dream—full of cataclysms and turmoil—and that I was waking up in a room which I did not recognize. Dawn was breaking: a faint diffused light outlined the foot of the iron bedstead, the table. I thought fearfully 'Where am I?' and realized that I did not know. I thought 'Who am I?' and I could not recognize myself. Fear grew within me. I thought, 'This distressing awakening is already hell, this awakening without a future will be my eternity.' Then I really awoke, trembling."

Not to know oneself, not to know one's destiny, that's certainly real hell. And man does not know himself. Now, the cheaper way is to create the ego, and the West has been following the cheaper way. And not only the West: the majority of people in the East too have been doing the same. Just leave a few enlightened people aside, and the whole world has been doing the same.

The West consists of ninety-nine point nine percent of the people in the world; the East consists of only a few people, they can be counted on the fingers. To me, the East and the West are not geographical: they are spiritual dimensions. Gautam Buddha, Lao Tzu, Zarathustra, Abraham,

Moses, Christ, St Francis—the East consists of these people. Where they were born is immaterial, is irrelevant. Certainly St Francis was not born in the East, but I count him as part of the East.

The spiritual dimension, the dimension where the inner sun rises, is the East. And the dark night of the soul, which knows nothing of the sunrise, is the West. You don't become religious just by being born in India. Religion is not that cheap. It is the costliest thing in existence, because it is the *most* precious. There is no shortcut to it, and those who seek shortcuts are bound to be deceived by somebody. They will be given toys, and you can go on believing in toys because you don't want to risk an adventure into the unknown.

The greatest unknown exists within you. The most uncharted sea is your consciousness, and the most dangerous too. Because when you start moving inwards, you start falling into an emptiness...and great fear arises, the fear of going mad, the fear of losing your identity. Because you have known yourself as the name, you have known yourself as a particular person—you have known yourself as a doctor, as an engineer, as a businessman; you have known yourself as an Indian, a German, a Chinese; you have known yourself as black or white, you have known yourself as man or woman, you have known yourself as educated or uneducated...all these categories start disappearing.

As you move inwards, you are neither man nor woman: *neti, neti*—neither this nor that, neither white nor black! neither Hindu nor Muslim, neither Indian nor Pakistani. As you move inwards, all these categories start slipping out of your hands. Then who are you? You start losing track of your ego, and a great fear arises; the fear of nothingness. You are falling into infinity. Who knows whether you will be able to come back or not? And who knows what is going to be the outcome of this exploration? The coward clings to the shore and forgets all about the sea.

That's what is happening all over the world. People cling to the ego because ego gives you a certain idea of who you are, gives you a certain clarity. But the ego is false, and the clarity is false. It is better to be confused with reality than to be clear with unreality.

ARADHANA, YOU ARE TRUE: WITH ME A GREAT confusion is bound to happen—because all your knowledge, slowly slowly, will be proved simple ignorance and nothing else. Hiding behind your knowledge is your ignorance. Hiding behind your cleverness is your stupid mind. And behind the ego there is nothing—it is a shadow.

Once this becomes clear to you, that you have been clinging to the shadow, a great fear and great confusion, a great chaos is bound to happen. But out of the chaos stars are born. One has to pass through such chaos; that is part of spiritual growth. You have to lose the false to get to the real. But between the two there will be an interval when the false will be gone and the true will not yet have arrived. Those are the moments, the most critical moments...these are the moments when you need a Master or a friend.

Just the other day, Buddha was saying, "A Master or a friend is needed." These are the moments when you will need somebody's hand who can hold you, who can support you, who can say, "Don't be afraid. This emptiness is going to disappear. Soon you will be overflowing—just a little waiting more, a little patience more." The Master cannot give you anything, but he can give you courage. He can give you his hand in those critical moments when your mind would like to go back, to turn back, to cling again to the shore.

The joy of the Master, his confidence, his authority... remember, when I say 'his authority' I don't mean that a Master is authoritarian. A Master is never authoritarian, but he has authority, because he is a witness to his own self. He *knows* about the other shore, he has *been* to the other shore. You have only *heard* about the other shore, you have read about it; you know only about this shore, and the comfort and the security, and the safety of this shore. And when the storms rage and when you start losing sight of *this* shore, and you are not able to see the other shore, your mind will say, "Go back! Go back as fast as possible! The old shore is disappearing and the new is not appearing. Maybe there is nothing on the other shore, maybe there is *no* other shore at all. And the storm is great!"

In those moments, if you are with a Master, and somebody is sitting in the boat silent, utterly calm and quiet, laughing and saying, "Don't be worried," playing on his flute, or singing a song, or telling you a joke, and he says, "Don't be worried. The other shore is—I know, I have been there. Just a little patience...."

Looking into his eyes, in his absolute confidence, will be the only help. Seeing his calmness, quietness, his integrity...he is not looking back, he is not afraid. He must have seen the other shore, he must have been there. His whole being says it, his whole being proves it. And when he holds your hand you can feel that his hand is not trembling, you can feel that whatsoever he is saying he is saying out of his own experience, not because it is written in the Bible, in the Gita, in the Dhammapada. He *knows* it on his own!—that is his authority.

Once his confidence, his trust, becomes contagious to

you, you will also start laughing. Of course, your laughter will have a little nervousness in it, but you will start laughing. You may start singing with him, maybe just to avoid fear, just as people whistle in the dark. You may join in his dance, just to forget all about what is happening. You don't want to see the storm that surrounds you, and you don't want to remember the past and you don't want to think about the future. It seems dark and dismal to you. You may join in his dance. . . .

Dancing with him, even if out of fear, singing with him even though your singing is bound to be nervous, laughing with him although your laughter is not total, the storm will be passed. Soon. The deeper your patience, the sooner it happens—you will be able to see the other shore. Because when the eyes are not troubled, when the eyes are not full of fear, they become perceptive. A seeing arises in you— you become a seer.

The other shore is not far away; just your eyes are so full of smoke that you cannot see. In fact, this very shore is the other shore—if your eyes are clear, if your perception is not clouded, if your insight has arisen in your being, if you can see and hear, this very shore is the other shore.

When one knows, one really laughs at the whole ridiculousness of life—because we have already got that for which we are longing. The treasure is with us and we are running hither and thither.

The ego has not to be created, because you have the supreme self within you. But your confusion, I can understand. Remain confused. Don't go back to your old clarity— it is deceptive. Be in this confusion, be with me a little while more, and soon the confusion will disperse and disappear. And then comes a totally new kind of clarity.

There are two kinds of clarity. One which is simply

intellectual, which any moment can be taken away, doubt can be created any moment. Intellect is full of doubt. Whatsoever you had heard and whatsoever you had been told has been taken away so easily by me, it was not of much value. Your whole life's training, and I have taken the earth from underneath your feet so easily... and you are confused. What value can such clarity have? If I can confuse you so easily, that means it was not real clarity. I will give you a new kind of clarity which cannot be confused.

Once a great philosopher went to see Ramakrishna. The philosopher argued against God, and he argued really well. His name was Keshavachandra Sen. Ramakrishna was utterly illiterate; he knew nothing of philosophy, he had never been to the university; he had only read up to the second standard. He could write and read Bengali a little bit.

The philosopher was well educated, world famous; he had written many books. He argued, and Ramakrishna laughed. And each time the philosopher gave a beautiful, profound argument against God, Ramakrishna would jump and hug him. A great crowd had gathered to see the scene, what was happening. The philosopher was very much embarrassed, because he had come to argue, and what kind of argument is this? This man laughs, dances! sometimes hugs.

The philosopher said, "Are you not disturbed by my arguments?"

Ramakrishna said, "How can I be disturbed? I am really enjoying your arguments. You *are* clever, you are intelligent, your arguments are beautiful—but what can I do? I know God! It is not a question of argument, it is not that I believe in God. Had I believed, you would have disturbed me, you would have taken all my clarity and you would have confused me. But I *know* he is!"

If you know, you know; there is no way of distracting you. I will give you *that* kind of clarity—which knows, and is not dependent on any argument but arises out of existential experience. Then you need not be taught to respect yourself or love yourself or feel worthwhile. Knowing oneself, one knows one is God. Now what more respect can you give to yourself? When this experience arises in you, "*Aham Brahmasmi!*—I am God!" what more respect can you give to yourself?

And who is there to give respect? Only God is . . . . . When in the deepest recesses of your being the realization happens, "*Ana'l Haq!*—I am truth!" what more worthwhileness do you need to feel? You have come to the ultimate, and you have come to know the ultimate as your innermost being, your interiority.

Yes, you have been told to be respectful to yourself because you don't know who you are. You have been told to feel worthwhile because you feel worthless. You have been told to love yourself because you hate yourself. And the strange thing is, the irony is, that it is the *same* people who have been doing both things to you.

The same people first make you feel worthless; this is the trade-secret of all the churches, of all the so-called religions, of all political ideologies, of all societies, civilizations and cultures, that have existed up to now. This is the trade secret: first they make you feel worthless; every child is made to feel worthless. He is told, "Unless you become this or that, you have no worth." When he starts feeling worthless, then we start telling him, "Feel worthwhile, feel some worth. If you cannot feel worthwhile, your life is wasted."

First we tell him to hate himself and condemn himself; everything that he does is wrong, hence he starts hating himself because he is not a beautiful person. The parents, the teachers, the priests, they are all joined in the conspiracy. Every child is reduced to such a condemnable state that he starts feeling, "I must be the ugliest person in the world, because I do things that should not be done, and I don't do things which should be done." And then one day we start telling the child, "Why don't you love yourself? Otherwise, how will you survive?"

We take all respect away from the child, and when he becomes disrespectful towards himself we start telling him to create respect. This is such an absurd situation! Each child is born with great respect for himself. Each child knows his worth, his intrinsic worth. He is not worthy because he is like Buddha or Krishna or Christ—he simply knows he has worth because he is, he has being. That's enough! And each child loves himself, respects himself.

It is you who teach him just the opposite. First you destroy all that is beautiful in him, and then you start painting a false picture. Destroy the natural beauty and then paint his face, make him absolutely false. But why is this done? Because only false people can be slaves, only false people can follow the stupid politicians, only false people can be victims of utterly ignorant priests. If people are real, they cannot be exploited and cannot be oppressed.

Aradhana, remain confused, it is good. It is good that you have come to this point where a great confusion has arisen in you—you can no more trust your ego, good! It is tremendously important, because now a second step becomes possible. I will give you your childhood back, your inner worth, which is not a created phenomenon; your natural love, which is not cultivated; your spontaneous respect, which arises only when you start feeling that you are part of God, that you are divine.

Remember, ego is comparative—it always compares itself with others—and the self is non-comparative. When you know yourself it is neither inferior nor superior in comparison to anybody—it is simply itself. But the ego is comparative. And remember: if you feel superior to somebody, you are bound to feel inferior to somebody else. So the ego is a very tricky phenomenon: on one hand it makes you feel superior, on the other hand it makes you feel inferior. It keeps you in a double bind, it goes on pulling you apart. It drives you crazy.

On the one hand you know that you are superior to your servant, but what about your boss? You force the servant to surrender to you, and you surrender to your boss. You force your servant or your wife or your children to be slaves to you, and then to your boss? You wag your tail there.

How can you be blissful? Both things are wrong. To make others feel inferior is violent, it is a crime against God; and to make yourself feel inferior before somebody is again a crime against God. When you know the real self, both things disappear. Then you are you, and the other is the other, and there is no comparison—nobody is superior and nobody is inferior.

This is what I call real spiritual communism, but this is possible only when self-knowledge has happened. Karl Marx or Friedrich Engels, Joseph Stalin or Mao Tse Tung, these are *not* the real communists. They live in the ego. The real communists are Gautam Buddha, Jesus, Lao

Tzu—nobody knows them as communists but they are
real communists. Because if you understand their vision,
all comparison disappears. And when there is no comparison, there is communism. Equality is possible only when
comparison disappears from the world.

Not knowing yourself, you are almost fast asleep; not
knowing yourself, you are like a drunkard who asks others
"Where is my home?" The drunkard sometimes even asks,
"Can you tell me, sir, who I am?"

Once a drunkard came back to the bartender and asked
him, "Have you seen my friend? Has he been here?"

The bartender said, "Yes, just a few minutes before, he
was here."

And the drunkard asked, "Will you be kind enough to
tell me: was I with him too?"

There was a drunk standing at a bar one day. He turned
to the man on his right and said, "Did you pour beer in
my pocket?"

"I certainly did not," said the man.

Then the drunk turned to the man on his left and said,
"Did you pour beer in my pocket?"

The man said, "I most certainly did not pour beer in
your pocket."

The drunk said, "Just like I thought—an inside job."

The second question

Bhagwan,
What is your vision for the new commune?

Krishna Prem,

THE NEW COMMUNE IS AN EXPERIMENT IN spiritual communism. The word 'communism' comes from 'commune'. There is only one possiblity of communism in the world and that possibility is through meditation. Communism is not possible through changing the economic structures of societies.

The change of economic structures of societies will only bring new classes; it cannot bring a classless society. The proletariat may disappear, the bourgeoisie may go, but then the ruler and the ruled—that's what has happened in Soviet Russia, that's what has happened in China. New distinctions, new classes have arisen.

Communism is basically a spiritual vision. It is not a question of changing the economic structures of the society, but changing people's spiritual vision. The new commune is going to be a space where we can create human beings who are not obsessed with comparison, who are not obsessed with the ego, who are not obsessed with the personality.

The new commune is going to be a context in which a new kind of man can become possible. Socrates says that the Master is a midwife, and he is right: all Masters are midwives. They always bring new humanities into existence. Through them a new man is born.

The old man is finished. The old man is no more valid. And with the old man, all that belonged to the old man has also become invalid, irrelevant. The old man was life-negative. The new commune will create a life-affirmative religiousness. The motto of the new commune is: This very body the Buddha, this very earth the Lotus Paradise.

The new commune is going to hallow the earth, to make everything sacred. We are not going to divide existence into this world and that world: we are going to live existence in its totality. We are going to live as scientists, as poets, as mystics—*all* together!

The scientist is partial: he believes only in the body, he cannot go beyond it; his vision is very limited, short-sighted. The poet clings to another aspect of humanity, the feeling part. He can see the beauty, but his beauty is very momentary. He has no idea of the eternal. The mystic lives in the being, he lives in the deathless, timeless state. Because he lives in the deathless, timeless state he becomes indifferent to the world of time and space. He becomes indifferent both to science and to poetry. These are all three aspects of reality, three faces of God, trinity, *trimurti*.

My effort in the new commune is to create a man who is not partial, who is total, whole, holy. A man should be all three together. He should be as accurate and objective as a scientist; and he should be as sensitive, as full of the heart, as the poet; and he should be as rooted deep down in his being as the mystic. He should not choose. He should allow all these three dimensions to exist together.

The East suffered because we became too much concerned with the being; we lost track of science, we lost track of art. The West has suffered, is suffering, because it has lost track of being. The East became inwardly rich but outwardly poor; the West has become outwardly rich, inwardly poor. The new commune is going to be rich in both ways.

I believe in richness. I am not a worshipper of poverty. That is simply stupid. I would like humanity to be rich in all possible ways: rich in science, rich in technology, rich in poetry, rich in music, rich in meditation, rich in mysticism. Life should be lived in its multi-dimensionality. God should be approached through all possible ways. Why impoverish your soul?

The new commune is going to create a space, a context, for this multi-dimensional human being to be born. And the future belongs to this new man.

The old man believed in renunciation; the old man believed that if you want to come closer to God you have to be away from the world, as if there is a conflict between God and the world. It is obviously wrong. The world exists through God! The world is God's body—there can't be any conflict! If there had been any conflict, then the world would have disappeared long ago.

The world breathes, is alive, and life is God. The tree is divine because it is alive, and the rock is divine because the rock is also alive in its own way, the rock also grows. The whole existence is full of life, overflowing with life. God is not against the world—how can the painter be against his painting? and how can the poet be against his poetry? and how can the musician be against his music? The world is his poetry, his painting, his music; it is his dance.

The old man lived in renunciation, escaped away from the world to the caves, to the monasteries, to the Himalayas. The old man was escapist, the old man was afraid to live; he was more ready to die. The old man was somehow suicidal.

My new man is going to be deep in love with life. And my religion is not of renunciation but of rejoicing. The new commune will create every possible opportunity to rejoice, sing, dance.

The new commune is going to be of a totally new kind

of religiousness, spirituality. Nobody is going to be a Hindu or a Mohammedan or a Christian or a Jaina, but everybody is going to be religious—just religious. To me, religion needs no adjectives. And the moment a religion becomes attached to an adjective, it is no more religion—it becomes politics.

Bayazid is not Mohammedan. Mohammed himself is not Mohammedan, cannot be. Christ is not Christian and Buddha is not Buddhist. They are simply religious. They have a certain flavour, a certain silence, a certain grace, surrounding them. They are windows to the beyond. Through them you can see the beyond; through them God goes on singing a thousand and one songs.

The new commune is not going to be of any religion. It will be religious. But the religion will not be unearthly, it will be very down-to-earth. Hence it will be creative; it will explore all possibilities of being creative. All kinds of creativity will be supported, nourished.

The real religious man has to contribute to the world. He has to make it a little more beautiful than he found it when he came into the world. He has to make it a little more joyous. He has to make it a little more perfumed. He has to make it a little more harmonious. That is going to be his contribution.

In the past we respected people for wrong reasons. We respected somebody because he was fasting. Now, fasting contributes nothing to the world. And the man who goes on long fasts is simply being violent with himself. To respect him is to respect violence, to respect him is to respect suicidal instincts, to respect him is to respect masochism. He is mentally ill! He is not natural, he is abnormal. He needs psychological treatment, he needs help. But you respect him, and because of your respect, his ego becomes puffed up. So if he was going to fast for one month, he will fast for three months. And the more he fasts, the more he tortures his body, the more respect you give to him.

The new commune will not respect any masochistic tendencies. It will not respect any asceticism, it will not respect any abnormal, unnatural tendencies—it will respect the natural man. It will respect the child in man, it will respect innocence, and it will respect creativity. It will respect a man who paints a beautiful picture, it will respect the man who plays beautifully on the flute. The flute-player will be religious, and the painter will be religious, and the dancer will be religious, not the man who goes on long fasts, who tortures his body, who lies down on a bed of thorns, who cripples himself.

It is going to be the beginning of a new humanity—it is needed, absolutely needed. If we cannot create the new man in the coming twenty years, by the end of this century, then humanity has no future. The old man has come to the end of his tether. The old man is ready to commit a global suicide. The third world war is going to be global suicide. It can be avoided only if a new kind of man can be created.

This is going to be an experiment, a great experiment, on which much is going to depend. It has tremendous implications for the future. Be ready for it. Be prepared for it. This ashram is just a launching pad.... On a small scale I am experimenting. The new commune will be on a big scale: ten thousand sannyasins living together as one body, one being. Nobody will possess anything; everybody will use everything, everybody will enjoy. Everybody is going to live as comfortably, as richly, as we can manage. But nobody will possess anything. Not only will things not be possessed, but persons also will not be possessed in the new commune. If you love a woman, live with her—out of sheer love, out of sheer joy—but you don't become her husband, you can't. You don't become a wife. To become a "wife" or a "husband" is ugly because it brings ownership; then the other is reduced to property.

The new commune is going to be non-possessive, full of love—living in love but with no possessiveness at all. Sharing all kinds of joys, making a pool of all the joys.... When ten thousand people contribute, it can become explosive. The rejoicing will be great.

Jesus says again and again: "Rejoice! Rejoice! Rejoice!" But he has not been heard yet. Christians look so serious, and they have painted Jesus also in such a way that it doesn't seem that he ever rejoiced himself. Christians say Jesus never laughed! This is ridiculous. The man who was saying "Rejoice!" the man who used to love good food, good wine, the man who used to feast and participate in festivals, the man around whom there was always feasting—he never laughed?

Christians have given a false Christ to the world.

In my commune, Buddha is going to laugh and dance, Christ is going to laugh and dance...poor fellows, nobody has allowed them up to now. Have compassion on them: let them dance and sing and play. My new commune is going to transform work into playfulness, it is going to transform life into love and laughter.

Remember the motto again—to hallow the earth, to make everything sacred, to transform the ordinary, mundane things into extraordinary, spiritual things. The whole of life has to be your temple, work has to be your worship, love has to be your prayer. This very body the Buddha, this very earth the Lotus Paradise.

The third question

Bhagwan,
I am a psychologist. I was hoping that studying psycho-
logy would help to change my life, but nothing like
that has happened. What should I do now?

PSYCHOLOGY IS STILL A VERY VERY IMMATURE
science. It is very rudimentary; it is only the beginning
It is not yet a way of life—it cannot transform you. It can
certainly give you a few insights into the mind, but those
insights are not going to be transforming. Why? Because
transformation always happens from a higher plane. Transformation never means solving problems remaining on
the same plane. That means adjustment, psychology is
still trying to help you adjust—to adjust to the society
which is itself insane, to adjust to the family, to adjust to
the ideas that are dominant around you. But all those ideas,
your family, your society, they themselves are ill, sick, and
to adjust to them will give you a certain normality, at least
a superficial appearance of health, but it is not going to
transform you.

Transformation means to change the plane of your
understanding. It comes through transcendence. If you
want to change your mind, you have to go to the state
of no-mind. Only from that height will you be able to
change your mind, because from that height you will be
the master. Remaining in the mind and trying to change
the mind by mind itself is a futile process. It is like pulling
yourself up by your own shoestrings. It is like a dog trying
to catch hold of its own tail; sometimes they do, sometimes they behave very humanly. The dog is sitting in
the warm sun early in the morning and he looks at the

tail just resting by his side—naturally, the curiosity arises: Why not catch hold of it? He tries, fails, feels offended, annoyed; tries hard, fails harder, becomes mad, crazy. But he will never be able to catch hold of the tail—it is his own tail. The more he jumps the more the tail will jump.

Psychology can give you a few insights into the mind, but because it cannot take you beyond the mind it can't be of any help.

Sam became a psychiatrist and began to prosper. He bought a big expensive limousine and drove it out for the first time. After riding for a few moments, another car slammed into him. He jumped out of his smashed Cadillac, went over to the car that had rammed his, shook his fist at it, and roared, "You idiot! You moron! You crook of a rat! You son of a...!" Then he suddenly remembered he was a psychiatrist and lowered his voice and softly asked, "Why do you hate your mother?"

Psychology cannot help. I have heard another story about this same Sam—a story of when he was no more in the world, he had died.

The widow was tending to the plants around her husband's grave. As she bent over, some blades of grass tickled the bare flesh under her skirt. Startled, she turned around quickly, but there was no one in sight. Sighing, she turned back to the grave and whispered, "Sam, behave yourself! And remember, you are supposed to be dead."

Neither in life nor in death is psychology going to help you much. You can be helped only by religion.

Now the psychologist is trying to play the role of the

Master, which is utterly pretentious. The psychologist, the psychoanalyst and the psychiatrist are not Masters! They don't know themselves. Yes, they have understood a little bit about the mechanism of the mind, they have studied, they are well informed. But information never changes anybody, it never brings any revolution. Deep down the person remains the same. He can talk beautifully, he can give you good advice, but he cannot follow his own advice.

The psychoanalyst cannot be the Master.

But in the West particularly he has become so successful professionally that even the priest is in tremendous awe. Even the priests—the Catholic and the Protestant—are studying psychoanalysis and other schools of psychology, because they see that people are not coming to the priest any more, they are going to the psychoanalyst. The priest is becoming afraid that he is losing his job.

The priest has dominated people for hundreds of years. He was the wise man—he has lost his attraction. And people cannot live without advisors; they need somebody to tell them what to do, because they never grow up; they are like small children, always in need of being told what to do and what not to do. Up to now the priest used to do that; now the priest has lost his charm, his validity. He is no more contemporary; he has become out of date. Now the psychoanalyst has taken his place: he is the priest now.

But as the priest was false, so is the psychoanalyst. The priest was using religious jargon to exploit people; the psychologist is using scientific jargon to exploit the same people. Neither was the priest awakened, nor is the psychoanalyst awakened. Man can be helped only by somebody who is a Buddha already, otherwise he cannot be helped.

All your advisors will make more and more mess out of

you. The more you listen to advisors, the more you will become messed up—because they don't know what they are saying! They don't even agree amongst themselves. Freud says one thing, Adler says another, Jung says still another. And now there are a thousand and one schools. And every school is fanatical about its philosophy, that it has the truth—the whole truth and nothing but the truth. Not only does it say that it is true; it says it has *the* truth, and everybody else is lying, deceiving.

If you listen to these psychoanalysts, if you go from one psychoanalyst to another, you will be more puzzled. The only help that they can give to you is that if you are intelligent enough you will become so fed up with them, so bored with them, that you will simply drop the idea of being transformed, and you may start living your life normally, without bothering much about transformation—*if* you are intelligent, which is very rare, because intelligence is crushed from the very beginning. You are made mediocres. From the *very* beginning, intelligence is destroyed. Only a few people somehow escape the society and remain intelligent.

Nagesh, you ask me:
What should I do now?

My suggestion is: you have done enough. Now learn something which is not doing but non-doing. Be here, and learn *not* to do but to be. Sit·silently, doing nothing. Within three to nine months, if one is patient enough, and if one can simply go on sitting for hours together every day, as much as one can find time just sit.... In the beginning, great turmoil will arise in your mind; everything from the unconscious will start surfacing. You will see it as if you are going mad. Go on watching, don't be worried. You cannot go mad because you are already mad, so there is nothing to lose and nothing to fear.

A politician, a great politician, was consulting a psychoanalyst. The politician was suffering from an inferiority complex—all politicians suffer from inferiority complexes. If they don't suffer from inferiority complexes, they will not be politicians in the first place. To be a politician means striving to be superior, to be in power, so one can prove to others and to oneself, "I am not inferior. Look! I am the prime minister. Look! Only I am the prime minister of the country and nobody else—how can I be inferior?"

Politics arises out of the inferiority complex—all power politics arises out of the inferiority complex. So it was not rare that the politician was suffering from an inferiority complex. The psychoanalyst worked on the politician year in, year out. After two or three years, listening to all his gibberish nonsense...because what can a politician say? For hours together he would lie down on the couch and talk nonsense.

After three years, one day when he came, the psychoanalyst received him with great joy and said, "I am glad to declare, after three years research on you that you don't suffer from an inferiority complex. I have come to this conclusion after such a long effort that it can't be wrong: you don't suffer from an inferiority complex—simply forget all about it."

The politician was very happy and he said, "I am grateful to you, but can you tell me how you arrived at this conclusion?"

The psychoanalyst said, "Because you are simply inferior—how can you suffer from an inferiority complex?"

Nagesh, you need not be worried. If sitting silently

you start feeling madness arising, don't be worried—you can't be more mad than you already are. Man cannot fall more. He has fallen to the rock bottom. Now there is no further to fall.

Sitting silently you will see madness arising in you, because it has remained repressed. And you keep occupied with things—psychology etc.—now you will become occupied with meditation and sannyas, but these are all occupations and you are not allowing your unconscious to reveal itself to you. It is frightening.

My suggestion to you is: just sit silently as much as you can find time to. Zen people sit silently at least six to eight hours per day. In the beginning it is really maddening. The mind plays so many tricks on you, tries to drive you crazy, creates imaginary fears, hallucinations. The body starts playing tricks on you…all kinds of things will happen. But if you can go on witnessing, within three to nine months, everything settles, and settles of its own accord—not because you have to do something. Without your doing, it simply settles, and when a stillness arises, uncultivated, unpractised, it is something superb, something tremendously graceful, exquisite. You have never tasted anything like it before—it is pure nectar.

You have transcended the mind! All mind problems are solved. Not that you have found a solution, but simply they have fallen by themselves—by witnessing, but just witnessing.

You are already too knowledgeable, no more knowledge is needed You need unlearning. Knowledgeable people are very cunning people; they can always go on finding excuses to remain the same.

A professor of philosophy and psychology was addicted

to moonshine whisky. One night, after guzzling a large amount, he went into his cabin, undressed for bed, and tried to blow out the candle. His alcoholic breath burst into flame.

Sadly shaken by the experience, he called out to his wife, "Bring me the Bible, Martha. This here has been a terrible lesson to me. I am going to swear off."

The happy housewife brought the Bible in a hurry, stood by while her man put his hand on it and looked heavenward: "I swear by all that is holy," intoned he, "that I will never again blow on a lighted candle."

Mind is cunning. You have to go beyond mind—that's what meditation is all about.

The last question

Bhagwan,
You seem to be the first enlightened Master who tells jokes—why is it so?

Garima,

I WILL TELL YOU A STORY. THE FOLLOWING story in the Talmud was particularly cherished by the great Hassid Master, Baal Shem.

Rabbi Beroka used to visit the marketplace where the Prophet Elijah often appeared to him. It was believed that he appeared to some saintly men to offer them spiritual guidance.

Once Beroka asked the Prophet, "Is there anyone here who has a share in the world to come?"

He replied, "No."

While they were conversing, two men passed by and Elijah remarked, "These two men have a share in the world to come."

Rabbi Beroka then approached and asked them, "What is your occupation?"

They replied, "We are jesters. When we see men depressed we cheer them up."

God loves laughter, God loves cheerful people. God is not interested in seeing you with long faces.

When Baal Shem was dying, somebody asked, "Are you prepared to meet the Lord?"

He said, "I have always been ready. It is not a question of becoming ready now—I have always been ready. Any moment he could have called me!"

The man asked, "What is your readiness?"

Baal Shem said, "I know a few beautiful jokes—I will tell him those jokes. And I know he will enjoy them and he will laugh with me. And what else can I offer to him? The whole world is his, the whole universe is his, I am his, so what can I offer to him? Just a few jokes."

Baal Shem is one of the great Buddhas who has come out of the Jewish tradition, one of the most loved by his disciples. He was the founder of Hassidism.

And remember, I am not the first to tell you jokes. There have been many.... But people are so sad that they forget about people who have been sources of laughter and joy— they remember only sad people. People are sad, hence they find a certain affinity with sad people. You remember only sad Buddhas—even if they were not sad, you make them sad. In your mind you fabricate stories, you manufacture ideas, and you make them look sad.

Now, a Jaina will be very much offended if I say that Mahavira laughed. Laughter seems to be so mundane, so worldly. How can Mahavira laugh? If I say Buddha laughed, Buddhists, particularly the Hinayana Buddhists, will be angry. I have been in tremendous love with Buddha; I think there is no other man on the earth today who has loved Buddha as much as I. But just the other day I was reading in the newspapers: the president of the Buddhist Society of India is going to raise questions against me in the Parliament in the coming session. I can understand; these people must be feeling very much offended, because I am giving Buddha a new colour—*his* colour, Buddha's colour. I am trying to bring his reality to you. And these people have distorted his image totally; they have made him look so sad, they won't allow him to laugh. If he laughs, they will raise questions against him in the Parliament.

I am offending people because I am trying to live religion not according to their ideas. I tell you, privately of course, that Jesus used to joke—but don't tell it to Christians, they will not understand. They can understand only the Jesus crucified. In fact, they are worshipping death, not Jesus; they are worshipping the cross not Christ. Hence I call Christianity Crossianity—it has nothing to do with Christ. I know the man, I personally know the man!

He used to love all the good things of life. How can he avoid joking? He loved to gossip, and they say he was only delivering gospels! He was a very very earth-rooted man. He moved with gamblers, with drunkards, with prostitutes too. He was not afraid of all these fools—that's why he had to suffer.

That's why *I* am to suffer. . . .

For a while the fool's mischief
Tastes sweet, sweet as honey.
But in the end it turns bitter.
And how bitterly he suffers!

For months the fool may fast,
Eating from the tip of a grass blade.
Still he is not worth a penny
Beside the master whose food is the way.

Fresh milk takes time to sour.
So a fool's mischief
Takes time to catch up with him.
Like the embers of a fire
It smoulders within him.

Whatever a fool learns,
It only makes him duller.
Knowledge cleaves his head.

For then he wants recognition.
A place before other people,
A place over other people.

"Let them know my work,
Let everyone look to me for direction."
Such are his desires,
Such is his swelling pride.

One way leads to wealth and fame,
The other to the end of the way.

Look not for recognition
But follow the awakened
And set yourself free.

July 9

Sowing Seeds of Bliss

THE LAST WORDS OF GAUTAM THE BUDDHA on the earth were: Be a light unto yourself. Do not follow others, do not imitate, because imitation, following, creates stupidity. You are born with a tremendous possibility of intelligence. You are born with a light within you. Listen to the still small voice within, and that will guide you. Nobody else can guide you; nobody else can become a model for your life— because you are unique. Nobody has there been ever who was exactly like you, and nobody is ever going to be there again who will be exactly like you. This is your glory, your grandeur, that you are utterly irreplaceable, that you are just yourself and nobody else.

The person who follows others becomes false, he becomes pseudo, he becomes mechanical. He can be a great saint in the eyes of others, but deep down, he is simply unintelligent and nothing else. He may have a very respectable character but that is only the surface; it is not even skin deep. Scratch him a little and you will be surprised that inside he is a totally different person, just the opposite of his outside.

By following others you can cultivate a beautiful character, but you cannot have a beautiful consciousness. And unless you have a beautiful consciousness you can never be free. You can go on changing your prisons, you can go on changing your bondages, your slaveries. You can be a Hindu or a Mohammedan or a Christian or a Jaina—that is not going to help you. To be a Jaina means to follow Mahavira as the model. Now, there is nobody who is like Mahavira or ever can be. Following Mahavira you will become a false entity. You will lose all reality, you will lose all sincerity, you will be untrue to yourself. And you will become artificial, unnatural. And to be artificial, to be unnatural, is the way of the mediocre, the stupid, the fool.

Buddha defines wisdom as living in the light of your own consciousness, and foolishness as following others, imitating others, becoming a shadow to somebody else.

The real Master creates masters, not followers. The real Master throws you back to yourself. His whole effort is to make you independent of him, because dependent you have been for centuries, and it has not led you anywhere. You still continue to stumble in the dark night of the soul.

Only your inner light can become the sunrise. The false Master persuades you to follow him, to imitate him, to be just a carbon copy of him; the real Master will not allow you to be a carbon copy, he wants you to be the original. He loves you! How can he make you imitative? He has compassion for you, he would like you to be utterly free—free from all outer dependencies.

But the ordinary human being does not want to be free. He wants to be dependent. He wants somebody else to guide him. Why? Because then he can throw the whole responsibility on the shoulders of somebody else. And the more responsibility you throw away onto somebody else's shoulders, the less is the possibility of your ever becoming intelligent. It is responsibility, the challenge of responsibility, that creates wisdom.

One has to accept life with all its problems. One has to go through life unprotected; one has to seek and search one's way. Life is an opportunity, a challenge, to find yourself. But the fool does not want to go the hard way; the fool chooses the shortcut. He says to himself, "Buddha has attained—why should I bother? I will just watch his behaviour and imitate. Jesus has attained, so why should I search and seek? I can simply become a shadow to Jesus. I can simply go on following him wherever he goes."

But following somebody else, how are you going to become intelligent? You will not give any chance for your intelligence to explode. It needs a challenging life, an adventurous life, a life that knows how to risk and how to go into the unknown, for intelligence to arise. And only intelligence can save you—nobody else—your own intelligence, mind you, your own awareness, can become your nirvana.

Be a light unto yourself and you will be wise; and let others become your leaders, your guides, and you will remain stupid, and you will go on missing all the treasures of life—which were yours! And how can you decide that the other's character is a right character for you to follow?

A Buddha lives in his own way, a Mahavira in his, a Jesus still different; a Mohammed *is* Mohammed, he is *not* Mahavira. Whom are you going to follow? Just by the accidents of birth you are going to decide your life, your destiny? Then you will remain accidental. And the fool *is* accidental. The wise man never lives by accidents. He does not become a Hindu because he is born in a Hindu family; he does not become a Christian because his parents are Christian; he does not become a communist because he is born in Russia. He seeks, he enquires.

Life is a tremendously beautiful pilgrimage, but only for those who are ready to seek and search.

Jesus says: Seek and ye shall find, ask and it shall be given to you, knock and the doors shall be opened unto you.

He is not saying: Follow, imitate. He is not saying: Be a Christian and the doors shall be opened unto you. He is not saying: I have knocked on the doors and opened them for you. He is saying: Knock and the doors shall be opened unto you. And everybody has to knock, because everybody has to enter by different doors. People are so unique, people are individuals.

This is your glory. Don't deny it, otherwise you will remain a fool. That does not mean don't learn from the Buddhas, the awakened ones—learn! Imbibe the spirit! Drink out of their springs, fresh springs of joy. Be in their company, become attuned to their inner music, listen to their harmony. And be filled with great joy that a man like you, just like you, has achieved, so you can also achieve. Become thrilled that a man just like you, made of blood and bones, has become enlightened, so you can also become enlightened.

A Buddha has not to be followed but understood. A Buddha has not to be imitated but listened to—listened to in tremendous silence, love, trust. And the more you understand a Buddha, the more you will feel he is speaking not from the outside but from within, from the very core of your being. He is a mirror who reflects your original face—but he is only a mirror. All great Masters are mirrors, they reflect your original face. But don't cling to the mirror. The mirror is not your face!

These sutras of Buddha are of immense value. Go into them meditatively. And when I say go into them meditatively, I mean don't be in an argumentative mood—that is not the way to listen. Be in a receptive mood, be feminine. Don't be on guard, don't be defensive. Don't hide behind armours. Don't bring your mind in to interpret what is being said. Put the mind aside and let the heart dance with these sutras. That's what I mean when I say listen meditatively. Let the heart rejoice. And in that rejoicing is a totally different kind of understanding—not of the intellect but of intelligence.

You will not become knowledgeable if you listen from the heart; you will become more and more wise. If you listen from the head, in the first place your listening will be distorted because all your prejudices will become mingled with it, and all your *a priori* conclusions will be a distraction, and your mind will give its colour to what is told to you. In the first place you won't listen to what is being said; your mind will make much noise and you will listen to your own noise. In the second place, whatsoever you gather will become knowledge, not wisdom. Knowledge is superficial; it does not go deep, it cannot go deep. Knowledge is a way to hide your ignorance; it does not destroy it. Wisdom is a light; it dispels darkness.

But wisdom is *always* of the heart, remember; it is never of the head. When you come to a Buddha, forget all about your head. It is a totally different approach to your being—through the heart. Listen through the heartbeats, become attuned—as if you are listening to great music. It *is* great music; in fact, what greater music can there be?

These sutras are the greatest poetry: the poetry of the ultimate being. These sutras are the lotus flowers, born in the lake of a consciousness of one who is awakened. Listen attentively, meditatively, lovingly, in deep trust, and you will be immensely benefitted blessed.

The first sutra:

For a while the fool's mischief
Tastes sweet, sweet as honey.
But in the end it turns bitter.
And how bitterly he suffers!

THERE IS A FAMOUS BUDDHIST PARABLE. BUDDHA loved to tell it again and again:

A man is being chased by his enemies. They are coming closer and closer; he can hear the sound of the hooves of the horses coming closer and closer every moment. It is death! And there seems to be no way to escape, because he has come to a cul-de-sac, the road ends. He is facing a great abyss. If he jumps he is bound to die. He cannot turn back because the enemy is going to kill him. He was hoping that there may be one chance if he jumps—he may become crippled, but maybe, by a miracle, he may survive—but that too seems to be impossible because he sees deep in the abyss two lions looking up at him, ready to devour him.

Finding no other way, cannot go back, cannot go ahead,

he hangs by the roots of a tree, just in the middle. It is a cold morning; his hands are becoming frozen. He knows within minutes he will not be able to hold the roots at all; his hands are slipping, he is losing his grip. He knows death is becoming more certain every moment.

And then he sees that two mice, one black, one white, are eating the root, cutting the root. Those two mice represent day and night—they represent time, which is cutting everybody's life root. Day and night, death is coming closer. So now it becomes even more absolutely certain that it is only a question of moments and he will be gone.

The root is becoming weaker every moment, thinner every moment. The mice are at work. And his hands are getting frozen and he can hear the lions roaring deep in the valley and he can hear the enemy approaching closer and closer. You can understand that man's plight.

And then suddenly he sees that just on the top of the tree there is a bees' nest, and a drop of honey is just slipping out of the nest. He forgets all about the enemies, all about the roaring lions, the white and black mice, his hands getting frozen—in a moment, he completely forgets everything. His whole mind becomes focussed on that drop of honey. He opens his mouth, the honey drops on his tongue . . .and it is so sweet.

This is the situation of the fool. This is the situation of every man on the earth. How sweet it tastes! But how long can this taste remain? Soon death is arriving, from all directions. But that's how we go on living—living for momentary pleasures, indulgence, food, sex, money, power, prestige. . .just drops of honey. And how sweet it tastes, and in that moment we completely forget what is going to happen. The moment takes possession of us and we become oblivious of the reality of life: that it is rooted in death, that it is going to disappear.

Buddha says:

For a while the fool's mischief
Tastes sweet, sweet as honey.
But in the end it turns bitter.
And how bitterly he suffers!

Watch yourself: what are you doing here on the earth? What have you done up to now? What does your life consist of? Have you done anything really real, or have you just been living in dreams? Have you approached in any way the eternal? Or are you too much occupied with the momentary? Have you made any plans, any projects, for the ultimate truth? Or are you just remaining drunk with the mundane, with the ordinary? going into the same rut every day, moving in the same rut every day? The morning comes and you rush to the marketplace, and the evening comes and you are tired and you come home... and the same circle goes on moving, the same wheel. And this has been going on and on for so many lives. When are you going to become bored with it? When are you going to become a little more alert about what you are doing to your life? This is a sheer wastage.

But Buddha says: Certainly, there is some sweetness, momentary, and one suffers for that sweetness. It turns, inevitably, into bitterness. Watch your life. You can earn much money, and while you are earning it tastes sweet. But you are not aware that you are losing your life in earning rubbish, that life is slipping out of your hands, that it is a very costly affair that you are pursuing, utterly foolish, stupid.

The life cannot be bought back; not even a single moment with all your wealth can you purchase back. It cannot be claimed back. Such precious time being wasted! And you are piling up wealth which will be taken away by death. And you will go empty-handed—as empty-handed as you had come to the earth. Then you will feel the bitterness of it, that you wasted your whole life for something which is not going to be with you. You wasted your whole life in power, politics; you wasted your whole life in becoming respectable, and now death has come and all will be taken away. And you have not tasted a single moment of your eternal reality—you have not tasted anything deathless.

This is what Buddha calls the fool's approach towards life. Everything turns bitter: your love, your friendship, your family, your business, your politics...everything, finally, proves to be poisonous, turns into bitterness. One who is wise will become aware while there is still time and something can be done.

> *For months a fool may fast,*
> *Eating from the tip of a grass blade.*
> *Still he is not worth a penny*
> *Beside the master whose food is the way.*

BUDDHA IS NOT SAYING BECOME AN ASCETIC. Buddha is not saying renounce the world, renounce food, starve yourself, fast, torture your body—he is not saying that. He cannot say it. He has learnt a lesson, a great lesson by doing all these things himself.

When he left his palace he followed the traditional path for six years, torturing himself, fasting, destroying his body. He came to a point when he was almost on the verge of death—he had tortured himself too much. In that moment he became aware, "What am I doing? First I was indulging, my whole day and night was devoted to indulgence: women, wine, good food, clothes, palaces, golden chariots, hunting...that was my life, the life of a prince. I was doing something which proved futile."

He was only twenty-nine when he left his palace—must have been a man of great intelligence. There are people who are seventy or seventy-nine and they have not yet become aware of the foolishness of their lives. He was only twenty-nine. Must have been a man of rare insight. Must have been watching, looking at what he was doing, meditating over things. Suddenly he became aware, "This whole thing is rubbish—all these women, all this wine, hunting, all this indulgence is not going to give me anything eternal."

The East has always been in search of the eternal; the definition of truth in the East is: that which is eternal. And the definition of untruth?—that which is momentary. When the Eastern mystics say that something is illusory, they mean it is momentary. They don't mean that it is not. They know it is, but it is only for the moment, like a soap bubble. It is! And sometimes a soap bubble can look really beautiful. If sunrays pass through it, it can be surrounded by a rainbow, all the colours. And a soap bubble *is*, but its isness is so momentary, so deceptive, that it is better to say that it is not. Hence the Eastern mystics say the world is *maya*—illusory. *Not* that it is not, but it is so momentary that it is almost pointless whether it is or it is not. It is better to call it illusory, because that will make you alert, wakeful.

Those twenty-nine years were enough to make him aware that he was playing with soap bubbles. He escaped, he renounced the kingdom. But as it almost always happens, mind moves to the opposite. Mind is like the pendulum of an old clock: goes from right to left, from left to right—to the opposite. It never stays in the middle. And in the middle is the secret. If the pendulum stops in the middle, the clock stops, time stops, the world stops. But the pendulum goes from the left to the right, from the right to the left, and it keeps the clock running, it keeps the clock moving—it keeps *time* alive. And time is the world.

To go beyond time is to know something deathless. Hence, in India, for time and death we use the same word, *kal*—the same word for time and the same word for death. It is not coincidental; it has a significance. Time is death, because in time everything is momentary, everything is going to die. One moment it is, another moment it is gone, and gone forever. The moment you go beyond time, you go beyond death.

But just as the mind functions—it moves to the opposite—Buddha's mind also moved to the opposite. He escaped from the palace. Up to now he had cared about his body; now he started torturing the body. Up to now he was too obsessed with good food; now he started fasting, long fasts. He became a famous ascetic. People started respecting him, people started following him. He was a beautiful man, one of the most beautiful who has ever walked on the earth, but these six years of self-torture and masochism destroyed his body. He became dark, he became thin, he became ugly.

But one day the great insight arose in him, "What am I doing? First I was obsessed with food, now I am obsessed with fasting—basically I am still obsessed with food. First it was a positive obsession, now it is a negative obsession. But I have not changed a little bit. First I was obsessed with women, now I am obsessed with *brahmacharya*—celibacy. Basically I have not changed—I am still obsessed with sex. First I was running towards sex, now I am running away from sex, but sex remains the center of my being."

The revelation was great. That very revelation created the context in which he became enlightened. The evening he understood this, something tremendously important happened to him. He laughed at the whole ridiculousness of his mind. He laughed at the tricky mind, that he was thinking that he was going against mind, but he was not going against mind—mind had played a trick. Mind had befooled him, mind had cheated him. Mind had come from the back door. First it was coming from the front door, now it was coming from the back door, and it is more dangerous when it comes from the back door. By the front door at least you are aware of what you are doing. When it comes from the back door, indirectly, in a subtle way, hiding, comes hidden behind a façade...mind is so cunning that it can hide in the garments of its very opposite. From indulgence it can become asceticism, from being a materialist it can become a spiritualist, from being worldly it can become other-worldly. But mind *is* mind—whether you are for the world or against the world you remain encaged in the mind. For or against, both are parts of the mind.

When mind disappears, mind disappears in a choiceless awareness—when you stop choosing, when you are neither for nor against, that is stopping in the middle. One choice leads to the left, one extreme; another choice leads to the right, the other extreme. If you don't choose, you are exactly in the middle. That is relaxation, that is rest. That is *true* renunciation. It is not opposed to the world, it is not opposed to the body—it has nothing to do with the body;

it is sheer awakening of consciousness. You become choice-less, unobsessed. And in that state of unobsessed, choice-less consciousness, intelligence arises which has been lying deep, dormant in your being. You become a light unto yourself. You are no more a fool.

FROM INDULGENCE YOU CAN MOVE TO REPRESSION; that is not going to help. That's where all the religions have got hooked.

The head nun is held up one evening while coming back from the bank where she has deposited the charity collection of the week. "You are wasting your time, young man," she tells the robber. "I have no money. I put it all in in the night deposit at the bank."

"We will see about that," he says grimly, and begins rumpling up under her black gown to search for the money.

"Oh! What are you doing?" she cries. "Oh! Oh!! Oh, Jesus, Mary! Don't stop now—I will write you a cheque!"

Repression is not the way, cannot be the way. All that you have repressed is waiting for its opportunity. It has simply gone into the unconscious; it can come back any moment. Any provocation and it will surface. You are not free of it. Repression is not the way to freedom. Repression is a far worse kind of bondage than indulgence, because through indulgence one becomes tired sooner or later, but through repression one never becomes tired.

See the point: indulgence is *bound* to tire you and bore you; sooner or later you will start thinking how to get rid of it all. But repression will keep things alive. Because you have not *lived*—how can you be bored? You have not lived—how can you be fed up? Because you have not lived, the charm continues, the hypnosis continues. Deep down, it waits.

And the people who indulge are in a way normal compared to the people who repress. The repressing person becomes pathological; the indulgent is at least natural. That's how nature has made you, but to repress is to become unnatural. It is easy to go from lower nature to higher nature. It is very difficult to go from being unnatural to higher nature. Buddha calls the ultimate truth 'ultimate nature'— *ais dhammo sanantano*. This is the ultimate nature, the ultimate law, he declares. What is the ultimate law? The eternal, the undying, the pure consciousness.

It is easy to reach this eternal law from nature, because nature *is* lower, but still it is nature. And from the lower to the higher you can step; the lower can become a stepping stone. But the moment you become unnatural it becomes very difficult. From being unnatural, there is no way to supreme nature.

Hence, my suggestion is: if you are going to choose, choose indulgence rather than repression. The best thing is *not* to choose, to remain choiceless, to be just a witness, to see your instincts, desires, and not get identified with them, for or against; the best thing is just to be a witness, because in witnessing, in the fire of witnessing, all desires are burnt—not only desires, but the very seeds of desires are burnt. One becomes *nirbeej*—seedless.

But don't choose the negative. Once you become repressive, you become pathological, you are ill. In fact, only pathological people become interested in repressive systems of thought.

All the nuns but one in a Belgian nunnery are found to

be pregnant just after the war. The cardinal makes a personal enquiry and learns that the nuns have all been raped by German soldiers.

"But why didn't they rape you?" he asks of the one thin, little, ugly and repulsive looking nun who is not pregnant.

"Who, me?" she says, "I resisted!"

The pathological can also find rationalizations. You know the old Aesop's fable?

The fox says, "The grapes are sour," because the fox could not get to the grapes—they were too high. She looked around, she tried hard to reach, but the grapes were too high, beyond her reach. She looked around, there was nobody; she walked away, but a hare was watching, hidden behind a bush. And the hare said, "Aunt, what happened? Couldn't you get to the grapes?"

The fox said, "No, it is not a question of getting to the grapes—they are not yet ripe, they are very sour."

The people who cannot get to the grapes can rationalize that they are sour. But these rationalizations may deceive others—how can they deceive you? The fox knows perfectly well that she had not been able to reach. Now, it is a rationalization, and mind is very clever in rationalizing.

Jake came home in the middle of the afternoon. He was met at the door by his wife and his son. His son exclaimed, "Dad, there is a bogeyman in the closet!"

Jake rushed to the closet and flung the door open. There, huddled among the coats was his partner, Sam. "Sam," shrieked Jake, "why in hell do you come here in the afternoon and scare my kid?"

Mind is very cunning and clever in rationalizing things,

in finding ways and means.... The mind can suggest repression to you very easily, because if you repress you will be far more in the power of the mind than you ever were when you were in the life of indulgence. And the mind will have a far stronger grip on you.

Buddha learnt it through his own experience. Six years of great torture. With Buddha the world entered into a new phase of religiousness. Before Buddha nobody had said this: that repressiveness, austerities, fasting, torturing your body, is not going to help. With Buddha humanity entered into a new phase, a higher phase.

Buddha is a very very significant milestone in the evolution of human consciousness, but he has not been understood rightly, because again the interpreters were those old scholars, pundits, priests. They again interpreted Buddha in such a way...they started interpreting Buddha almost completely against his own experience. They started talking much about those six years; Buddhist scriptures are full of the description of those six years. And if you read Buddhist scriptures you will find that it seems as if it is because of those six years of austerities that he attained enlightenment. It is not so. It is not by those six years of austerities that he attained enlightenment; he attained enlightenment the day he dropped all those austerities. It was by dropping them that he attained enlightenment, not by or through them.

But if you read the scriptures, particularly those written in India, you will be given a totally false impression. They make it appear as if Buddha has not contributed anything new to human consciousness, as if he is just the old type of ascetic—maybe far more intelligent in expressing, far more convincing, logical, far more deep-going in his insight, but nothing new. It is the same old religion which he has brought in new words, with new logic; the same old wine in a new bottle, that's all. That's what Indians have made Buddha look like. That is a falsification. Buddha does not represent the old. He is a stepping beyond the old. He is a new phase.

And just as he took a new step, again another step is needed. Twenty-five centuries have passed. My new commune is going to be that new step—a further step in human evolution, in human consciousness. Although Buddha dropped asceticism, he did not talk much against it; he could not, because he had to communicate with people who were full of the ancient lore and the ancient ideology. He had to talk to people who would have been absolutely incapable of understanding if he had talked like me. Even I am not comprehensible to people. Twenty-five centuries have passed and people are stuck still.

It is very rare to find a contemporary. People *are* in the twentieth century, but only physically; spiritually they are thousands of years back. Buddha could not even make an effort. He did say to his closest disciples, "It is not through asceticism that I have attained. I have attained by dropping asceticism—that was all foolishness." These sutras were given to his closest disciples.

He says:

For months the fool may fast,
Eating from the tip of a grass blade.
Still he is not worth a penny
Beside the master whose food is the way.

IF YOU REALLY WANT A TRANSFORMATION, then make Dhamma your food—let the very way to God be your food. Nourish yourself on it! Jesus says in another way: Eat me! He says to his disciples. Drink me! Absorb me, digest me!

Buddha says:

... whose food is the way.

The way means Dhamma, religion, the ultimate law, that keeps the whole world in harmony. One who starts eating out of this harmony, that one attains—not by fasting. It is not by fasting from the gross food, but by eating the subtle food that one attains.

Yes, there is a subtle food available. When you look at a roseflower, just watch. Let the beauty of the rose be absorbed in you, and you will feel nourished. You have not eaten the rose but something subtle that surrounds the rose, the aura of the rose, the dance of the rose in the wind, the fragrance which is invisible. Have you not felt it? Seeing a beautiful flower, suddenly you feel saturated, contented. Looking at the sky full of stars, have you not felt nourished? Watching the sunrise or the sunset, or just listening to the faraway call of a cuckoo, a distant song, have you not felt yourself becoming full of something unknown...?

Your body needs food, your soul also needs food. The bodily food is gross, obviously; the body is part of the gross world. The spiritual food is invisible. In music, in poetry, in beauty, in dance, in song, in prayer, in meditation...and you go deeper and deeper towards the spritual nourishment.

Buddha says: It is *not* by dropping the gross food, by fasting, that one attains, but by eating the way. A strange expression—by eating Dhamma. What is Dhamma? Just the other day somebody asked: "Bhagwan, I love it when you say '*Ais dhammo sanantano*,' but what exactly does it mean?" It means the harmony of existence, it means the melody of existence, it means the ultimate dance that is going on and on. It means the celebration that is everywhere. The trees are celebrating and the birds and the animals and the rivers and the mountains...this whole existence is made of the stuff called bliss.

That's what Buddha means when he says: *Ais dhammo sanantano*—this is the ultimate law, inexhaustible. You can go on eating out of it, but you cannot exhaust it. And the more you eat, the more soul you will have. The more you eat it, the more divine you become. Buddha is saying: "I am not teaching fasting—I am teaching you a new way of indulgence, a higher kind of indulgence." He is not saying it exactly in that way, but I am saying it. I am teaching you a higher way of love, a higher way of rejoicing, a higher way of dance, a higher way of absorbing God's energy into yourself—becoming more and more receptive and feminine so you can be pregnant with God.

He calls the man a fool who goes on fasting, but those fools are worshipped in India, and not only in India— almost all over the world. In fact, the majority of the crowd consists of fools; hence, whenever a fool starts following the rotten, trodden path, the traditional path of the crowds, the crowds are very much thrilled. Their egos are very much satisfied. This man proves that they have been right, their parents have been right; their heritage is proved right: "Look, this man is fasting! And spiritual people have always been fasting"—that is their idea.

Yes, sometimes it has happened that a spiritual person *has* fasted, but the reason is totally different from what you think. Mahavira fasted, and fasted for twelve years, and for long long periods. It is said that in those twelve years he took food for only three hundred and sixty-five days—that means only one year. One month he would fast and he would take food for one day; in twelve years, one year means that mostly after twelve days he ate on one day—average. That was his way of fasting.

But Mahavira never became tired and Buddha became tired after six years. What was the matter? And he attained! as much as Buddha attained. Buddha attained by dropping his fasting and austerity; Mahavira never dropped it. Now, both cannot be right—and I say to you both are right. But the reasons are so different, almost inconceivable.

Mahavira's fast has a totally different quality. He is not an ascetic, he is not fasting—in fact, he is eating so much of God that he does not feel the need to eat. His soul is so overflowing with subtle energies that his body feels satisfied. He does not feel the need to eat. In fact, to say that he fasts is not right. If I am allowed then I will say: he cannot eat. And you have also sometimes observed it.

When I used to come to Poona, I used to stay with Sohan. And she was very much puzzled. One day she asked me, "What is the matter? Once or twice a year you come to Poona. I wait the whole year long—you will be coming, you will be coming—and then for three or four days you come. For these three or four days I cannot eat at all. What is the reason why I can't eat? I am not fasting," she told me. "I want to eat, but I simply can't eat. I feel so full."

I told her, "Whenever you are tremendously happy, you will not be able to eat. Your blissfulness is so over-flowing it leaves no appetite, it leaves no emptiness in you. Not only is your soul overflowing, your body starts being affected by the soul. Your body is a shadow to your soul."

You will be surprised: miserable people eat more, happy

people less. A miserable person feels so empty that he wants to fill himself, stuff himself with something or other. The miserable person goes on eating; he goes on stuffing this and that inside. He feels so utterly empty and lost that he does not know what to do. It seems easy to go to the fridge and eat something more; maybe that will give you a feeling of fullness. And certainly it does give, on the very gross level, a feeling of fullness.

Now America suffers most from overeating, and the reason is simple: America is now suffering from great inner emptiness. The reason is spiritual, hence no dieting can help; and how long can you diet? You can diet for a few days with great will-power; you have to force yourself, and then after a few days you become tired of making the effort and then you jump upon food with a vengeance. And you will gain more weight than you had lost by dieting.

In America this is a problem; in all rich countries this is going to be a problem, because you have food and you have emptiness both available. Only food is left to fill yourself with, sex is left to fill yourself with. Go on purchasing new gadgets, new things; if you cannot have anything else you can at least go on accumulating furniture. You can fill the house if you cannot fill your being. Just a vicarious way of feeling full. Just the opposite happens when you are really happy, joyous, when you are flying, when you are feeling weightless.

I told Sohan, "This is perfectly logical. This is real fasting!"

In Sanskrit, the word for 'fast' has a beauty of its own. The English word does not have that quality. The English word 'fast' simply means starving through will-power. The Sanskrit word is *upawas*—it means 'being close to God'. Literally it means being close to God; it has nothing to do with fasting. It means being so close to God, so full of God, that you forget all about your body, that you forget all about your body nourishment. You are so nourished by the subtle food, the subtle energy, that goes on showering on you.

Mahavira was not fasting in the same way that Buddha was; Mahavira was eating God, and Buddha was simply fasting. Mahavira's fast was *upawas*—being close to God. His fast was what it means in Sanskrit; Buddha's fast was what it means in English—just starving. Hence Mahavira attained without dropping his fast. It was not fasting in the first place; there was no need to drop it. Buddha had to drop it; it was just the opposite of indulgence. He was simply starving himself with the motive that by starvation one can attain.

How can you attain God by starving the body? What logic is this? What scientific reasoning is there in it? Do you think God is someone like Adolf Hilter who enjoys your tortures? who enjoys seeing his children hungry and dreaming of food? who enjoys seeing people becoming ugly, ill? God is compassion, God is love. He would like you to be full of him. And when you are full of him you may not feel the need to eat.

Mahavira was not fasting, he was simply not feeling like eating, that's all. And that's a great difference.

Buddha says:

For months the fool may fast,
Eating from the tip of a grass blade.
Still he is not worth a penny
Beside the master whose food is the way.

275

One day he discovered that there is another kind of food: one can eat out of the harmony of existence, one can become part of the harmony, one can become part of the celebration, the festivity that goes on and on, with no beginning and no end. Then you are full and fulfilled.

> *Fresh milk takes time to sour.*
> *So a fool's mischief*
> *Takes time to catch up with him.*
> *Like the embers of a fire*
> *It smoulders within him.*

IF YOU DO SOMETHING, IT TAKES TIME FOR ITS result to come. And you may not even be able to connect the two, the cause and the effect.

Do you know that in Africa, still there are primitive tribes which have no conception that the birth of a child has anything to do with intercourse—because the gap is so big, nine months. And not only is the gap so big...and they have no way of calculating time, so for them nine months is really a long time; they cannot keep track of time. They have no calendar, no watches, no idea of time at all. They live in a really primitive world where time has not been invented yet, so how can they conceive that the intercourse between a man and a woman can be the cause of the birth of a child?

And then there are other reasons: it doesn't always happen. You may make love to a woman and there may come no child, so it is not an inevitable thing. Then how is the child born? The child is born not by intercourse, not by sexual relationship, it has no biology behind it—it comes as a gift from God, whomsoever he chooses. If you follow the tribe's religion, you will be blessed with children; otherwise there is no possibility.

When Christian missionaries for the first time discovered this tribe, they could not believe that these people for centuries have lived, given birth to children, and have no idea at all of cause and effect. And that's how we all are, in so many ways, primitive.

Today suddenly you start feeling sad for no reason at all; you cannot find any reason in close proximity— nothing has happened. In the night when you had gone to bed, everything was good; you were flowing, glowing, and in the morning you are suddenly sad. Nobody has insulted you, nothing has happened, no bad news has arrived ... why? From where has this sadness come? You must have done something; maybe there is a time gap, maybe three months' gap or three years. And those who have gone deep into this phenomenon, they say maybe even in the past life...sometimes a few seeds take very long to sprout.

And, because of this, the fool goes on living in the same way, in the same foolish way, because he cannot see that his life's suffering is caused by his own choices. Those choices may have been made long before. You may have thrown the seeds a year before, and then you have completely forgotten about those seeds. And rains come, and the seeds start sprouting, and you are surprised—from where?! From where are these plants coming up? And, of course, the seeds that we go on sowing in our souls are very very invisible. You may have been angry, violent, jealous, and it has remained inside you.

Buddha says:

Like the embers of a fire
It smoulders within him.

It goes on inside you, getting ready, waiting for the spring to come, and then it explodes suddenly. Man is responsible for whatsoever happens to him. The wise man becomes aware of it and stops sowing seeds of misery and starts sowing seeds of joy. Sooner or later you will be ready to reap the harvest.

That's what heaven is: a wise man sowing seeds of bliss, love, compassion. And one day the garden is ready. Do you know?—the word 'paradise' comes from Persian, has a beautiful meaning. In Persian it is *firdaus;* from *firdaus* it has become 'paradise' in English. *Firdaus* means a walled garden of truth. If you go on sowing seeds of joy, beauty, dance, song, meditation, prayer, soon you will create a walled garden of truth—that is paradise. Otherwise, you are bound to create hell. Live unconsciously, live mechanically, live foolishly, and hell is going to be the outcome of it.

> *Whatever a fool learns,*
> *It only makes him duller.*
> *Knowledge cleaves his head.*

The fool is not very much interested in becoming intelligent, because intelligence is dangerous. Intelligence is rebellious, hence it is dangerous. Intelligence brings individuality to you, and the moment you become an integrated individual the crowds start turning against you; they cannot tolerate an individual. They cannot forgive a Jesus or a Buddha. They are very happy with the fools, because the fools are just like them—in fact, a little more magnified, a little more decorated, a little more sophisticated. They are very happy with the fools. They are happy with politicians, they are happy with professors, they are happy with pundits, but they are not happy with a Jesus or a Socrates or a Buddha. Why? Because the presence of a Buddha makes them look stupid. The very presence of a Buddha and they start feeling silly. How can they forgive him?

And they don't want to be intelligent themselves, because it is a long journey and there is no shortcut to it. It is hard, arduous. To become intelligent means to sharpen your consciousness continuously; to become intelligent means to be full of love. Love is the center of intelligence, logic the center of intellectuality.

The fool becomes intellectual; then he can brag that he knows. He is interested in knowledge. He will read the Bible and the Vedas and the Koran; he will cram information. He turns his mind into a computer; he becomes a walking Encyclopaedia Britannica. That is easy, that is simple; that can be done by a machine; it does not need any intelligence. And your schools, colleges and universities only make people computers.

We have yet to create universities where intelligence is sharpened. Our universities only dull the intelligence, because they prepare slaves for the society. The universities are in the service of the vested interests; they are agents of the established status quo. They don't serve the future of humanity; they serve the past, they serve the dead. They are not interested in creating people who are intelligent, creative, alert, aware; they are interested in people who are dull, stupid, but efficient. Clerks, deputy collectors, station masters—efficient! They can just do their work very efficiently. And remember, machines are more efficient than men, so they are not interested in men: they are interested in reducing men to machines.

Buddha says:

Whatever a fool learns,
It only makes him duller.

The more knowledge he gathers, the more dull he becomes, the more stupid he becomes. And that is my observation too. I have seen ignorant villagers far more intelligent than the so–called Ph.D.'s and D.Litt.'s and professors of the universities, deans, vice chancellors and chancellors. They seem to be the dullest people in the world.

A villager, a woodcutter, seems to be far more intelligent. He has no information, of course; he is not knowledgeable—but he is innocent. And innocence is part of intelligence.

To be knowledgeable is to be machinelike—and machines *are* dull. Have you ever seen any machine which is intelligent? Just look at the machine, and look at the dean and the vice chancellor...! In fact, the duller you are, the greater is the possibility that you will become a vice chancellor—because the politicians will not like a Buddha to become a vice chancellor, they will not allow Socrates to become a vice chancellor. This was the crime Socrates was accused of, that he was corrupting youth. Socrates, and corrupting youth, and these fools—the magistrates and the vice chancellors and the prime ministers and the presidents—these fools are not corrupting? Socrates is corrupting the youth—what do they mean by it? In a way, they are true: he is corrupting the youth because he is preparing them for the future. He has to destroy the past; he has to create doubt, enquiry; he has to create seekers, not believers. And the society wants believers, and the dull people are good believers. A Mohammedan, a Christian, a Hindu, a Jaina— the duller they are, the more they believe, the better they believe. Because the dull person cannot enquire, he cannot risk. He is afraid; he knows that he is not capable of knowing the truth on his own. He has to believe somebody else.

> *Knowledge cleaves his head,*
> says Buddha.

Knowledge does not help him but becomes a burden, a Himalayan weight on his being.

> *For then he wants recognition,*
> *A place before other people,*
> *A place over other people.*

His whole knowledge becomes an ego trip, and the ego is the greatest bondage there is. To be free of ego is to be redeemed. But the fool learns just to become famous, to be recognized as an authority, to be an expert. The fool accumulates knowledge so that he can brag and exhibit, so that he can show people how intelligent he is. And intelligence is not of the ego; intelligence comes only when you are in a deep egoless state. Intelligence is the disappearance of ego, meeting and merging with the whole, forgetting your separation, becoming a wave in the ocean of God—then you are intelligent.

> *"Let them know my work,*
> *Let everyone look to me for direction."*
> *Such are his desires,*
> *Such is his swelling pride.*

> *One way leads to wealth and fame...*

BUDDHA SAYS: BUT LET ME MAKE YOU AWARE that if you want wealth and fame, then follow the way of the fool—because the foolish person is capable of becoming famous more easily than the intelligent person. If the intelligent person becomes famous, that is just accidental; he never tries. If the intelligent person is well known, that is not because of his effort. His fragrance may have reached people, but there is no positive effort on his side to be recognized. He knows his being; he does not depend on others' recognition. He knows who he is; he does not need anybody else's certificate.

When I came out of the university I went to see the education minister. I told him, "These are my qualifications. If you can give me some place anywhere, any place will be okay." He looked at my qualifications, was very much impressed—people are impressed by nonsense—because I was a gold-medallist, first class first. He was very much impressed. He said, "Immediately I will appoint you as a lecturer. But one thing you will have to do: have you got a character certificate?"

I said, "I have got a character, but no character certificate. Look into my eyes, hold my hand! I can hug you . . . !"

He said, "But that . . . that is not the point. Where is the character certificate?"

I said, "I have got no character certificate."

He said, "You can go to the vice chancellor, or the head of your department—just one character certificate. It is a formality."

I said, "I cannot ask the vice chancellor, because I don't believe that he has any character at all! What weight will his certificate carry? And the head of my department?—I know him more than he knows himself. I cannot give him a character certificate!"

He was very much puzzled. He really wanted to help.

In fact, he became really interested in me also; he had never come across such a man—so many people must have approached him, but nobody had said, "Look into my eyes, or hold my hand and feel! Or I can come and live with you for one week, in your house. Just see my character in every possible way. I will not even lock the door of my bathroom; I will keep everything open, so you can just go on watching....!"

He said, "These things are not needed at all! Just a simple character certificate."

So I said, "Then I can write a simple character certificate to myself"—and that's what I did. I wrote a certificate, in front of him, and he said, "What are you doing? But this has never been done: you yourself giving a character certificate to yourself? Somebody else's signature is needed!"

So I said, "Okay, then I will sign for the head of my department, on his behalf. This is a true copy," I told him, "and the original I will take from the head of my department."

So I went to the head of my department. I said, "I have given this character certificate in your name—you please give the original."

He said, "This is strange! The original is needed *first*." But he loved the idea and he gave me an original.

One way leads to wealth and fame ...

If you follow the fool's way, you can become very rich, you can become famous. You can become a president of a country, a prime minister of a country—you can become anything. You can have as much wealth as you want— just follow the fool's way. Don't be intelligent, remain stupid, because in fact except for a stupid person who wants to run after money? Yes, sometimes it happens, money comes to the intelligent person; but it comes running after him, he does not go.... Fame also sometimes comes to the intelligent person; it comes on its own. He is not interested at all.

> ... *The other to the end of the way.*

But if you want to end this whole nonsense that has persisted down the ages, for so many lives, the same repetitive wheel of birth and death moving, if you want to stop it, then the other, the way of the intelligent person, the way of the wise: be a light unto yourself.

> *Look not for recognition*
> *But follow the awakened*
> *And set yourself free.*

Don't be bothered, don't desire recognition. If millions of fools recognize you, what does it matter? Millions of fools recognizing you simply proves that you are a greater fool than them. Nothing else is proved.

> *But follow the awakened* ...

What does Buddha mean when he says "follow the awakened"? He does not mean imitate. He simply means: become awakened as the awakened has become awakened. Be awake—that is following the awakened. Not following in the details: how he lives, what he eats, when he goes to sleep—that is stupidity. Follow the awakened in becoming awake.

> ... *And set yourself free.*

Because it is only awareness, the state of an awakened consciousness that brings freedom. Intelligence is freedom.

Meditation is freedom. Awareness is freedom. And those who live mechanically, unconsciously, unintelligently, they live in prisons. And to live in a prison is to suffer.

Freedom is the ultimate value of life.

> *. . . follow the awakened*
> *And set yourself free.*

Ais dhammo sanantano . . . .

what do you mean by
the dimension of music?

is spontaneity compatible
with watching?

nobody likes to be criticized yet
everybody loves to criticize—why?

why do I feel helpless
to surrender to you?

have I been a Jew in my past life?

why don't I understand you?

July 10

Law — Ancient and Inexhaustible

The first question

Bhagwan,
Please tell us more about what you mean by the
dimension of music.

Yoga Chinmaya,

LIFE CAN BE LIVED IN TWO WAYS: EITHER as calculation or as poetry. Man has two sides to his inner being: the calculative side that creates science, business, politics; and the non-calculative side, which creates poetry, scuplture, music. These two sides have not yet been bridged; they have separate existences. Because of this man is immensely impoverished, remains unnecessarily lop-sided—they have to be bridged.

In scientific language it is said that your brain has two hemispheres. The left-side hemisphere calculates, is mathematical, is prose; and the right-side hemisphere of the brain is poetry, is love, is song. One side is logic, the other side is love. One side is syllogism, the other side is song. And they are not really bridged, hence man lives in a kind of split.

My effort here is to bridge these two hemispheres. Man should be as scientific as possible, as far as the objective world is concerned, and as musical as possible as far as the world of relationship is concerned.

There are two worlds outside you. One is the world of objects: the house, the money, the furniture. The other is the world of persons: the wife, the husband, the mother, the children, the friend. With the objects be scientific; never be scientific with persons. If you are scientific with persons you reduce them to objects, and that is one of the greatest crimes one can commit. If you treat your wife only as an object, as a sexual object, then you are behaving in a very ugly way. If you treat your husband only as a financial support, as a means, then this is immoral, then this relationship is immoral—it is prostitution, pure prostitution and nothing else.

Don't treat persons as means: they are ends unto themselves. Relate to them—in love, in respect. Never possess them and never be possessed by them. Don't be dependent on them and don't make persons around you dependent. Don't create dependence in any way; remain independent and let them remain independent.

This is music. This dimension I call the dimension of music. And if you can be as scientific as possible with objects, your life will be rich, affluent; if you can be as musical as possible, your life will have beauty. And there is a third dimension also, which is beyond the mind. These two belong to the mind: the scientist and the artist. There is a third dimension, invisible: the dimension of no-mind.

That belongs to the mystic. That is available through meditation.

Hence, I say these three words have to be remembered—three M's like three R's: mathematics, the lowest; music, just in the middle; and meditation, the highest. A perfect human being is scientific about objects, is aesthetic, musical, poetic, about persons, and is meditative about himself. Where all these three meet, great rejoicing happens.

This is the real trinity, *trimurti*. In the East, particularly in India, we worship a place where three rivers meet—we call it a *sangam*, the meeting place. And the greatest of all of them is Preyag where the Ganges and Jamuna and Saraswati meet. Now, you can see the Ganges and you can see Jamuna, but Saraswati is invisible—you cannot see it. It is a metaphor! It simply represents, symbolically, the inner meeting of the three. You can see mathematics, you can see music, but you cannot see meditation. You can see the scientist; his work is outside. You can see the artist; his work is also outside. But you cannot see the mystic; his work is subjective. That is *saraswati*—the invisible river.

You can become a sacred place, you can hallow this body and this earth: this very body the Buddha, this very earth the Lotus Paradise. This is my slogan for the sannyasins. A sannyasin has to be the ultimate synthesis of all that God is.

God is known only when you have come to this synthesis. Otherwise, you can believe in God, but you will not know. And belief is just hiding your ignorance. Knowing is transforming, only knowledge brings understanding. And knowledge is not information: knowledge is the synthesis, integration, of all your potential.

Where the scientist and the poet and the mystic meet and become one—when this great synthesis happens, when all the three faces of God are expressed in you—*you* become a God. Then you can declare *"Aham Brahmasmi!* I am God!" Then you can say to the winds and the moon and to the rains and to the sun *"Ana'l Haq!* I am the truth!" Before that, you are only a seed.

When this synthesis happens, you have bloomed, blossomed—you have become the one-thousand-petalled lotus, the golden lotus, the eternal lotus, that never dies: *ais dhammo sanantano.* This is the inexhaustible law that all the Buddhas have been teaching down the ages.

The second question

Bhagwan,
In the West we are constantly drilled with the aphorism:
Don't just stand there—do something! Yet, Buddha
would say: Don't just do something—stand there!
The unconscious man reacts while the wise man watches.
But what about spontaneity? Is spontaneity compatible
with watching?

BUDDHA CERTAINLY SAYS: DON'T JUST DO something—stand there! But that is only the beginning of the pilgrimage, not the end. When you have learnt how to stand, when you have learnt how to be utterly silent, unmoving, undisturbed, when you know how to just sit... sitting silently, doing nothing, the spring comes and the grass grows by itself. But the grass grows, remember!

Action does not disappear: the grass grows by itself. The Buddha does not become inactive; *great* action happens through him, although there is no doer any more. The doer disappears, the doing continues. And when there is no doer, the doing *is* spontaneous. It cannot be otherwise. It is the doer that does not allow spontaneity.

The doer means the ego, the ego means the past. When you act, you are always acting through the past, you are acting out of the experience that you have accumulated, you are acting out of the conclusions that you have arrived at in the past. How can you be spontaneous? The past dominates, and because of the past you cannot even see the present. Your eyes are so full of the past, the smoke of the past is so much, that seeing is impossible. You cannot see! You are almost completely blind—blind because of the smoke, blind because of the past conclusions, blind because of knowledge.

The knowledgeable man is the most blind man in the world. Because he functions out of his knowledge, he does not see what the case is. He simply goes on functioning mechanically. He has learnt something; it has become a ready-made mechanism in him...he acts out of it.

There is a famous story:

There were two temples in Japan, both enemies to each other, as temples have always been down the ages. The priests were so antagonistic that they had stopped even looking at each other. If they came across each other on the road, they would not look at each other. They had stopped talking; for centuries those two temples and their priests had not talked. But both the priests had two small boys—to serve them, just for running errands. And both the priests were afraid that boys, after all, will be boys, and they might start becoming friends to each other.

The one priest said to his boy, "Remember, the other

temple is our enemy. Never talk to the boy of the other temple! They are dangerous people—avoid them as one avoids a disease, as one avoids the plague. Avoid them!"

The boy was always interested, because he used to get tired of listening to great sermons; he could not understand them. Strange scriptures were read; he could not understand the language. Great, ultimate problems were discussed. There was nobody to play with, nobody even to talk with. And when he was told, "Don't talk to the boy of the other temple," great temptation arose in him. That's how temptation arises.

That day he could not avoid talking to the other boy When he saw him on the road he asked him, "Where are you going?"

The other boy was a little philosophical; listening to great philosophy he had become philosophical. He said, "Going? There is nobody who comes and goes! It is happening—wherever the wind takes me. . . ." He had heard the master say many times that that's how a Buddha lives, like a dead leaf: wherever the wind takes it, it goes. So the boy said, "I am not! There is no doer. So how can I go? What nonsense are you talking? I am a dead leaf. Wherever the wind takes me. . . ."

The other boy was dumb. He could not even answer. He could not find what to say. He was really embarrassed, ashamed, and felt also, "My master was right not to talk with these people—these are dangerous people! What kind of talk is this? I had asked a simple question: 'Where are you going?' In fact I already knew where he was going, because we were both going to purchase vegetables in the market. A simple answer would have done."

He went back, told his master, "I am sorry, excuse me. You *had* prohibited me; I didn't listen to you. In fact, because of your prohibition I was tempted. This is the first time I have talked to those dangerous people. I just asked a simple question, 'Where are you going?' and he started saying strange things: 'There is no going, no coming. Who comes? Who goes? I am utter emptiness,' he was saying, 'just a dead leaf in the wind. And wherever the wind takes me....' "

The master said, "I had told you before! Now, tomorrow stand in the same place and when he comes ask him again, 'Where are you going?' And when he says these things, you simply say, 'That's true. Yes, you are a dead leaf, so am I. But when the wind is not blowing, where are you going? Then where can you go?' Just say that, and that will embarrass him—and he has to be embarrassed, he has to be defeated. We have been constantly quarrelling, and those people have not been able to defeat us in any debate. So tomorrow it has to be done!"

Early the boy got up, prepared his answer, repeated it many times before he went. Then he stood in the place where the boy used to cross the road, repeated again and again, prepared himself, and then he saw the boy coming. He said, "Okay, now!"

The boy came. He asked, "Where are you going?" And he was hoping that now the opportunity would come....

But the boy said, "Wherever the legs will take me...." No mention of wind! No talk of nothingness! No question of the non-doer! Now what to do? His whole ready-made answer looked absurd. Now to talk about the wind would be irrelevant.

Again crestfallen, now *really* ashamed that he was simply stupid: "And this boy certainly knows some strange things— now he says, 'Wherever the legs take me....' "

He went back to the master. The master said, "I have told you *not* to talk with those people—they *are* dangerous! This is our centuries' long experience. But now something has to be done. So tomorrow you ask again, 'Where are you going?' and when he says, 'Wherever my legs take me,' tell him, 'If you had no legs, then. . . ?' He has to be silenced some way or other!"

So the next day he asked again, "Where are you going?" and waited.

And the boy said, "I am going to the market to fetch vegetables."

Man ordinarily functions out of the past, and life goes on changing. Life has no obligation to fit with your conclusions. That's why life is very confusing—confusing to the knowledgeable person. He has all ready-made answers: the Bhagavad Gita, the holy Koran, the Bible, the Vedas. He has everything crammed; he knows all the answers. But life never raises the same question again! Hence the knowledgeable person always falls short.

Buddha certainly says: "Know how to sit silently." That does not mean that he says: "Go on sitting silently forever." He is not saying you have to become inactive; on the contrary, it is only out of silence that action arises. If you are not silent, if you don't know how to sit silently, or stand silently, in deep meditation, whatsoever you go on doing is reaction, not action. You react.

Somebody insults you, pushes a button, and you react: you are angry, you jump on him—and you call it action? It is not action, mind you, it is reaction. He is the manipulator and you are the manipulated. He has pushed a button and you have functioned like a machine. Just like you push a button and the light goes on, and you push the button and the light goes off—that's what people are doing to you: they put you on, they put you off.

Somebody comes and praises you and puffs up your ego, and you feel so great; and then somebody comes and punctures you, and you are simply flat on the ground. You are not your own master: anybody can insult you and make you sad, angry, irritated, annoyed, violent, mad. And anybody can praise you and make you feel at the heights, can make you feel that you are the greatest—that Alexander the Great was nothing compared to you.

And you act according to others' manipulations. This is not real action.

BUDDHA WAS PASSING THROUGH A VILLAGE and the people came and they insulted him. And they used *all* the insulting words that they could use—all the four-letter words that they knew. And Buddha stood there, listened silently, very attentively, and then said, "Thank you for coming to me, but I am in a hurry. I have to reach the next village; people will be waiting for me there. I cannot devote more time to you today, but tomorrow coming back I will have more time. You can gather again, and tomorrow if something is left which you wanted to say and have not been able to say, you can say it to me. But today, excuse me."

Those people could not believe their ears, their eyes. "This man has remained utterly unaffected, undistracted." One of them asked, "Have you not heard us? We have been abusing you like anything, and you have not even answered!"

Buddha said, "If you wanted an answer then you have come too late. You should have come ten years ago, then I would have answered you. But for these ten years I have stopped being manipulated by others; I am no more a slave: I am my own master. I act according to myself, not according to anybody else. I act according to my inner need. You cannot force me to do anything. It's perfectly good! You wanted to abuse me, you abused me! Feel fulfilled. You have done your work perfectly well. But as far as I am concerned, I don't take your insults. And unless I take them, they are meaningless."

When somebody insults you, you have to become a receiver, you have to accept what he says; only then can you react. But if you don't accept, if you simply remain detached, if you keep the distance, if you remain cool, what can he do?

Buddha said, "Somebody can throw a burning torch into the river. It will remain fire up till it reaches the river; the moment it falls into the river, all fire is gone. The river cools it. I have become a river. You throw abuses at me. They are fire when you throw them, but the moment they reach me, in my coolness, their fire is lost. They no longer hurt. You throw thorns—falling in my silence they become flowers.

"I act out of my own intrinsic nature."

This is spontaneity. The man of awareness, understanding, acts. Then man who is unaware, unconscious, mechanical, robotlike, reacts.

Curtis, you ask me:
The unconscious man reacts while the wise man watches.

It is not that he simply watches—watching is one aspect of his being. He does not act without watching, but don't misunderstand the Buddha. The Buddhas have always been misunderstood; you are not the first to misunderstand. This whole country has been misunderstanding the Buddha; hence the whole country has become inactive. Thinking that all the great Masters say "Sit silently," the country has become lazy, lousy; the country has lost energy, vitality, life. It has become utterly dull, unintelligent, because intelligence becomes sharpened only when you act.

And when you act moment-to-moment out of your awareness and watchfulness, great intelligence arises. You start shining, glowing, you become luminous. But it happens through two things: watching, and *action out of that watching*. If watching becomes inaction, you are committing suicide. Watching should lead you into action, a new kind of action; a new quality is brought to action.

You watch, you are utterly quiet and silent. You see what the situation is, and out of that seeing you respond. The man of awareness responds, he is responsible—literally! He is responsive, he does not react. His action is born *out* of his awareness, not out of your manipulation. That is the difference. Hence there is no question of there being any incompatibility between watching and spontaneity. Watching is the beginning of spontaneity: spontaneity is the fulfillment of watching.

The real man of understanding acts—acts tremendously, acts totally, but he acts in the moment, out of his consciousness. He is like a mirror. The ordinary man, the unconscious man, is not like a mirror, he is like a photoplate. What is the difference between a mirror and a photoplate?

A photoplate, once exposed, becomes useless. It receives the impression, becomes impressed by it: it carries the picture. But remember, the picture is not reality—the reality goes on growing. You can go into the garden and you can take a picture of a rosebush. Tomorrow the picture will be the same, the day after tomorrow also the picture will be the same. Go again and see the rosebush: it is no more the same. The roses have gone, or new roses have arrived. A thousand and one things have happened.

It is said that once a realist philosopher went to see the famous painter, Picasso. The philosopher believed in realism and he had come to criticize Picasso because Picasso's paintings are abstract, they are not realistic. They don't depict reality as it is. On the contrary, they are symbolic, have a totally different dimension—they are symbolistic.

The realist said, "I don't like your paintings. A painting should be real! If you paint my wife, then your painting should *look* like my wife." And he took out a picture of his wife and said, "Look at this picture! The painting should be like this."

Picasso looked at the picture and said, "This is your wife?"

He said, "Yes, this is my wife!"

Picasso said, "I am surprised: she is very small and flat."

The picture cannot be the wife!

Another story is told:

A beautiful woman came to Picasso and said, "Just the other day I saw your self-portrait in a friend's home. It was so beautiful, I was so influenced, almost hypnotized, that I hugged the picture and kissed it."

Picasso said, "Really! And then what did the picture do to you? Did the picture kiss you back?"

The woman said, "Are you mad?! The picture did not kiss me back."

Picasso said, "Then it was not me."

A picture is a dead thing. The camera, the photoplate,

catches only a static phenomenon. And life is never static. It goes on changing. Your mind functions like a camera, it goes on collecting pictures—it is an album. And then out of those pictures you go on reacting. Hence, you are never true to life, because whatsoever you do is wrong; *whatsoever*, I say, you do is wrong. It never fits.

A woman was showing the family album to her child, and they came across a picture of a beautiful man: long hair, beard, very young, very alive. And the boy asked, "Mummy, who is this man?"

And the woman said, "Can't you recognize him? He is your daddy!"

The boy looked puzzled and said, "If *he* is my daddy, then who is that bald man who lives with us?"

A picture is static. It remains as it is. It never changes. The unconscious mind functions like a camera, it functions like a photoplate. The watchful mind, the meditative mind, functions like a mirror. It catches no impression; it remains utterly empty, always empty. So whatsoever comes in front of the mirror, it is reflected. If you are standing before the mirror, it reflects you. If you are gone, don't say that the mirror betrays you. The mirror is simply a mirror. When you are gone, it no longer reflects you; it has no obligation to reflect you any more. Now somebody else is facing it— it reflects somebody else. If nobody is there, it reflects nothing. It is always true to life.

The photoplate is never true to life. Even if your photo is taken right now, by the time the photographer has taken it out of the camera, you are no more the same! Much water has already gone down the Ganges. You have grown, changed, you have become older. Maybe only one minute has passed, but one minute can be a great thing—you may be dead! Just one minute before, you were alive; after one minute, you may be dead. The picture will never die.

But in the mirror, if you are alive, you are alive, if you are dead, you are dead.

Buddha says: Learn sitting silently—become a mirror. Silence makes a mirror out of your consciousness, and then you function moment-to-moment. You reflect life. You don't carry an album within your head. Then your eyes are clear and innocent, you have clarity, you have vision, and you are never untrue to life.

This is authentic living.

The third question

Bhagwan,
Why is it that nobody likes to be criticized, and yet everybody loves to criticize others?

Gayatri,

THE EGO IS VERY SENSITIVE AND VERY FRAGILE, and is very afraid of criticism. The ego depends on others' opinions. It has *no* reality of its own. It is not a real entity, it is not substantial—it is just a collection of others' opinions. Somebody says, "You are beautiful," and you collect it. Somebody says, "You are intelligent," and you collect it. And somebody says, "I have never come across such a unique person," and you collect it. And then one day a person comes and he says, "You are repulsive!" Now how can you accept criticism? It goes against the image that you have been creating of yourself. You will retaliate, you will fight tooth and nail. But whatsoever you do, the mind has taken the impression of this opinion too. Then somebody says, "You are ugly," and somebody says, "You are stupid." And there are millions of people in the world and they all have their own opinions, likes and dislikes.

Hence your ego becomes a hodge-podge thing, a very contradictory phenomenon. One fragment says, "You are beautiful!" another fragment says, "Nonsense, you are ugly!" One fragment says, "You are intelligent," another fragment says, "Keep quiet! Shut your big mouth! You are just plain stupid and nothing else!"

Hence people live in a confused state. They don't know who they are, whether they are intelligent or stupid, beautiful or ugly, good or bad, saint or sinner—because one person may call you a saint, another person may call you a sinner. There are different values and different criterions in the world; there are different moralities in the world.

Your neighbour may be a Christian and you may be a Jaina. Now the Christian has no problem with drinking wine; in fact, Christ himself loved to drink wine. But the Jaina cannot conceive, even in his dreams, Mahavira drinking wine. That's impossible...the very idea is inconceivable. But to the Christian the greatest miracle that Jesus did was to turn water into wine. If Mahavira had been around, he would have done just the opposite miracle immediately! He would have turned the wine again into water.

Now, if you drink wine once in a while, are you a saint or a sinner? Different people will say different things. In Mahatma Gandhi's ashram tea was prohibited. What to say about wine? Tea, poor tea, innocent tea was prohibited! And all the Buddhist monks down the ages have been drinking tea. In fact they think that it helps meditation. And there may be a grain of truth in it, because it keeps you awake. And the Buddhist meditation is such that you tend to doze off: sitting for hours in a single posture.... Just try it. After ten minutes you will start dreaming. After one hour it it impossible to keep awake.

Tea may have helped. In fact tea was discovered by Buddhists. One of the greatest Buddhist Masters, Bodhidharma, discovered tea. The name comes from a monastery, Ta, in which Bodhidharma used to live in China. That monastery was on top of the hill, Ta. In China 'ta' can be pronounced in two ways: either it can be pronounced as 'ta' or as 'cha'—hence the Hindi 'chai', the Marathi 'cha', and the English 'tea'. Bodhidharma, the great founder of Zen, discovered it.

And wine has been made in Catholic monasteries down the ages. You will be surprised to know that the best wine has been made by Catholic monks and nuns. The oldest wine is available only in the cellars of ancient monasteries in Europe, the oldest and the best. Wine, made in monasteries? What kind of monasteries are these? Who is going to decide?

In fact, again there is a grain of truth in it. Buddhist meditation means watchfulness, and tea has some chemicals in it which help watchfulness—it has a stimulant. Now some day it is possible that another Bodhidharma will come and say, "Smoking is good," because tobacco also has a stimulant—nicotine. Smoking can also help meditation if tea can help it. Smoking is still waiting for its Bodhidharma to appear. Then you will be able to smoke and feel very virtuous: the more you will smoke the more saintly you will be!

It is not accidental that wine became part of the monastery's creativity. Jesus says: "To be drowned in God is prayer." Jesus' path is that of love. Buddha's path is that of meditation, hence Buddha will never agree to wine, but to tea he may agree. Jesus agrees to wine because wine gives you a taste of being utterly lost, of being drowned, of getting out of the ego, of forgetting the ego and all its worries. It gives you a taste, a glimpse of the unknown.

But who is going to decide about who is right and who is wrong? All these things are there in the atmosphere, and you catch them. Out of these things you make some kind of image—it is bound to remain hodge-podge. It can't be clear-cut. Hence you are very much afraid of somebody criticizing you because he brings your hodge-podgeness to the surface. It is not his criticism that you are against; you are against the fact that he brings problems to the surface which you are somehow repressing within yourself. He makes you aware of the problems and nobody wants to be aware of the problems, because problems then want to be solved, and it is a complex and arduous affair. It needs guts to solve problems. You may not like to solve problems in fact, because you may have some investment in your problems—you *must* have, because you have lived with them for so long that you must have invested in them. You may not like to change your lifestyle. If you are miserable you may like to remain miserable, whatsoever you say on the surface—that's another matter. Notwithstanding what you say, deep down you may still like to remain miserable.

For example: a wife knows that only when she is ill is the husband loving towards her. Whenever she is healthy he simply forgets all about her, he never takes any care when she is healthy. When she is ill, out of sheer duty, responsibility, he comes, sits by her side, puts his hand on her head— otherwise he does not give her even a look. Ask husbands, "How long has it been since you have seen your wife's face face-to-face?" You may be able to recognize your dog if it is lost, but if your wife is lost you will have to ask the neighbours because they will recognize her better—just as you will recognize the neighbour's wife better. Who looks at his own wife?

Mulla Naruddin had gone to see a play. A man was in such great love in the play, he was acting so romantically that Nasruddin said to his wife, "This man is a great actor."

The wife said, "And do you know?—the woman he's acting with is really his wife in actual life."

Nasruddin said "Then he is the greatest actor in the world!"

To show so much romance to one's own wife. . . it is next to impossible.

I was travelling for twenty years in this country. I was staying in thousands of homes, and I saw it continuously: when the husband is not in the house, the wife seems to be very cheerful, very happy; the *moment* the husband enters the house she has a headache, and she lies down on the bed. And I was watching, because I was just staying in the house. Just a moment before, everything was okay—as if the husband has not entered but a headache has entered.

Slowly slowly I understood the logic. There is a great investment in it. And, remember, I am not saying that she is simply pretending. If you pretend too long it can become a reality, it can become an autohypnosis. I'm not saying that she is *not* suffering from a headache, remember. She *may* be suffering: just the face of the husband is enough to trigger the process! It has happened so many times that now it has become an automatic process. So I am not saying that she is deceiving the husband. She is deceived by her *own* investments.

You have a certain image and you don't want it to be changed, and criticism means again a disturbance.

You surely know the story of Little Red Riding Hood: This little girl had gone to see her grandmother who lived in the woods. The bad wolf, who wanted to eat her up, took the grandma's place in the bed after having devoured her in one gulp. So he was under the blankets with grandma's nightie and nightcap on.

When Little Red Riding Hood arrived, she noticed something different, and looking the grandmother in the eye, she asked:

"But, granny, what big eyes you have!"

"It is to see you better, my dear."

"But granny, what a big nose you have!"

"It is to smell you better, my dear."

"But granny, what big arms you have!"

"It is to hug you better, my dear."

"But granny, what hairy hands you have!"

"Hey! Have you come around just to criticize?"

There is a limit. Beyond that nobody likes to be criticized. But the other side of the story is that everybody likes to criticize others; that gives you a good feeling. If others are bad, vicariously it helps you to feel good. If everybody is a cheat, a hypocrite, dishonest, cunning, it gives you a good feeling: you are not *that* bad, you are not *that* dishonest. The comparison relaxes you. It helps you to remain dishonest because people are more dishonest than you are. In this dishonest world how can you survive? You have to play the game.

Every morning, early in the morning, when you read the

newspapers it always gives you a good feeling—so much happening all over the world, so many ugly things, so much violence, murder, suicide, rape, robbery, that compared to all this you are a saint. Hence people don't like to read the Bible in the morning, or the Gita, but the newspaper! Because reading the Gita you feel like a sinner, reading the Bible you start feeling a trembling, that hell is bound to happen to you, that you are on the way. And the scriptures depict hell so vividly, with such colour that it can make anybody afraid. And one thing seems to be certain: that you cannot reach heaven. It seems to be impossible; it demands impossibilities.

Nobody likes to read the scriptures, nobody likes to listen to the scriptures. That's why if you go to the temple you will find almost everybody fast asleep. There are physicians I know who send people to religious discourses if they suffer from insomnia. If no tranquillizer works, don't be worried, go to a religious discourse; it is the ultimate in tranquillizers. Up to now nothing has been able to defeat it. Listening to religious scriptures one starts falling asleep. It is a protection, it is to avoid. Otherwise, it becomes absolutely certain that heaven is not for you, you are meant for hell. And it stirs your heart, raises great fear, and there seems to be no way to escape from it.

Hence, everybody likes to criticize, and not only to criticize—everybody likes to magnify others' faults. You try to make others' faults as big as possible because then, in comparison, your faults are negligible. And God is compassionate: Rahim, Rehman! God is compassion! And you have only small faults, and looking at the world where so many sinners exist. . . .

When the Day of Judgement comes you can be perfectly

certain that your number is not going to be called, you will not be called. The queue will be too long, and it has to be decided within twenty-four hours. One Day of Judgement, and millions and millions of people—Tamerlaine and Genghis Khan and Alexander the Great, and Adolf Hitler and Mussolini and Josef Stalin and Mao Tse Tung—these will be the people standing in front. You will be the *last* in the queue. Your number is not going to come. You can be certain of it if you look at people with a magnifying glass.

After running into a wild crowd at a basketball game one evening, the referee picked up his wife and told her it might be better if she stayed away from the remaining games to which he was assigned. "After all," he said, "it must have been pretty embarrassing to you when everyone stood up and booed me."

"It was not so bad," she replied, "I stood up and booed too."

Ego does not want to be criticized *and* wants to criticize everybody. Become aware of the strategy of the ego, how it nourishes itself, how it protects itself. Unless you become absolutely aware of all the cunning devices of the ego, you will never be able to get rid of it. And to get rid of it is the beginning of a religious life, is the beginning of sannyas. Then you are no more worried what others say about you.

Just look at me.... The whole world goes on saying things about me. I don't even read them. Every day Laxmi brings hundreds of reports appearing in different languages from different countries. Who cares? If they are enjoying rumours, let them enjoy; they don't have anything else to enjoy in their lives. Let them have a little fun. Nothing is wrong in it. They cannot harm me. They can destroy my body, but they cannot harm *me*. And I have no image of my own; they cannot destroy it either.

And I don't react, I act. My action springs out of my self, it is not to be manipulated by others. I am a free man, freedom. I act of my own accord. Learn the art of acting of your own accord. Don't be worried about criticisms and don't be interested in praises. If you are interested in being praised by others, then you cannot be unconcerned about criticism. Remain aloof. Praise or criticism, it is all alike. Success or failure, it is all alike. *Ais dhammo sanantano.*

The fourth question

Bhagwan,
Although I want to surrender myself to you and take sannyas, I feel helpless to do so. Why is it so? Please clarify this.

S.D. Prasad,

IT IS VERY SIMPLE, THERE IS NOTHING TO CLARIFY. You are afraid of people, you are afraid of the society; you are afraid of the established church, the established religion, the priests, the politicians—you are simply afraid. It is fear that is preventing you. Sannyas needs courage, sannyas needs guts, particularly my sannyas.

The old sannyas needs no guts any more, because it is already part of the status quo. It is accepted, respected. If you become an oldstyle sannyasin people will worship you. If you become *my* sannyasin you will be in constant danger.

People will think you are mad, people will think you are hypnotized. People will think that something has gone wrong—that you have gone nuts. People will say, "Such a good man. We had never ever thought, dreamt that this was going to happen to you."

People will laugh, rumour about you, gossip about you, will create a thousand and one kinds of troubles for you. And you have to exist with people, you have to live with them. On each step they will create barriers and they will put rocks in your path. And not only those who are part of the greater society, but even those who are very close: your wife may create so much trouble for you...your children, your parents. From every nook and corner you will have to face difficulties.

You are afraid. Just try to understand your fear, and then it is very easy. Once you see that it is fear, drop it. In spite of all fears, jump into sannyas. Because to remain in fear is to become a coward, to remain in fear is to miss the whole joy of life. Life belongs to those who know how to risk. Life belongs to the adventurous, and sannyas is the greatest adventure there is. And because I am bringing a totally new concept of sannyas into the world...a sannyas that is not escapist, a sannyas that does not believe in renunciation, a sannyas that believes in rejoicing, a sannyas that wants to live in the world and yet be not of it.

The old sannyas is easy: you escape from the world, you leave the opportunities where temptation is possible, you escape to the Himalayan caves. Sitting there you will be a saint, because you don't have any other opportunity. You *have* to be a saint. What else can you do there?

In the world all kinds of temptations exist. To be a saint in the world is something superb, something extraordinary.

If there is no woman in the Himalayan caves...and I don't think there is. Women have never been so foolish; they are more earthly. They are more intuitive, they are not intellectuals. They are very realistic; they don't go after words and theories and philosophies. It is man who becomes very much attracted by abstractions. Woman does not bother much about the other world, she wants a beautiful sari here*now*! You are a fool if you are waiting for some beautiful woman in heaven.

The feminine mind does not bother much about the other world. The feminine mind says, "We will see. If we can manage here, we will manage there too. If we can find a fool here, the same fools will be available there too. So why be worried about the other world?"

But man lives in abstractions. That is the masculine mind's greatest flaw. It lives in theories. It becomes so much hypnotized by words that it is ready to sacrifice life itself. It is ready to go to the caves, to renounce this life in order to attain the other life. It lives in the past, it lives in the future. Woman lives more in the present. Hence, there have been no women in the Himalayan caves. You can go and sit there and dream all kinds of dreams, but no opportunity is there. Money is not there, power is not there, beauty is not there—nothing is there! Sitting in your cave you become more and more dull. Slowly slowly...it is a kind of gradual suicide.

My sannyas is not dropping out of the world but getting deeper into it, getting to the very core of it, because God *is* at the very core of the world. God is the soul of the world. You cannot find him by escaping from the world. You can find him only by going deeper and deeper into the world. When you reach the very center of existence, you will find him. He is hidden in the world; the whole world is permeated by him. He is in the trees and in the rocks and in the birds and in the people. Yes, he is in your wife, in your husband and in your children. He is in you! And the best possibility to find him is in the world, not out of the world.

To go out of the world has been a great attraction; that too because of fear. The escapist is a coward; he cannot be watchful enough to live in the world and yet be unaffected by it. He cannot be so watchful—he does not have that much intelligence, he cannot make that great effort to be awake—hence he escapes. He is a coward.

So the old sannyas, S. D. Prasad, may fit you perfectly, but it is not going to help. You will remain a coward, and you will remain fear oriented.

On the surface it appears that the sannyasin who is leaving the world is very brave. It is not so. Don't be deceived by the appearances. The soldier who is going to war looks so brave—don't be deceived by the appearances—deep down he is trembling, he's afraid.

Adolf Hitler was preparing his wardrobe for a second dismal winter on the frozen front in Russia.

"Mein Führer," suggested one of his suite, "remember what Napoleon did when he was in Russia. He wore a bright red uniform so that in case he was wounded his men would not notice the fact that he was bleeding."

"Excellent idea! Excellent idea!" ruminated Adolf. "Just throw me my brown pants."

Don't be deceived by the appearances. Even people like Adolf Hitler are tremendously afraid, trembling. And your so-called sannyasins who have escaped from the world have escaped out of fear.

I teach you the way of fearlessness. It is simply fear and

nothing else that is preventing you, although you will not feel very happy with my answer. You must have been expecting that I would say something very gratifying to your ego. Excuse me, I cannot speak any untruth. I can only speak the true, even if it hurts, it hurts. It is only through truth that light starts entering into your being. So if you feel wounded...because your name seems unfamiliar to me, you must be new. And with new people I am never so rude, but I see a possibility in you, hence I am so hard.

Whenever I see a possibility in a man, I become hard. Whenever I see no possibility I remain very polite. If I am polite, that simply means I want to get rid of you. If I am hard, if I hammer hard on your head, that means I have already started respecting you.

The fifth question

Bhagwan,
I am very greedy for money. Do you think I have been a Jew in my past life?

Suresh,

WHY IN A PAST LIFE? YOU ARE A JEW RIGHT NOW! Just by being born in India, just by being born in a Hindu family, does not make any difference. 'Jew' does not mean a race, it is a psychology, it is a metaphysics. The *marwari* is a Jew—the Indian Jew. In fact, anybody who is greedy is Jewish—greed is Jewish.

Jesus is not a Jew although he was born a Jew—he is not Jewish at all. When I use words like 'Jew', remember always that I'm not talking about races. I'm not interested in blood. The Jewish blood and the Christian blood and the Hindu blood are all alike. You can take a few samples—you can get all kinds of samples here—you can take a few samples to the doctor and ask him which blood is Jewish and which blood is Hindu and which blood is Buddhist, and he will be at a loss. He cannot find any way to figure it out—blood is blood! Of course there are types in blood, but they are not Jewish and Hindu and Buddhist.

'Jew' is nothing but another name for greed. In that sense the whole world consists of Jews, except for a few exceptional people. Almost everybody is a Jew! Either you are a Jesus or you are a Jew—these are the only alternatives. If you don't want to be a Jew then be a Jesus. And don't try to console yourself that in a past life.... Those are tricky inventions of the human mind: "In the past life maybe I was a Jew." You are a Jew right now. Throwing the responsibility on the past life keeps you intact, then you can continue as you are.

An old Jew offers to pay a prostitute double her demanded fee if she will keep both hands on his head during love-making. Afterwards she asks him what special thrill he got out of this.

"No thrill," he says, taking a large roll of bills out of his pocket, "but for two bucks extra I know your hands are on my head and not in my pockets!"

Another story for you Suresh:

A retired Jewish businessman is nearly ruined by his sons' demands for money to pay off the girls whom they have seduced and made pregnant. But he pays in order to keep from seeing the family name disgraced.

A few days later his daughter comes to him and confesses, "Papa, I am pregnant."

"Thank God, business is picking up," says the old man.

And the third story:

A room full of Jews are discussing what business is best. Finally one bearded old man says, "Let us stop lying to each other. The whorehouse business is the best: they got it, they sell it, they still got it."

"What are you saying?" cries another horrified old man.

"What am I saying? I'm saying: no overhead, no upkeep, no inventory—who can beat it? And, yes, it is all wholesale."

Greed is Jewish, and everybody is a Jew in that sense. And remember that greed is a projection of fear. It is because of fear that man becomes greedy. He's so much afraid that he wants to accumulate for the future. He's so afraid that he sacrifices his today for tomorrow, and the tomorrow never comes. The greedy man is the most foolish man in the world. 'The fool' Buddha calls him—the fool par excellence, because he goes on sacrificing the present for the future which never comes.

He accumulates money but he cannot use it; he remains poor. The greedy man never becomes rich. He may have the whole world at his disposal, but he remains poor; he cannot enjoy it. His greed won't allow that. He remains miserly. He always remains in such fear of the future that he cannot part from his money. He accumulates, accumulates, wastes his whole life and one day dies. A poor man he was his whole life—empty-handed he had come, empty-handed he has gone. And his whole life went down the drain with no significance.

Don't try to console yourself that in the past life you

were a Jew. Look into your being! You are a Jew. And then there is a possibility that you will see it. "I am a Jew, I am greedy. From where is my greed coming?" Go deeper into greed, analyse greed and you will find fear. And when you find fear you have come to a very fundamental thing.

There are only two ways to live life: one is that of fear and the other is that of love. The man who lives out of fear becomes greedy, becomes aggressive, becomes violent, becomes egoistic. And the man who lives out of love is out of necessity non-greedy, because love knows how to share. Love enjoys sharing; love knows no greater joy than sharing. Whatsoever love has, love shares. And love comes to know a great secret: that the more you share the more love energy goes on reaching you, welling up from some unknown, inexhaustible source—*ais dhammo sanantano.*

The more you love, the more you are prayerful. The more you love, the more God gives you, because you are giving. Whatsoever you do to people, God goes on doing to you. If you are miserly, God becomes miserly towards you. If you are sharing, God is sharing. Existence is only a mirror, it reflects your face, it echoes your being. Live through love and you will be a Jesus.

Jesus says: "God is love." Live through fear and you are a Jew. You may be a Hindu Jew or a Muslim Jew or a Christian Jew—it doesn't matter. Adjectives don't matter.

The last question

Bhagwan,
Why don't I understand you?

Ram Gopal,

UNDERSTANDING IS A SECOND STEP. THE FIRST
is hearing. You don't hear me. You miss the first step, then
the second is not possible.

While you are listening to me, a thousand and one
thoughts are roaming in your mind. They keep you deaf.
My words never reach you intact, in their purity. They
are distorted, they are coloured by your thoughts, by your
prejudices, by your already arrived at conclusions. You
listen to me through your knowledge—that's why you
really *don't* listen. And whatsoever reaches you is something totally different than what was conveyed. I'm saying
one thing, you go on hearing something else. Hence the
misunderstanding. That's why you don't understand me.
Otherwise I am using very simple words.

I'm not using any intellectual jargon. I'm using the day-
to-day language, I never use big words. My words are
simple, as simple as they can be. If you don't understand,
that simply means that somehow you are inwardly deaf.
A great clamour of words and thoughts and conclusions
and theories and prejudices and knowledge and experience—
the Hindu, the Mohammedan, the Christian, the Jew—
they are all there inside. It is very difficult for me to find
a way to you. It is almost impossible to reach you.

It is not a question of understanding. Understanding will
flower of its own accord if you can do one thing: if you can
listen, if you can allow me to reach you, if you can open

your heart, if you are not deaf—then understanding is bound to happen. Truth heard is understood, is bound to be understood. Understanding needs no other effort, it simply needs an opening, a vulnerability. Just open a window to me, just a window will do, and I can steal into you. Just a window will do. If you cannot open the front door, don't be worried, the back door will do. But open some door to me, let me come in, and then it is impossible not to understand, it is impossible to misunderstand.

Truth has such clarity that once understood it transforms your life. Once heard, it is understood. Truth has a very simple process: once heard, it is understood; once understood, it transforms your life. If rightly heard you never ask how to understand. If rightly understood you never ask, "Now what should I do to transform my life according to it?" Truth transforms, truth liberates.

Meditate over this small anecdote:

A man walked into a New York bar and ordered two whiskies, one for himself and one for his friend. The barman produced the whiskies and the man poured some whisky into a thimble which he placed on a perfect miniature grand piano, which he took from his briefcase. He also took from his briefcase a twelve-inch-high man in evening dress, who sat down in front of the piano and commenced playing "The Moonlight Sonata."

The barman was incredulous and demanded to know where the little man had come from.

The man explained, "I was just looking through a junk shop when I found an old oil lamp. I rubbed it with my sleeve a little in order to examine it better when there was a flash and a genie appeared saying he was the slave of the lamp and any wish of mine was his task to fulfill. So I told him I wanted a twelve-inch penis, and this is what the deaf sonofabitch gave me!"

He heard 'a pianist' and missed the whole point.

You go on hearing what you can hear. You go on hearing things which are not said at all. And then you interpret them, and all interpretations are misinterpretations. And whatsoever you do you will feel frustrated, because your misinterpretations cannot bring you to truth. Truth is a communion.

Buddha says, "Find a friend, find a Master and be in communion with the Master." What is communion? Communion means withdrawing all conditions, withdrawing all prejudices, becoming innocent with somebody who has arrived, becoming a child again in front of one who has become awakened. Listen like a small child: alert, full of awe, wonder, and your heart will immediately be penetrated. I will reach you like an arrow.

Yes, there will be a little pain too, but very sweet. So sweet that you have never known anything more sweet than that. Yes, when for the first time the truth penetrates your heart like an arrow, it kills you—it kills you as an ego. It is a crucifixion. But immediately there is a resurrection. On the one hand you die as you have been up to now, on the other hand you are born again. You become a twice-born, a *dwija;* you become a brahmin, you become one who knows.

But knowing needs a great love affair between the disciple and the Master. Knowing is possible only when the love affair is total, when the commitment is total, when the involvement is total. If you listen just like a spectator, you will go on missing. If you listen only out of curiosity, you will go on missing. If you listen with all your ideas and philosophies, you will hear something else which has not been said.

It is not a question of understanding my words: it is a question of understanding my presence. Only the disciple is blessed.

Ram Gopal, you are still not a disciple. You are curious. You have come to see what is happening. You are not yet committed. You listen to me, but you keep a distance, so that if things become too much you can escape easily. You remain on the periphery, you have not entered into the circle.

Enter the circle—I give you the invitation. Become my guest: let me be your host. Drink out of me and you will be drowned, and you will be transformed. It is a promise.

BOOKS PUBLISHED BY
RAJNEESH FOUNDATION
INTERNATIONAL

For a complete catalog of all the books published by
Rajneesh Foundation International, contact:

Rajneesh Foundation International
P.O. Box 9
Rajneeshpuram, Oregon 97741 USA
(503) 489-3462

EARLY DISCOURSES

A Cup of Tea
letters to disciples

From Sex to Superconsciousness

THE BAULS

The Beloved (2 volumes)

BUDDHA

The Book of the Books (volume 1)
the Dhammapada

The Diamond Sutra
the Vajrachchedika Prajnaparamita Sutra

The Discipline of Transcendence (4 volumes)
the Sutra of 42 Chapters

The Heart Sutra
the Prajnaparamita Hridayam Sutra

BUDDHIST MASTERS

The Book of Wisdom (volume 1)
Atisha's Seven Points of Mind Training

The White Lotus
the sayings of Bodhidharma

HASIDISM

The Art of Dying

The True Sage

JESUS

Come Follow Me (4 volumes)
the sayings of Jesus

I Say Unto You (2 volumes)
the sayings of Jesus

KABIR

The Divine Melody

Ecstasy: The Forgotten Language

The Fish in the Sea is Not Thirsty

The Guest

The Path of Love

The Revolution

RESPONSES TO QUESTIONS

Be Still and Know

The Goose is Out

My Way: The Way of the White Clouds

Walking in Zen, Sitting in Zen

Walk Without Feet, Fly Without Wings
and Think Without Mind

Zen: Zest, Zip, Zap and Zing

SUFISM

Just Like That

The Perfect Master (2 volumes)

The Secret

Sufis: The People of the Path (2 volumes)

Unio Mystica (2 volumes)
the Hadiqa of Hakim Sanai

Until You Die

The Wisdom of the Sands (2 volumes)

TANTRA

The Book of the Secrets (volumes 4 & 5)
Vigyana Bhairava Tantra

Tantra, Spirituality & Sex
Excerpts from The Book of the Secrets

The Tantra Vision (2 volumes)
the Royal Song of Saraha

TAO

The Empty Boat
the stories of Chuang Tzu

The Secret of Secrets (2 volumes)
the Secret of the Golden Flower

Tao: The Pathless Path (2 volumes)
the stories of Lieh Tzu

Tao: The Three Treasures (4 volumes)
the Tao Te Ching of Lao Tzu

When The Shoe Fits
the stories of Chuang Tzu

THE UPANISHADS

The Ultimate Alchemy (2 volumes)
Atma Pooja Upanishad

Vedanta: Seven Steps to Samadhi
Akshya Upanishad

Philosophia Ultima
Mandukya Upanishad

WESTERN MYSTICS

The Hidden Harmony
the fragments of Heraclitus

The New Alchemy: To Turn You On
Mabel Collins' Light on the Path

Philosophia Perennis (2 volumes)
the Golden Verses of Pythagoras

Guida Spirituale
the Desiderata

Theologia Mystica
the treatise of St. Dionysius

YOGA

Yoga: The Alpha and the Omega
(10 volumes)
the Yoga Sutras of Patanjali

ZEN

Ah, This!

Ancient Music in the Pines

And the Flowers Showered

Dang Dang Doko Dang

The First Principle

The Grass Grows By Itself

Nirvana: the Last Nightmare

No Water, No Moon

Returning to the Source

A Sudden Clash of Thunder

The Sun Rises in the Evening

Zen: The Path of Paradox (3 volumes)

ZEN MASTERS

Hsin Hsin Ming: The Book of Nothing
Discourses on the faith-mind of Sosan

The Search
the Ten Bulls of Zen

Take It Easy (2 volumes)
poems of Ikkyu

This Very Body the Buddha
Hakuin's Song of Meditation

INITIATION TALKS
between Master disciple

Hammer On The Rock
(December 10, 1975 - January 15, 1976)

Above All Don't Wobble
(January 16 - February 12, 1976)

Nothing To Lose But Your Head
(February 13 - March 12, 1976)

Be Realistic: Plan For a Miracle
(March 13 - April 6, 1976)

Get Out of Your Own Way
(April 7 - May 2, 1976)

Beloved of My Heart
(May 3 - 28, 1976)

The Cypress in the Courtyard
(May 29 - June 27, 1976)

A Rose is a Rose is a Rose
(June 28 - July 27, 1976)

Dance Your Way to God
(July 28 - August 20, 1976)

The Passion for the Impossible
(August 21 - September 18, 1976)

The Open Door
(December 1977)

The Sun Behind the Sun Behind the Sun
(January 1978)

Believing the Impossible Before Breakfast
(February 1978)

Don't Bite My Finger, Look Where I am Pointing
(March 1978)

Let Go!
(April 1978)

The Ninety-Nine Names of Nothingness
(May 1978)

The Madman's Guide to Enlightenment
(June 1978)

Don't Look Before You Leap
(July 1978)

Hallelujah!
(August 1978)

God's Got a Thing About You
(September 1978)

The Tongue-Tip Taste of Tao
(October 1978)

The Sacred Yes
(November 1978)

Turn On, Tune In, and Drop the Lot
(December 1978)

Zorba the Buddha
(January 1979)

Won't You Join the Dance?
(February 1979)

The Sound of One Hand Clapping
(March 1981)

OTHER TITLES

Rajneeshism
an introduction to Bhagwan Shree Rajneesh and His religion

The Sound of Running Water
a photobiography of
Bhagwan Shree Rajneesh and His work

The Orange Book
the meditation techniques of
Bhagwan Shree Rajneesh

BOOKS FROM OTHER PUBLISHERS

ENGLISH EDITIONS
UNITED KINGDOM

The Art of Dying
(Sheldon Press)

The Book of the Secrets (volume 1)
(Thames & Hudson)

Dimensions Beyond the Known
(Sheldon Press)

The Hidden Harmony
(Sheldon Press)

Meditation: The Art of Ecstasy
(Sheldon Press)

The Mustard Seed
(Sheldon Press)

Neither This Nor That
(Sheldon Press)

No Water, No Moon
(Sheldon Press)

Roots and Wings
(Routledge & Kegan Paul)

Straight to Freedom (Original title:
Until You Die)
(Sheldon Press)

The Supreme Doctrine
(Routledge & Kegan Paul)

The Supreme Understanding (Original title:
Tantra: The Supreme Understanding)
(Sheldon Press)

Tao: The Three Treasures (volume 1)
(Wildwood House)

UNITED STATES OF AMERICA

The Book of the Secrets (volumes 1-3)
(Harper & Row)

The Great Challenge
(Grove Press)

Hammer on the Rock
(Grove Press)

I Am The Gate
(Harper & Row)

Journey Toward the Heart (Original title:
Until You Die)
(Harper & Row)

Meditation: The Art of Ecstasy
(Harper & Row)

The Mustard Seed
(Harper & Row)

My Way: The Way of the White Clouds
(Grove Press)

Only One Sky (Original title:
Tantra: The Supreme Understanding)
(Dutton)

The Psychology of the Esoteric
(Harper & Row)

Roots and Wings
(Routledge & Kegan Paul)

The Supreme Doctrine
(Routledge & Kegan Paul)

Words Like Fire (Original title:
Come Follow Me, volume 1)
(Harper & Row)

BOOKS ON BHAGWAN

The Awakened One: The Life and Work
of Bhagwan Shree Rajneesh
by Swami Satya Vedant
(Harper & Row)

Death Comes Dancing: Celebrating Life
with Bhagwan Shree Rajneesh
by Ma Satya Bharti
(Routledge & Kegan Paul)

Drunk On The Divine
by Ma Satya Bharti
(Grove Press)

The Ultimate Risk
by Ma Satya Bharti
(Routledge & Kegan Paul)

Dying For Enlightenment
by Bernard Gunther (Swami Deva Amitprem)
(Harper & Row)

Neo-Tantra
by Bernard Gunther (Swami Deva Amitprem)
(Harper & Row)

FOREIGN LANGUAGE EDITIONS
DANISH

TRANSLATIONS

Hemmelighedernes Bog (volume 1)
(Borgens Forlag)

Hu-Meditation Og Kosmisk Orgasme
(Borgens Forlag)

BOOKS ON BHAGWAN

Sjælens Oprør
by Swami Deva Satyarthi
(Borgens Forlag)

DUTCH

TRANSLATIONS

Drink Mij
(Ankh-Hermes)

Het Boek Der Geheimen (volumes 1-4)
(Mirananda)

Geen Water, Geen Maan
(Mirananda)

Gezaaid In Goede Aarde
(Ankh-Hermes)

Ik Ben De Poort
(Ankh-Hermes)

Ik Ben De Zee Die Je Zoekt
(Ankh-Hermes)

Meditatie: De Kunst van Innerlijke Extase
(Mirananda)

Mijn Weg, De Weg van de Witte Wolk
(Arcanum)

Het Mosterdzaad (volumes 1 & 2)
(Mirananda)

Het Oranje Meditatieboek
(Ankh-Hermes)

Psychologie en Evolutie
(Ankh-Hermes)

Tantra: Het Allerhoogste Inzicht
(Ankh-Hermes)

Tantra, Spiritualiteit en Seks
(Ankh-Hermes)

De Tantra Visie (volume 1)
(Arcanum)

Tau
(Ankh-Hermes)

Totdat Je Sterft
(Ankh-Hermes)

De Verborgen Harmonie
(Mirananda)

Volg Mij
(Ankh-Hermes)

Zoeken naar de Stier
(Ankh-Hermes)

BOOKS ON BHAGWAN

Bhagwan: Notities van Een Discipel
by Swami Deva Amrito (Jan Foudraine)
(Ankh-Hermes)

Bhagwan Shree Rajneesh: De Laatste Gok
by Ma Satya Bharti
(Mirananda)

Oorspronkelijk Gezicht,
Een Gang Naar Huis
by Swami Deva Amrito (Jan Foudraine)
(Ambo)

FRENCH

TRANSLATIONS

L'éveil à la Conscience Cosmique
(Dangles)

Je Suis La Porte
(EPI)

Le Livre Des Secrets (volume 1)
(Soleil Orange)

La Meditation Dynamique
(Dangles)

GERMAN

TRANSLATIONS

Auf der Suche
(Sambuddha Verlag)

Das Buch der Geheimnisse (volume 1)
(Heyne Verlag)

Das Orangene Buch
(Sambuddha Verlag)

Der Freund
(Sannyas Verlag)

Reise ins Unbekannte
(Sannyas Verlag)

Ekstase: Die vergessene Sprache
(Herzschlag Verlag, formerly Ki-Buch)

Esoterische Pyschologie
(Sannyas Verlag)

Die Rebellion der Seele
(Sannyas Verlag)

Ich bin der Weg
(Rajneesh Verlag)

Intelligenz des Herzens
(Herzschlag Verlag, formerly Ki-Buch)

Jesus aber Schwieg
(Sannyas Verlag)

Kein Wasser Kein Mond
(Herzschlag Verlag, formerly Ki-Buch)

Komm und folge mir
(Sannyas Verlag)

Meditation: Die Kunst zu sich selbst zu finden
(Heyne Verlag)

Mein Weg: Der Weg der weissen Wolke
(Herzschlag Verlag, formerly Ki-Buch)

Mit Wurzeln und mit Flügeln
(Edition Lotus)

Nicht bevor du stirbst
(Edition Gyandip, Switzerland)

Die Schuhe auf dem Kopf
(Edition Lotus)

Das Klatschen der einen Hand
(Edition Gyandip, Switzerland)

Spirituelle Entwicklung
(Fischer)

Sprengt den Fels der Unbewusstheit
(Fischer)

Tantra: Die höchste Einsicht
(Sambuddha Verlag)

Tantrische Liebeskunst
(Sannyas Verlag)

Die Alchemie der Verwandlung
(Edition Lotus)

Die verborgene Harmonie
(Sannyas Verlag)

Was ist Meditation?
(Sannyas Verlag)

BOOKS ON BHAGWAN

Begegnung mit Niemand
by Mascha Rabben (Ma Hari Chetana)
(Herzschlag Verlag)

Ganz entspannt im Hier und Jetzt
by Swami Satyananda
(Rowohlt)

Im Grunde ist alles ganz einfach
by Swami Satyananda
(Ullstein)

Wagnis Orange
by Ma Satya Bharti
(Fachbuchhandlung at für Psychologie)

Wenn das Herz frei wird
by Ma Prem Gayan (Silvie Winter)
(Herbig)

GREEK

TRANSLATION

I Krifi Armonia (The Hidden Harmony)
(Emmanual Rassoulis)

HEBREW

TRANSLATION

Tantra: The Supreme Understanding
(Massada)

ITALIAN

TRANSLATIONS

L'Armonia Nascosta (volumes 1 & 2)
(Re Nudo)

Dieci Storie Zen di Bhagwan Shree Rajneesh
(Né Acqua, Né Luna)
(Il Fiore d'Oro)

La Dottrina Suprema
(Rizzoli)

Dimensioni Oltre il Conosciuto
(Mediterranee)

Io Sono La Soglia
(Mediterranee)

Il Libro Arancione
(Mediterranee)

Il Libro dei Segreti
(Bompiani)

Meditazione Dinamica:
L'Arte dell'Estasi Interiore
(Mediterranee)

La Nuova Alchimia
(Psiche)

La Rivoluzione Interiore
(Armenia)

La Ricerca
(La Salamandra)

Il Seme della Ribellione (volumes 1-3)
(Re Nudo)

Tantra: La Comprensione Suprema
(Bompiani)

Tao: I Tre Tesori (volumes 1-3)
(Re Nudo)

Tecniche di Liberazione
(La Salamandra)

Semi di Saggezza
(SugarCo)

BOOKS ON BHAGWAN

Alla Ricerca del Dio Perduto
by Swami Deva Majid
(SugarCo)

Il Grande Esperimento:
   Meditazioni E Terapie Nell'ashram
Di Bhagwan Shree Rajneesh
by Ma Satya Bharti
(Armenia)

L'Incanto D'Arancio
by Swami Swatantra Sarjano
(Savelli)

JAPANESE

TRANSLATIONS

Dance Your Way to God
(Rajneesh Publications)

The Empty Boat (volumes 1 & 2)
(Rajneesh Publications)

From Sex to Superconsciousness
(Rajneesh Publications)

The Grass Grows by Itself
(Fumikura)

The Heart Sutra
(Merkmal)

Meditation: The Art of Ecstasy
(Merkmal)

The Mustard Seed
(Merkmal)

My Way: The Way of the White Clouds
(Rajneesh Publications)

The Orange Book
(Wholistic Therapy Institute)

The Search
(Merkmal)

The Beloved
(Merkmal)

Take It Easy (volume 1)
(Merkmal)

Tantra: The Supreme Understanding
(Merkmal)

Tao: The Three Treasures (volumes 1-4)
(Merkmal)

Until You Due
(Fumikura)

PORTUGUESE (BRAZIL)

TRANSLATIONS

O Cipreste No Jardim
(Soma)

Dimensões Além do Conhecido
(Soma)

O Livro Dos Segredos (volume 1)
(Maha Lakshmi Editora)

Eu Sou A Porta
(Pensamento)

A Harmonia Oculta
(Pensamento)

Meditacão: A Arte Do Extase
(Cultrix)

Meu Caminho:
   O Comainho Das Nuvens Brancas
(Tao Livraria & Editora)

Nem Agua, Nem Lua
(Pensamento)

O Livro Orange
(Soma)

Palavras De Fogo
(Global/Ground)

A Psicologia Do Esotérico
(Tao Livraria & Editora)

A Semente De Mostarda (volumes 1 & 2)
(Tao Livraria & Editora)

Tantra: Sexo E Espiritualidade
(Agora)

Tantra: A Supreme Comprensao
(Cultrix)

Antes Que Voce Morra
(Maha Lakshmi Editora)

SPANISH

TRANSLATIONS

Introducción al Mundo del Tantra
(Collección Tantra)

Meditación: El Arte del Extasis
(Collección Tantra)

Psicológia de lo Esotérico:
La Nueva Evolución del Hombre
(Cuatro Vientos Editorial)

¿Qué Es Meditación?
(Koan/Roselló Impresions)

Yo Soy La Puerta
(Editorial Diana)

Sòlo Un Cielo (volumes 1 & 2)
(Colección Tantra)

RAJNEESH MEDITATION CENTERS, ASHRAMS AND COMMUNES

There are hundreds of Rajneesh meditation centers throughout the world. These are some of the main ones, which can be contacted for the name and address of the center nearest you. They can also tell you about the availability of the books of Bhagwan Shree Rajneesh – in English or in foreign language editions. General information is available from Rajneesh Foundation International.

A wide range of meditation and inner growth programs is available throughout the year at Rajneesh International Meditation University.

For further information and a complete listing of programs, write or call:

Rajneesh International Meditation University
P.O. Box 5, Rajneeshpuram, OR 97741 USA
Phone: (503) 489-3328

USA

RAJNEESH FOUNDATION INTERNATIONAL
P.O. Box 9, Rajneeshpuram, Oregon 97741.
Tel: (503) 489-3301

SAMBODHI RAJNEESH SANNYAS ASHRAM
Conomo Point Road, Essex, MA 01929. Tel: (617) 768-7640

UTSAVA RAJNEESH MEDITATION CENTER
20062 Laguna Canyon, Laguna Beach, CA 92651.
Tel: (714) 497-4877

DEVADEEP RAJNEESH SANNYAS ASHRAM
1430 Longfellow St., N.W., Washington, D.C. 20011.
Tel: (202) 723-2186

CANADA

ARVIND RAJNEESH SANNYAS ASHRAM
2807 W. 16th Ave., Vancouver, B.C. V6K 3C5.
Tel: (604) 734-4681

SHANTI SADAN RAJNEESH MEDITATION CENTER
1817 Rosemont, Montreal, Quebec H2G 1S5.
Tel: (514) 272-4566

AUSTRALIA

PREMDWEEP RAJNEESH MEDITATION CENTER
64 Fullarton Rd., Norwood, S.A. 5067. Tel: 08-423388

SATPRAKASH RAJNEESH MEDITATION CENTER
108 Oxford Street, Darlinghurst 2010, N.S.W.
Tel: (02) 336570

SAHAJAM RAJNEESH SANNYAS ASHRAM
6 Collie Street, Fremantle 6160, W.A.
Tel: (09) 336-2422

SVARUP RAJNEESH MEDITATION CENTER
169 Elgin St., Carlton 3053, Victoria. Tel: 347-6274

AUSTRIA

PRADEEP RAJNEESH MEDITATION CENTER
Siebenbrunnenfeldgasse 4, 1050 Vienna. Tel: 542-860

BELGIUM

VADAN RAJNEESH MEDITATION CENTER
Platte-Lo-Straat 65, 3200 Leuven (Kessel-Lo).
Tel: 016/25-1487

BRAZIL

PRASTHAN RAJNEESH MEDITATION CENTER
R. Paulos Matos 121, Rio de Janeiro, R.J. 20251.
Tel: 222-9476

PURNAM RAJNEESH MEDITATION CENTER
Caixa Postal 1946, Porto Alegre, RS 90000.

CHILE

SAGARO RAJNEESH MEDITATION CENTER
Golfo de Darien 10217, Las Condas, Santiago.
Tel: 472476

DENMARK

ANAND NIKETAN RAJNEESH MEDITATION CENTER
Strøget, Frederiksberggade 15, 1459 Copenhagen K.
Tel: (01) 139940

EAST AFRICA

ANAND NEED RAJNEESH MEDITATION CENTER
Kitisuru Estate, P.O. Box 72424, Nairobi, Kenya.
Tel: 582600

AMBHOJ RAJNEESH MEDITATION CENTER
P.O. Box 10256, Nairobi, Kenya

FRANCE

PRADIP RAJNEESH MEDITATION CENTER
23 Rue Cecile, Maisons Alfoet, 94700 Paris.
Tel: 3531190

GREAT BRITAIN

MEDINA RAJNEESH NEO-SANNYAS COMMUNE
Herringswell, Bury St. Edmunds, Suffolk 1P28 6SW.
Tel: (0638) 750234

MEDINA RAJNEESH BODY CENTER
81 Belsize Park Gardens, London NW3.
Tel: (01) 722-8220, 722-6404

HOLLAND

DE STAD RAJNEESH NEO-SANNYAS COMMUNE
Kamperweg 80-86 8191 KC Heerde. Tel: 05207-1261

GRADA RAJNEESH NEO-SANNYAS COMMUNE
Prins Hendrikstraat 64, 1931 BK Egmond aan Zee.
Tel: 02206-4114

INDIA

RAJNEESHDHAM NEO-SANNYAS COMMUNE
17 Koregaon Park, Poona 411 001, MS. Tel: 28127

RAJ YOGA RAJNEESH MEDITATION CENTER
C5/44 Safdarjang Development Area, New Delhi 100 016.
Tel: 654533

ITALY

MIASTO RAJNEESH NEO-SANNYAS COMMUNE
Podere S. Giorgio, Cotorniano, 53010 Frosini (Siena).
Tel: 0577-960124

VIVEK RAJNEESH MEDITATION CENTER
Via San Marco 40/4, 20121 Milan. Tel: 659-5632

JAPAN

SHANTIYUGA RAJNEESH MEDITATION CENTER
Sky Mansion 2F, 1-34-1 Ookayama, Meguro-ku, Tokyo 152.
Tel: (03) 724-9631

UTSAVA RAJNEESH MEDITATION CENTER
2-9-8 Hattori-Motomachi, Toyonaki-shi, Osaka 561.
Tel: 06-863-4246

NEW ZEALAND

SHANTI NIKETAN RAJNEESH MEDITATION CENTER
115 Symonds Street, Auckland. Tel: 770-326

PUERTO RICO

BHAGWATAM RAJNEESH MEDITATION CENTER
Calle Sebastian 208 (Altos), Viejo San Juan, PR 00905.
Tel: 725-0593

SPAIN

SARVOGEET RAJNEESH MEDITATION CENTER
C. Titania 55, Madrid, 33. Tel: 200-0313

SWEDEN

DEEVA RAJNEESH MEDITATION CENTER
Surbrunnsgatan 60, 11327 Stockholm. Tel: (08) 327788

SWITZERLAND

GYANDIP RAJNEESH MEDITATION CENTER
Baumackerstr. 42, 8050 Zurich. Tel: (01) 312 1600

WEST GERMANY

ANAND SAGAR RAJNEESH MEDITATION CENTER
Lutticherstr. 33/35, 5000 Cologne 1. Tel: 0221-517199

BAILE RAJNEESH NEO-SANNYAS COMMUNE
Karolinenstr. 7-9, 2000 Hamburg 6. Tel: (040) 432140

RAJNEESHSTADT NEO-SANNYAS COMMUNE
Schloss Wolfsbrunnen, 3446 Meinhard-Schwebda.
Tel: (05651) 70044

SATDHARMA RAJNEESH MEDITATION CENTER
Klenzestr. 41, 8000 Munich 5. Tel: (089) 269-077

DORFCHEN RAJNEESH NEO-SANNYAS
Urbanstr. 64, 1000 Berlin 61. Tel: (030) 691-7917